Re-visioning Science Education from Feminist Perspectives

CULTURAL PERPECTIVES IN SCIENCE EDUCATION:
DISTINGUISHED CONTRIBUTORS

Series Editors

Kenneth Tobin
The Graduate Center, City University of New York

Catherine Milne
New York University

Cultural Perspectives in Science Education consists of handbooks and books that employ sociocultural theory and related methods to explicate key issues in science education. The series embraces diverse perspectives, endeavoring to learn from difference, polysemia and polyphonia, and resisting a tendency to emphasize one preferred form of scholarship. The series presents cutting edge theory and research, historical perspectives, biographies and syntheses of research that are germane to different geographical regions. The strength deriving from differences in science education is evident in the works of scholars from the expanding international community in which science education is practiced. Through research in science education, each volume in the series seeks to make a difference to critical issues that face humanity, examining scientific literacies and their role in sustaining life in a diverse, dynamic ecosystem.

Re-visioning Science Education from Feminist Perspectives

Challenges, Choices and Careers

Kathryn Scantlebury
University of Delaware

Jane Butler Kahle
Miami University

Sonya N. Martin
Drexel University

SENSE PUBLISHERS
ROTTERDAM/BOSTON/TAIPEI

A C.I.P. record for this book is available from the Library of Congress.

ISBN: 978-94-6091-084-5 (paperback)
ISBN: 978-94-6091-085-2 (hardback)
ISBN: 978-94-6091-086-9 (e-book)

Published by: Sense Publishers,
P.O. Box 21858
3001 AW Rotterdam
The Netherlands
http://www.sensepublishers.com

Printed on acid-free paper

CONTENTS

SECTION I: INTRODUCTION

The genesis for this book happened on a Sunday afternoon, Ken Tobin had emailed Kate and others in our wider network of scholars and friends to ask if we would send a supportive email to a female, untenured colleague whose department chair had questioned the value of her research contributions, implied that her upcoming tenure review would be unsuccessful, and that although she was 'a good teacher', that was the extent of her value to his department, the college and the university. Kate sent the email to her female colleagues and also began a conversation with Ken about how several other junior female colleagues in science education had been subjected to sexism, racism, and tokenism. From their personal stories, we noted inequities with negotiating for salaries and start-up costs, teaching loads and assignments, and the expectation from university administrators and senior colleagues who expected these beginning female scholars to prioritize others' needs before their own.

In subsequent conversations, Kate began discussing these issues with other women colleagues who were at different stages of their academic careers and had a plethora of stories to tell and experiences to share. Issues of discrimination and inequitable treatment are pervasive in all areas of academia, however, the sciences, and by extension science education, are reinforced by the gendered nature of science as a male-dominated discipline, which reinforces a White, male hegemony. Expanded conversations with multiple cross-generational colleagues revealed that, even in 2009, women continue to be faced with challenges similar to those who entered the academy over forty years ago! As a result of these conversations, Kate invited Jane Butler Kahle, a senior colleague and Sonya Martin, a junior colleague, to join her in editing a collection of works from academic women in science education.

Specifically, we invited women who represent diverse perspectives and experiences on the issues facing them in science education. We asked that contributors share from a personal perspective the challenges and choices they have navigated throughout their academic careers and that they do so from a feminist perspective. We recognize that there is no single feminist perspective, and after reading and editing these collected chapters, we have been impressed by the diversity of thought as it relates to feminism and science education. We expected that women from different parts of the world, who vary with regards to race, ethnicity, religion, class, and sexual orientation would necessarily have different experiences to share and would do so using differing feminist theoretical lens. Some interesting differences we noted from reading these chapters is that the role feminism has played in the lives of these women has been largely informed by the greater socio-historical context of the time period in which these women have begun their careers. The role feminism has played in the life of a woman whom graduated college in 1955 is radically different than for a woman who graduated in 2005. Because we have chosen to elicit a variety of stories from women who are differently positioned with respect to varying feminist theories and ideologies, we will examine what it means historically to be a feminist and how this identity and terminology continues to evolve.

1. WOMEN IN SCIENCE EDUCATION

Introduction and Historical Overview

WHAT IS A FEMINIST PERSPECTIVE?

In this section, we provide a brief historical overview of Western feminism to serve as a backdrop for considering the lived experiences of women academics over time. Feminists and feminist scholars have divided the history of Western feminism into three waves. The term wave describes the transition of the feminist movement's focus from gaining the right to vote, to fighting social and cultural inequalities, and to critically examining the power dynamics between different peoples (across race, gender, class, ability, sexual orientation, etc.) and in the context of trans-national and global politics.

First wave feminism generally refers to action/thought in relation to the suffragist movement of late 1880s-1930s in the United States and other Western countries. This first wave of feminism 'ended' as women attained suffrage, however, well into the 20th century, and in some countries the 21st century, Black, Middle Eastern or illiterate women did not have voting rights. Second-wave feminism refers to the women's rights movement of 1960s through the late 1980s, where advocates sought equity for women within societal institutions such as education, business, career paths and health care. Second-wave feminists focused primarily on identity politics where race, ethnicity, class, and sexual orientation became a focus for discussing women's rights within the context of cultural identity and issues. The third wave of feminism began in the early 1990's and has been described by some as a response to perceived failures of the second wave and as a backlash against initiatives and movements started by second wave feminists (Krolokke & Sorensen, 2005). Third-wave feminists often focus on trans-national politics, seek to challenge notions of femininity and gender as defined by the second-wavers, and have tended to take critical approaches to previous feminist discourses, which are criticized for ignoring or marginalizing the experiences of non-White, middle class women.

Some scholars indicate that the second and third waves concurrently co-exist as a range of feminist theory standpoints (Harding, 2004) which stem from differing ideologies and include examples such as, liberal feminism, radical feminism, Black feminism, postcolonial feminism, post-structural feminism, socialist feminism, multiracial feminism, ecofeminism, and critical feminism, to name a few. We offer this overview to underscore the fact that there are many

K. Scantlebury, J. Butler Kahle and S. N. Martin (eds.) Re-visioning Science Education from Feminist Perspectives: Challenges, Choices and Careers, 3–7.

feminist perspectives that are reflected by our invited authors. An interesting observation we have made from reading these chapters is related to how individual women place their lived experiences within the greater socio-historical context of the feminist movement. Where women find themselves within this continuum has implications for the perspective or lens from which they analyze their experiences as women. The editors of this book illustrate this point. Jane, who completed her doctorate in 1972, intimately experienced the early U.S. women's liberation movement throughout the 1960s and has engaged with feminism throughout her career. Kate's introduction to feminism began in Australia during the 1970's and 80's and has informed and framed her scholarship. Sonya's engagement with the movement is different still, as it was not until she moved from rural Georgia to attend a women's college in the early 1990's that she considered the role of feminism in her life.

Where we place along this continuum of experience with feminism and the women's movement is significant, because the struggles that young women who have come of age primarily within the third wave of feminism, do so with many privileges in place that are not always recognized as being hard won rights by women who lived and experienced the women's movement of the 1960s-1980s and earlier. Thus, the stories of our contributors may resonate with women differently, depending on their individual experiences with not only the choices and challenges being described, but with understanding of the context of the lived experience. We raise this point because we want our readers to be cognizant that while they are reading the text, the reader is simultaneously layering the text of their own lived experience. So for those women who identify more with the politics of third wave feminism, the challenges women describe from their experiences in academia in the 1960s and 1970s are part of the history and in some circumstances viewed as irrelevant to today's academic climate, work environment and politics.

As women representing experiences from across differing eras, race, ethnicity, class, religious beliefs, and sexual identity, we believe it is also necessary for us to preserve our individual voices. As such, we asked contributors to determine for themselves how they wanted to author their stories, choosing when and how to be inclusive of others, and when and how to separate and tease out their own individual stories. We have found many authors have chosen to utilize genres that both seek to merge voices and/or maintain individual perspectives. Some authors chose to deliberately blend their voices and some felt they were more empowered to maintain independent representation through metalogues, internal dialogues within the text in which authors critically examine and interact with one another through the text. For example, Molly and Bambi's chapter that share their experiences of being Southern White women or the different life experience for Eileen and Felicia as African American women. Other authors have chosen to use biographical narratives, and have employed components of autobiography to share their experiences. Thus, some co-authored chapters represent contributions to authorship alphabetically so that the name order listed is not necessarily indicative of a lead author, but of co-authors. In the same spirit, throughout this and the concluding chapter, we editors have chosen to employ a blend of these writing styles, sometimes choosing to blend our thoughts and perspectives into one voice. In other instances, we have chosen to preserve our individual perspectives, using metalogues to respond to and explore issues raised within the book's subsections.

While many of the chapters are autobiographical in nature – meaning they tell the story of an individual woman, they are also biographical in that the experiences of these individuals are representative of the collective – of women in academia everywhere. Thus, we invite you to engage with these chapters from the multiple perspectives offered and from your own. For example, we invite the reader to consider in what way her lived experience as a young Hispanic woman from a wealthy family from the north-eastern United States informs her perspective as she reads a narrative account from a woman recounting her journey from her elementary school days in Jamaica to her career as an organic chemistry professor in a large university in New York City. Thus, we ask that you take into account the socio-historical context of your lived experience in the world as you interact with the texts of these women's lives and we ask you to consider the ways in which your lived experience informs the way in which you see and make sense of the different these accounts of life in academia. We encourage female and male readers to learn from the experiences these authors share and that you individually reflect upon your own such that we can continue these conversations in the academy and actively work together to effect transformation that expands opportunities for everyone.

LOOKING AHEAD

The editors and authors of *Re-visioning Science Education from Feminist Perspectives: Choices, Challenges, and Careers* have contrasting but complementary experiences and expertise in science education. Several authors began their academic careers in science and moved into education. Others "worked their way up the ranks" beginning their careers as elementary, middle or high school science teachers before moving into the academy. Their experience in science education ranges from over fifty years to those at the start of their academic careers. The range of age, race, class, geographic location, education, and life experiences inform the individual perspectives of each author around feminism and feminist thought as related to their personal stories and to the common story of women who share their experiences in the academy.

Thus, the book's contributors span a temporal and spatial continuum, with each chapter focusing on a variety of issues related to paradoxes for academic women in science education. Topics discussed include how engagement with science has shaped the career trajectories of women, including re-directing some from science to science education. Several authors examine the nexus of gender, culture, race, and class as an influencing factor on their career trajectories. Other contributors explore the dialectical relationship between women's private/public lives and their agency (collective and individual) in the academy and its enactment within different academic fields. Although contributors speak from different theoretical standpoints as related to their personal experience as a woman who has come from specific socioeconomic circumstances, geographical locations, racial and ethnic backgrounds, and who holds certain religious beliefs, we have noted similar themes emerge across all of these works. For example, women's careers are impacted by their reproductive choices and many women claim they struggle to maintain positive relationships with their family members without sacrificing their academic careers. In addition, our contributors offer readers their differing perspectives caring for elderly parents and dealing with life's changing circumstances. Thus, these chapters provide analysis of experiences relevant to women who are in various stages of their careers, including those just starting out in academe and those who may be transitioning into administrative positions, retirement, or a new stage in their careers.

The chapters are organized into five sections. We begin each section with a brief introduction to describe the connections between the chapters and to provide a description of each chapter in the context of the identified themes. The first section contextualizes the role, careers, and trajectories of women across several generations, across race, class, and geographical location. From these stories, we seek to explore some of the individual/collective issues faced by women in science and science education in general, including women feeling pushed to the margins of science culture, feeling alienated from their families due to their successes in science, or learning to balance the pursuit of a family life with their career. The second section offers chapters by women who have pursued careers as academics in the sciences and who have transitioned into science education. The third section offers readers examples of the ways in which women in science education are transforming their experiences and the experiences of others in the academy through actions that promote equity, question the status quo, and serve as role models for other women academics who seek to expand learning opportunities for all students. The fourth section explores some of the ways in which women are working to define new expectations for themselves, their colleagues, and their institutions, with regards to scholarship, teaching, and the pursuit of fulfilling social lives outside of academia. The final section contains one chapter in which we, as the editors, identify patterns and contradictions, raise issues for further consideration, and discuss the implications of these works for current and future research and practice.

We expect the chapters in this book will resonate with a wide variety of readers, including those who are interested in pursuing careers in academia, conducting gender studies research, or who are interested in finding ways to transform structures that limit women from gaining equitable access to resources that will enable them to be successful in academia. Undergraduate and graduate students will find these stories informative, not only as historical accounts of the challenges women have faced in academia, but also as examples of issues with which women continue to struggle. Senior colleagues and junior colleagues in academia, both male and female, may consider their own role and responsibility to expand opportunities for women in academia, a chance to re-examine unconscious stereotypic biases towards female academics.

REFERENCES

Battercharjee, Y. (2004). Family matters: Stopping the tenure clock may not be enough. *Science, 306,* 2031–2032.

Harding, S. (2004). *The feminist standpoint theory reader: Intellectual and political controversies.* New York: Routledge.

Krolokke, C., & Sorensen, A. S. (2005). *Gender communication theories and analyses: From silence to performance.* New York: Sage Publications.

Mason, M., & Goulden, M. (2002). Do babies matter? The effect of family formation on the lifelong careers of academic men and women. *Academe, 90*(6), 11–16.

AFFILIATIONS

Kathryn Scantlebury
Department of Chemistry and Biochemistry,
University of Delaware

Sonya N. Martin
School of Education,
Drexel University

Jane Butler Kahle
Condit Endowed Professor, Emerita
Miami University

SECTION II: ONGOING ISSUES FOR FEMALE SCIENCE EDUCATORS IN ACADEME

In this section, we seek to explore some of the individual/collective issues faced by women in science and science education to contextualize the different trajectories of women in academia. This section foregrounds a variety of issues and challenges that academic women face.

In this section's five chapters the contributors each employ a variety of writing styles within the genre of auto/biography and auto/ethnography. The authors utilize a variety of methods to share their individual accounts, including using episodic stories, short vignettes, and autobiographical accounts interwoven with analytical responses from the perspective of the co-author, none of which conform to conventional writing formats. The first four chapters are each co-authored such that the contributors blend their voices to share and analyze their experiences as women in science from perspectives that range across generations, race, class, and geographical location. The final chapter is a solo contribution examining the ways in which science can serve to both liberate women from social constraints and alienate them from others as a result of their liberation.

Eileen Carlton Parsons and Felicia Moore Mensah (Chapter 2) offer a unique pairing of episodic snapshots from similar time periods in their lives to compare and contrast their experiences as African American women navigating their way through school and academia in the southern United States. From these snapshots, Parsons and Mensah then engage in a dialogue within the text, using Black Feminist theory (Collins, 1990) as a framework for examining common themes that emerge from their experiences and to highlight the ways in which their experiences have differed. They draw attention to the concept of intersectionality (Collins, 1990) exploring how race and gender are intersecting oppressions for Black women in society and how Black feminist thought, a critical social theory committed to justice for U.S. Black women as a collectivity, provides a backdrop for the articulation of their shared experiences as Black women in academia.

Chapter 3 provides yet another example of multi-voiced text in which Rose Pringle narrates major life experiences that have shaped and reshaped her identity as an educator as she has moved from high school science teacher in her home country of Jamaica to becoming an elementary science educator at a large university in Florida. Interwoven within her narrative is a paired metalogue, written by co-author Rowhea Elmesky. Elmesky provides a reflective voice and theoretical understandings as she analyzes Rose's lived experiences through the frameworks of empowerment, structure and agency (Sewell, 1992), and identity (Roth, 2006). Utilizing these lenses, Elmesky reframes the discussion of Pringle's challenges as a complex interplay between schema (beliefs and values of Pringle and others) and resources (including Pringle's access to human, material, and symbolic resources) to provide the reader with a theorized account of the structures that both afforded and truncated Pringle's access and appropriation of resources as she has transitioned from a classroom teacher into academia. Thus, Pringle provides a personalized account of her experiences and

Elmesky parlays this account into a generalizable depiction of the experiences of many women in academia, particularly those who are racial minorities and immigrants.

The chapter that follows by Gale Seiler and Gale Blunck (Chapter 4) offers the reader a blend of individual autobiographical accounts along with a metalogic narrative in which each author responds to the other, providing critical discussion of the individual and shared events of their lives. Specifically, Seiler and Blunck embrace a notion asserted by sociocultural theorists that a person's perspective changes as experiences change. Seiler and Blunck explore their trajectories into science education careers by first sharing a vignette from a lived experience of their past and then analyze these actions from their present perspective. As such, this chapter offers readers a temporal and phenomenological analysis of experiences from critical points in the careers of these two authors from a first person (past) and third person (present) perspective.

Using bell hooks' (1984) notion of center and margin shifts, Molly Weinburgh and Bambi Bailey, weave an auto/biographical account their personal/public struggles to move from the margins of undergraduate science classrooms in the 1970s, where male professors held power over female students and discouraged them from advancing in science, to the center of their own classrooms where they actively seek to support and promote women in science. In Chapter 5, the authors draw attention to the role of privilege and power and the notion of center and margin shifts as they each discuss the privilege associated with being White in academia, thus shifting them to the center in some respects, but as women, they found themselves pushed yet again to the margins. This shift is demonstrated by Weinburgh and Bailey's description of the significance of gender in academic social settings, where the "Good Old Boy" network provided opportunities for junior male faculty to make important social connections, but because they were excluded as women, they often were not informed about or invited to collaborate with colleagues on new projects. Weinburg and Bailey both discuss the significant role mentors, both male and female, have had in advancing their careers in academia and how they each have assumed the responsibility to be mentors to junior colleagues as a way to help shift more women from the margins to the center.

The final chapter (Chapter 6) in this section examines the role Nancy Brickhouse's father, who was a scientist, enculturated her into science, and how her early experiences with science at home with her father and in school, have shaped her identity as a science learner and a researcher. Brickhouse examines her early experiences with science in relation to her gender and the expectations family, teacher, and society held for her as a young girl growing up in a small town in northeast Texas in the 1960s and 1970s. Her account traces the distance, both physically and philosophically, that a career in science has placed between her and the friends and family in the small town where she once lived. Specifically, Brickhouse explores her autobiographical experiences in relation to gender and her development of a science-related identity, which continues to inform and shape her research on gender and science learning in her career today, an identity which has, in some ways, separated her from her family and friends.

REFERENCES

Collins, P. H. (1990). *Black feminist thought: Knowledge, consciousness, and the politics of empowerment*. New York: Routledge.

hooks, b. (1984). *Feminist theory: From margin to center*. Boston: South End Press.

EILEEN CARLTON PARSONS AND FELICIA MOORE MENSAH

2. BLACK FEMINIST THOUGHT

The Lived Experiences of Two Black Female Science Educators

INTRODUCTION

As Black females from working class origins in the rural South, we encounter a myriad of challenges and tensions in science education, a field that is predominantly White, male, and middle class. Even in writing this chapter, we struggled: Are we at liberty to use the communicative practices of our cultural communities? Do we structure our sharing in a manner that is more acceptable to the field? We decided to employ both communicative repertoires in the form of personal stories and conversation framed by theory. Within our stories, we relay episodic snippets of our childhood and adolescence as well as our years as undergraduates at The University of North Carolina at Chapel Hill (UNC). In our conversation, we discursively discuss our careers in relation to our worldviews. At the outset, we conform to the standard in the field by contextualizing our personal histories and dialogue within a conceptual framework, Black feminist thought.

THEORETICAL POSITIONING OF OUR ARTICULATIONS

Collins (2000) described oppression as unjust situations where another group systematically denies one group's access to a society's resources over an extended period of time. In the United States (U.S.), major forms of oppression stem from race, gender, and class. According to Collins (2000), these oppressions affect Black women in many ways; the impact most relevant to our articulations is intersectionality.

Intersectionality refers to particular suppressive forms that are manifested by the overlapping or intersection of oppressions. For example, race and gender are intersecting oppressions for Black women in a society where full membership is based upon Whiteness for feminist thought, maleness for Black social and political thought, and a combination of both for maximum participation in the mainstream (Collins, 2000; Frankenberg, 2003). The individual and collective experiences we share in our stories and discuss in our conversation demonstrate these intersecting oppressions. These intersecting oppressions like the ones we highlight in our articulations give rise to Black feminist thought, a critical social theory committed to justice for U.S. Black women as a collectivity.

K. Scantlebury, J. Butler Kahle and S. N. Martin (eds.) Re-visioning Science Education from Feminist Perspectives: Challenges, Choices and Careers, 13–24.

As described by Collins (2000), targeting U.S. Black women as a collectivity is founded upon the premise that the group shares common histories (e.g., legacies of struggle) and faces similar oppressions (e.g., differential treatment) but this collectivity does not presume homogeneity among Black women. African American women may not experience all the same oppressions and they may not perceive and feel them in the same way. Notwithstanding the variability among African American women, Black women occupy an outsider social location in the U.S. (Collins, 1986). Our varying stances highlight the significance of gender in the interpretation of our experiences; the convergence and divergence of our personal histories; and the past and present complementary and contradictory meanings we construct about and from them exemplify this collectivity-individuality/homogeneity-heterogeneity dialectic within Black feminist thought. Furthermore, in our stories and conversation, we attest to Black women's outsider social location but within the context of science education. Being neither White nor male in a society where either one is accompanied by certain exclusive privileges necessitates Black feminist thought, a distinctive consciousness among Black women regarding their overall experiences in such a space.

Six features characterize Black feminist thought (Collins, 2000). First, the overarching purpose of Black feminist thought is to resist oppression by way of activism. This activism may be overt and confrontational or covert and subversive. Second, this activist stance against oppression is not delimited to the plight of U.S. Black women; it is part of a larger social justice project with the empowerment of the oppressed as its goal. Third, in order for Black feminist thought to function effectively within this wider social justice project, it must be fluid and adapt to the fluctuating social conditions that under gird and perpetuate oppression. The adaptability and fluidity of Black feminist thought is facilitated by heterogeneous collectivity, the fourth distinctive characteristic. Heterogeneous collectivity is the dialogical relationship among group knowledge and lived experiences. From this collectivity, a myriad of unique responses consisting of experience-based ideas emerges, the fifth distinguishing feature of Black feminist thought. Finally, the sixth distinctive characteristic of Black feminist thought is that African American women from all walks of life generate these experientially based ideas that may be used to resist oppression. Collins (2000) argues that "it is the convergence of these distinguishing features that gives U.S. Black feminist thought its distinctive contours" (p. 22), a gestalt embodied in our stories and conversation.

STORIES OF TWO AFRICANAMERICAN WOMEN SCIENCE EDUCATORS

Eileen

My story does not pivot around the activities of science but the circumstances in which I was born, reared, and educated. Life as part of the rural poor residing in Boomer,

Felicia

I suppose my story is similar to other women, yet uniquely different because of my early life experiences and the frameworks I use today to make meaning of them. These

North Carolina (NC). I developed a psychological and emotional toughness that serve me well as I, a Black woman, exists in the margins of higher education.

The Early Years

I am the youngest and only female child of six, born to parents who have less than a high school education. I learned much from my parents' fortitude to provide, under the direst of circumstances, the best life they could envision for their children.

Life Lesson #1

My mom worked outside the home in numerous blue-collar jobs. For several years, she worked as a domestic caring for a White family. After a full day of caring for another family, Mom returned to our home for round two. As I grew older, my mother spoke of her work as a domestic in order to convey the message: *You can always find the strength within to do what needs to be done.*

Life Lesson #2

During the elementary years, there was one memorable incident, one in which I was punished unfairly. One day in the 4th grade, a White male student who eventually became one of my closest friends called me a *nigger*. Without hesitation, I physically attacked him. The teacher attended to the other student's wounds and then deducted stars, rewards for academic success, from me but she did not punish the White male student. When I arrived home, I shared the incident with my mother.

meanings come not only from understanding my gender but also from being raised in the rural south, being African American from a working class family, and realizing a divine order to my life. These meanings enable me to survive and move forward in science education, where as an African American woman, I exist on the margins.

The Eldest Daughter

My early life experiences have been good, turbulent, and supportive. I grew up in Selma, North Carolina (NC) as the second born, yet eldest daughter, of five children; my brother is a couple of years older than I. I admit that the being the eldest daughter brings with it a great deal of responsibilities. As a young person I did not realize to what extent this meant for my family and my life now as an adult. The eldest position has and continues to shape the way I view the world.

The Country Was My Science Lab

I have always liked science, or nature. I would sit on the front porch morning, day, and night looking at the sky, making pictures out of the rolling clouds, imaging what it would be like to go to the moon, and dreaming about the stars in the sky at night. This was my quiet time to think, to escape, and to have time to be alone with my thoughts. I would catch bugs, dissect birds, and listen to sounds in the air–animals insects, the wind; eat from the plum trees that surrounded our house; the large pecan tree in the neighbor's backyard; and the blackberries, wild sweet weeds and honeysuckle in the fields down the

The next day, with me by her side, my mother visited the school armed with a less than professional demeanor. She demanded to speak with the principal and the teacher. Even though the Black male principal suggested that I wait in the reception area, my mother insisted that I attend the meeting because I needed to know about life as a Black woman in this world. By the end of the day, the teacher replaced my stars. Shortly after that incident, my mother talked to me about doing better than what she and my father had done, the importance of knowing who you are from the inside out, and not giving power to others to define who you are and what you can do. The life lesson I learned from that indelible 4th grade experience was that *being Black and female means that I must speak up, stand up, and fight for what is rightfully earned.*

The previously stated life lessons helped me to achieve what few could envision for a poor, Black girl from the mountains of NC.

Entry into Science

The journey to a better life not enjoyed by my parents began with a Black, female, middle school teacher's intervention, an individual I did not have for a class. Somehow, she knew about my tumultuous home circumstances, my destructive school behaviour (e.g., fighting peers outside of class), and my exceptional academic performance in the standard classes. One day, during my 9th grade year, she pulled me aside for a heart-to-heart, Black female-to-Black female conversation that literally changed the direction of my life. I began to

dirt road where I lived; run through the corn fields and watch tobacco grow. Therefore, living in the country was like a large laboratory of things to do, see, and imagine. For me, science was alive in nature—a natural place for my curiosities, questions, and excitement about the living world.

Part of my interest in science was to become a physician because I believed that the doctors who were treating my mother did not know what they were doing. I thought if I went to college and majored in science, since I already liked it, then I could treat my mother and she would get well. This was an influential decision regarding my life at age nine.

Moving Up & Out

I was promoted from a lower track to the upper honors/college track in school. It first happened in the 7th grade, and then again in the 12th grade when I was moved from Algebra 3 to Calculus and Trigonometry—a two-hour block course. I was the only African American student, and I felt so out of place. The mathematics teacher was an African American woman—older, tough, strong, and "mean." I felt it firsthand. As the only African American student in the class, I (and my classmates) felt like she picked on me. One day she called me to her room for a talk. Scared and nervous, I went. She said, in a very strong voice, leaning toward me, "Do you know why you are in **my** classroom?" I said, "No, ma'am." She said, "Because I put you in here." She went on to tell me that I was smart, that I could compete with the White students in my class. That conversation changed my life. I understood why consider my future, view school as an opportunity, and to change what was primarily within my control—my actions. At the end of that year, the school recognized me for numerous achievements including a 4.0 grade point average. However, I now know that stellar performance in the standard, academic track was not enough to achieve that better life elusive to my parents.

The following year, my White sophomore English teacher spearheaded an effort to move me to the academically gifted (AG) track where I would be one of two Black students. AG opened the door to fully funded years of studies in higher education at prestigious universities but, before I could enter, I needed to make up a lot of ground I unknowingly lost in middle school via my previous placement in the lower track. As a consequence, an overload in course work led to my enrolment in science courses and subsequently an interest in science.

My interest in science did not develop because of my performance. I did equally well in all my courses. I graduated as valedictorian of my predominantly White high school with a 4.0 grade point average. Also, the interest in science did not emerge because I simply enjoyed the content. My interest in science was sparked by the meaningful interactions I had with my high school science teachers, who were female, and one of who was Black. I also appreciated the intellectual challenge afforded by the subject matter. This intellectual stimulation continued at UNC by way of entrance to the honors' program.

I was moved from one track to the next, from one math classroom to the next. This teacher also helped me to get two scholarships to attend my undergraduate institution, UNC-Chapel Hill.

Confronting Difference

It was not until my undergraduate years that my dreams were met with opposition. As an undergraduate pre-med major, I met other people with different expectations, backgrounds, and ways of learning. I found myself among other students from the "top ten percent" of their graduating classes, and the level of competition among these students was high. Although my math teacher said I could compete, I was not sure that I could and or wanted to. I was naïve. College was different from high school, and I felt very alienated. I was able to find supportive networks of friends, but most friendships lasted the length of a semester and then people were off to their next course. With the few African American female friends I made in college, our similar goals helped to maintain our friendships.

Gender and Race in Science

As a result of both gender socialization and racial prejudice, I learned science from a distance (Moore, 2003). Still, I maintained my interest in science despite the opposing forces within the system. I spent a great deal of time studying alone, learning in silence; however, I was very observant, making sure to do what was required of me as a science major. These ways of being

As part of the honors' program, I attended small science classes where I, as the sole Black student, worked in isolation. I excelled in chemistry and took graduate level courses as an undergraduate; however, I did not see a science career as a viable avenue for directly impacting the lives of the impoverished. Inevitably, I pursued an undergraduate degree in science teaching and graduate degrees (M.S. and Ph.D.) in science education.

My Journey in Science Education

As I reflect upon my 10-year journey in science education, I am pleased with my successes (i.e., prestigious research grants, national and international publications) but perplexed by my lack of progress (i.e., perpetual status as an untenured assistant professor).

I received a Ph. D. from Cornell University in 1994, but my first college position in science education did not commence until 1995-1996. I accepted a tenure track assistant professor position at Lenoir-Rhyne, a liberal arts college located in North Carolina. After a Ford Postdoctoral fellowship followed by part-time employment at UNC-Charlotte, I accepted a tenure track position at North Carolina State University (NCSU).

During my four years at NCSU, my focus broadened from an exclusive emphasis upon science teacher preparation to include the preparation of science education researchers. While at NCSU, I did the kind of work I wanted to define my professional career. As doctoral chair of three Black females' committees, I became more conscious of my outsider allowed me to develop my own sense of identity as a female science major. Therefore, I look at my gender socialization in science as an African American woman equally as oppression and opportunity (Zinn & Dill, 1996). My gender and early childhood experiences afforded me the privilege to learn science in my own way.

During my senior year at UNC, I worked in a genetics lab within the science department. Working in the genetics lab was where I found my place in science. I was provided the opportunity to work on a research team, conduct experiments that involved my interests, and think of alternative ways of doing research. I met with the senior researcher to discuss what I was doing and how it was connected to the overall research project. Therefore, my experiences as a female scientist shaped the perspectives I have in understanding, learning, and doing science now as a science educator.

In a Position to Effect Change

My first academic position was at Michigan State University as a postdoctoral fellow (Moore, 2005). The experiences I had there were foundational for my current position at Teachers College, Columbia University. I often tell people, *"I love my job"* because I am living my life's purpose. At the same time, I am aware that my position is multiple, challenging, full of possibilities and contradictions. Nevertheless, I feel like that I am in a position to effect positive change in so many ways. One specific way is to change perceptions of African American women in positions of authority—who we are position in science education. From this increased awareness, I deemed it imperative to prepare the Black females for a world in which they would likely be marginalized by helping them to develop a strong sense of self and a self-reliant disposition to "go it alone if necessary." I attempted to develop the aforementioned by being supportive but very strict, brutally honest yet encouraging, and understanding but tough.

In yet another assistant professor position, I work to meet what I consider one of my life's divinely appointed purposes. As in the past, I am certain lessons learned earlier in life will facilitate my forward movement in science education even if it is relegated to the margins.

and what we can do. Thus, my research, teaching, advising, and service are similar to what Ladson-Billings says of her work: "I, too, share a concern for situating myself as researcher—who I am, what I believe, what experiences I have had all impact what, how, and why I research. What may make these research revelations more problematic for me is my own membership in a marginalized racial/cultural group" (1995, p. 470). Problematic is my research in the sense that my concerns and issues are marginalized. However, I am optimistic. I work in the margins—perfecting my craft, and waiting patiently for someone to notice. While I consider the margins to be (a)lone(ly) space, I also see it as a full of opportunity. I work quietly, being observant to the forces around me, and anticipating the moment where marginalization becomes a past notion.

CONSTRUCTING PRESENT MEANING FROM PAST EXPERIENCES

Eileen: The juxtaposition of our biographies is striking. We were reared among the working poor in two, small, rural towns of North Carolina—you in the east and I in the west. Although we studied in different science departments, we attended UNC-CH around the same time. Both of us elected to launch and continue our careers at predominately white institutions (PWIs), and we endured similar challenges along the way.

Felicia: Yes, our background experiences are very similar. For me, a similarity I see in our parallel stories is the influence of our families, our mothers in particular, and the way we approach life. We have developed a toughness to survive that we have garnered from our mothers' lives.

Eileen: I'm also taken aback by our roles within our families. Your experiences of caring for your family at an early age resemble the responsibilities I now manage. Because I'm the child most educationally, financially, and socially positioned to do so, I govern the affairs of my aging and chronically ill parents who continue to live in poverty.

Felicia: I think the centrality of our families in defining who we are may speak to our commonality as Black women. Even though I did not mention this in my personal history, another key factor in defining who I am is my religion. It is very influential in how I view life, respond to events in my life, and look to the future. With regard to religion, I feel like being in science education is what I'm supposed to be doing–what I am purposed to do– a divine assignment, not a job but a mission. Even when I see things happening around me, the good and the challenging, I take them as life lessons that I'm supposed to learn. I find and pull strength from my faith.

Eileen: The faith you mention is also at the core of who I am and what I do. Faith produces a confidence and certainty in how I act that others who do not share my faith cannot understand.

Felicia: Sometimes, others misinterpret having this assurance that things will work out for our benefit as arrogance.

Eileen: I agree. In your biography, I noticed you cited gender and then race. When I interpret my experiences and construct responses to them, race is more salient.

Felicia: Here is where we are uniquely different. First, gender is salient for me because gender was emphasized in my early home life as a major division of roles and expectations for members of the family. My father worked and my mother stayed at home; she worked outside of the home after my youngest sister started school. Even with a part-time job outside of the home, my mother still maintained duties within the home. In addition, my mother baked cupcakes for special occasions, like Christmas and Valentine's Day, for my elementary classmates. I suppose I grew up thinking that this was what mothers did; they kept the home and the fathers worked. In accordance to these gender roles in my household, my younger sisters and I had chores that centered on housework. I learned how to sew, go grocery shopping, to cook biscuits, cakes and other things from scratch as well as prepare meals, "do hair", and take care of my younger sisters. My father was the authority in the home, and we respected and loved him, and were obedient to what he required of us.

Eileen: My early life experiences did not distinguish between male and female roles. My mom worked outside and inside the home. During my early years, roles were not determined by societal expectations of what was appropriate and inappropriate for males and females but by need and who was best situated to address the need. For example, my brothers and I did so-called woman's work such as cooking, cleaning, and doing laundry. Need, expertise, and circumstance continue to dictate who does what in my personal life. For instance, my husband and I both do "male jobs" and "female jobs."

Felicia: Well, being single. I do it all! And I suppose this will not change too much as I begin to fulfill my marital duties in the home and also work outside of the home.

Eileen: I also think growing up in a male-dominated environment impacts how I view and enact myself as a female in science education. As I matured, my mom coached me on things like proper posturing etiquette, but, in areas where it mattered like standing up in face of opposition, she encouraged me to do it like the boys. Incidents of oppression in higher education also diminish (not eliminate) the prominence of gender in my worldview. As in my unforgettable 4th grade experience, racial oppression continues to be prominent in my current professional experiences. One event is especially memorable. During my employment at one institution, I was one among several female assistant professors. We primarily differed in race and number of years employed in higher education with me being the more senior in experience. Because we were in some regards "sisters", we on occasion discussed our tribulations. Through these conversations, I learned that we received conflicting information regarding career progression. They were coached on how to become a part of the profession's ruling class, and I was encouraged to be a dutiful worker. I also had the lowest salary. To me, race and perhaps social class were major factors that circumscribed the advice and compensation I received. In order to offset this differentiation in expectation, information shared, and treatment, I acted on my somewhat naïve belief that individuals will do what is just and fair if informed so I openly highlighted issues. Today, because the event altered how I perceive and, to some extent, interact with the world, I continue to feel the impact. I realize the naïveté of the belief that individuals will be fair and just if informed about oppression. Now I purposefully challenge oppressions by first naming them and then I work to create and support structures to circumvent them—all with the intent of improving conditions for a future generation. One example of supporting structures to circumvent oppression (limited access) is my participation in the preconference workshops held at the annual meetings of the National Association for Research in Science Teaching. These workshops provide pertinent information regarding career trajectories in academe often withheld from people of color.

Felicia: That is interesting, Eileen. I can see oppression through the women in my life, mainly my three biological sisters and my closest girlfriends. So, again gender is salient but definitely connected to race and social class issues. However, gender, to me, is still the major influence, though the others are closely connected. I am a member of Sisters of the Academy (SOTA). I started as a graduate student member and have remained with the organization since its short, five-year history, even serving on the executive board of the organization since the beginning. As a SOTA member, here is where I work to help other African American females to advance in academe and administration. Our mission is to support and nurture through education, scholarship, and service. Similar, to you Eileen, being involved in professional organizations allows me to build supportive structures and to be in positions where obtaining information and passing it along truly helps the next generation of Black women specifically, but for all who are marginalized generally.

Eileen: Your declaration, "gender is major," is not a sentiment common among Black women. How did you get to this place?

Felicia: My status as the eldest child is very influential and impacts what I do and how I interact with others. I do not want to say nurturing; but I am very supportive and helpful to everyone. This helpful, assisting kind of identity is a part of me, and it comes from my childhood. Because of my social class, I have learned how to make do with what I have, and I really have no desire to accumulate a lot. I don't work just to accumulate things. This influences what I do in science education and my research. For example, when I accepted my academic position I was given a budget for research to I buy what I needed. I just spent the last of the money after 4 years! I have learned to make good use of resources or work in ways that require very little financial resources.

Eileen: You seem to equate the significance of gender to a supportive, helpful, assisting role. Perhaps, it is this meaning being supportive, helpful, and assisting that gender is eminent but problematic for me. In my work with prospective science teachers, I am supportive, helpful, and assisting in a manner that is not stereotypical. My caring signifies the racial/cultural differences Siddle-Walker and Snarey (2004) discussed in their work. Particularly because we work in a field that is predominantly White and middle class, this expectation to mother students in a way that corresponds to the mainstream view of caring conjures unsettling images—historical caricatures like "Mammy" and real-life mental impressions of my mother as a domestic. Among my more pressing challenges in science education is balancing this external expectation to be a mother to students and my worldview indelibly shaped by the intersecting oppressions of race, social class, and gender I experience. Of the many reasons why I selected and continue to work at PWIs, projecting or reinforcing a mothering image is not one of them.

Felicia: Being at TC has been a blessing and a challenge in the sense of constructing the kind of image I want for myself as a faculty member. The most important reason for my selection of a PWI is being able to present an image that African American women can do research, can teach, and can be successful at a White institution. People are surprised by my success and sometimes my presence at one of the top, leading research institutions in the world. For me, it is not by accident. I am supposed to be here to do what I am supposed to do.

In the past, I tried this experiment; I would arrive to class before the students and sit in the audience. After everyone was present, I would stand up and say, "Hello, class, welcome to science education!" Eyes would get big; mouths would drop open. The students' surprise told me a great deal about the unexpectedness of having an African American female science education professor. Second, I feel that my position of power, as my minister says, is to be there for other African American students and other students of color to support them in their personal and professional growth. Because there are so few Black faculty, who will be there to support students of color? I want to be in a position to effect change and to change oppressive structures for students and faculty who are with me and those who will come after me.

Eileen: The reasons you articulate as well as the oppressions we face are my motives for working at PWIs and for persevering in science education. The often pursued tangibles of material accumulation, prestige, position, etc. are not my motivations for what I do and how I do it. Although the mission is costly in many ways, I hope that our presence, our actions, and that of others who resist oppression and empower the oppressed will change the landscape of science education such that the stories of the African American women behind us will herald more inclusive rather than marginalized experiences.

CONCLUSION

Comparisons and contrasts of our experiences as Black women in science education in the U.S. illustrate Collins' Black feminist theory. On one hand, as Black women we share common challenges in milieus where Whiteness and maleness maximize participation. These common experiences exemplify the collectivity and homogeneity domains of the collectivity-individuality and homogeneity-heterogeneity dialectics of Black feminist thought. On the other hand, our experiences are unique and different, diverging on the salience of various oppressions in our lives. As revealed in our stories and discussion of life events, how oppressions intersect in our lives as Black females in science education manifest differently and elicit characteristically distinctive responses. Nevertheless, aligning with the primary aim of Black feminist thought, each of us devotes our lives and our careers to actively resist oppressions.

Intent on confronting oppression, we have elected to establish our careers in science education at PWIs. We use our mere presence in the college classroom to question stereotypical and derogatory images of African American women. Additionally, we utilize our positions to facilitate the personal and professional growth of marginalized others in science education, as we continuously resist oppression. In the physical setting of PWIs and in the professional setting of science education, we employed and will continue to share what we have gained in the form of knowledge and expertise from our lived experiences as individuals and as a part of the Black women collectivity as ways to educate the oppressor, to empower the oppressed, and to disrupt and alter oppressive systems.

REFERENCES

Collins, P. H. (1986). Learning from the outsider within: The sociological significance of Black feminist thought. *Social Problems, 33*(6), 14–32.

Collins, P. H. (2000). Black feminist thought: Knowledge, consciousness, and the politics of empowerment (2nd ed.). New York: Routledge.

Frankenberg, R. (1993). *White women, race matters: The social construction of whiteness.* Minneapolis, MN: University of Minnesota Press.

Ladson-Billings, G. (1995). Toward a theory of culturally relevant pedagogy. *American Educational Research Journal, 32*(3), 465–491.

Moore, F. M. (2003). In the midst of it all: A feminist perspective on science and science teaching. In A. L. Green & L. V. Scott (Eds.), *Journey to the Ph.D.: How to navigate the process as African Americans* (pp. 104–121). Sterling, VA: Stylus.

Moore, F. M. (2005). The dissertation and graduation: Not just a black and white process—Mountain climbing, middle passage, and learning as a postdoctoral fellow. *ERIC Digest,* ED489985.

Siddle Walker, V., & Snarey, J. (2004). *Race-ing moral formation: African American perspectives on care and justice.* New York: Teachers College Press.

Zinn, M. B., & Dill, B. T. (1996). Theorizing difference from multiracial feminism. *Feminist Studies, 22*(2), 321–331.

AFFILIATIONS

Eileen Carlton Parsons
University of North Carolina at Chapel Hill,
Chapel Hill, North Carolina

Felicia M. Moore Mensah
Teachers College, Columbia University,
New York, New York

ROSE PRINGLE AND ROWHEA ELMESKY

3. MAINTAINING COMMITMENTS, SHIFTING IDENTIFIES, AND UNDERSTANDING CULTURAL CONFLICTS WHILE NAVIGATING THE RITE OF PASSAGE IN THE SCIENCE EDUCATION ACADEMY

INTRODUCTION

The purpose of this chapter is to narrate major life experiences that have shaped and reshaped my identity as an educator. Interwoven within my narrative, my co-author, Rowhea, provides a reflective voice and theoretical understandings through the frameworks of empowerment or agency, structure (Sewell, 1992) and identity (Roth, 2006). Our goal is that, through this chapter, others will come to better understand how one individual came to academia and the ways in which identity continuously forms and reforms as one experiences life within the collective. We envision identity as the ways in which one defines oneself as well as the ways in which others define us. Therefore, to understand identity on the individual level, one must understand what happens in the social realm as one interacts with others. These interactions impact the ways in which one perceives oneself and also shapes how personal goals shift and take different forms as they are socially mediated. I am currently an associate professor at the University of Florida in science education. Looking back, I now recognize that my work as a high school science teacher was the first step along the journey of my development from science teacher to science educator.

Born and raised in Jamaica, teaching was my first career choice. "Teaching is the noblest of profession and is the foundation for all other professions," my teacher in elementary school had told me, and I wholeheartedly embraced that ideology. At that time, I observed teachers being treated with much respect by everyone in the community. In fact, in my district, if you were a teacher, you were held in high esteem. Looking back, I became a teacher because I wanted to impact others and as my mother insisted, education opened the doors for a better way of life. She had instilled in her children the notion of education for social and economic mobility.

After graduating from the prestigious Mico Teachers' College, I set out to be the best high school teacher. My first and only teaching position was at the Queen's School, an elite high school for girls. The Queen's School was one of the few schools that catered to the offspring of the upper socio-economic Jamaicans. Although I did not belong to this social class but I had graduated from college with a distinction in teaching and the best teacher of science. These distinctions contributed to my first employment, and I was pleased to begin my work as an educator in that environment.

K. Scantlebury, J. Butler Kahle and S. N. Martin (eds.) Re-visioning Science Education from Feminist Perspectives: Challenges, Choices and Careers, 25–36.
© 2010 Sense Publishers. All rights reserved.

FROM SCIENCE TEACHER TO SCIENCE TEACHER EDUCATOR

While teaching high school science at The Queen's School, I assumed other responsibilities including monitoring and guiding preservice teachers interning in the school. In this new role, I began to question what was happening in the educational programs of the teachers' colleges. My observation of the preservice teachers overtime led me to examine the quality of beginning teachers who were entering our school system. In my teacher preparation, science was presented as a "doing" subject, yet I was observing beginning teachers who were comfortable assuming the role of lecturer in high school classrooms. I constantly remembered my internship supervisor's voice as he bellowed at our weekly seminars, "The chalk and talk teacher is the sign of weak pedagogy." We were told this and, to be assigned a passing grade for internship, you always had to assume that stance. The internship was crucial in the preparation program since, if you failed, you would have to repeat an entire academic year in college.

Since I was supervising preservice teachers who were comfortable with using the "chalk and talk" approach, interspersed with some science laboratory activities, I began to share some of the expectations I had learned during my own college experience and had been refining after being in the classroom for a number of years. I found myself really enjoying working with these new teachers! As I modeled different practices, I began to dream of becoming an educator at a teachers' college.

Rowhea: Rose, I think it is interesting to consider the ways in which you began to shift in your perceptions of your capabilities in education from that of science teacher to science teacher educator. Importantly, your perceptions of yourself as an educator were changing through your actual experiences and interactions with the preservice teachers; you were able to enact different roles that expanded beyond that of a science teacher. Through these expanded roles, you could begin to consider a different set of possibilities in terms of a professional career. Drawing upon Sewell's (1992) notions of agency and structure, we can better understand your shifting identity in terms of the ways in which you exercised agency (your sense of empowerment) as you worked with the preservice teachers. Agency can be understood in multiple ways, yet in this chapter, we can view the concept of agency as closely interwoven with understanding structures or schema and resources. As described by Sewell, schema can be rules, norms, recipes for action, notions and/or ideology (including hidden and oppressive hegemony). For example, understanding science teaching to forefront "doing" rather than lecturing illuminates a set of schema that you (and the teaching college institutions) held to define 'good' science teaching practices. It is in the process of transposing schema from one context to another that one may exercise agency. In the situation you describe, you carried schema that had been developed in another place and time (your college education) into the school where you taught. That is, you extended the concept that science should actively involve students into your mentorship of the new teachers entering the school. This transposition of schema represents agency in action and was triggered by the tension between your own notions and the practices you observed among the prospective teachers. In exercising agency, you were gradually expanding your capacity for action.

REACHING FOR AN OPPORTUNITY: GAINING A MASTER'S DEGREE IN SCIENCE EDUCATION

In recognition of my achievement as a science teacher, I was awarded a scholarship by United States Aids International Development (USAID) to complete a Masters at Florida State University (FSU). Before leaving Jamaica, I requested and was granted that my program included some courses or a minor in science education. During advisement at FSU, I was introduced to the science education program. It was all I thought that I needed, a masters in science education to equip me with the tools to be an effective science educator in a teachers' college. Over the next 16 months, a whole new world of opportunities opened. I worked with some of the best-known science educators and had experiences that I noted in my journal as being "out of a textbook." I was also exposed to the school system in Florida by being an assistant on the Statewide Systemic Initiative (SSI). There, I gained insights into the impact of Florida's Department of Education (DOE) and its role in directing science education in the state. As I traveled with the team from the DOE and listened to the range of stakeholders, I became more convinced that teachers, if given the right kinds of support, could make a difference in the lives of children and ultimately the well being of the state. As I engaged in these new experiences, I reflected upon the teachers in my hometown and thought about how they helped make a difference in my life. My passion for science teacher education was further fueled; I wanted to become more deeply engaged in science classrooms and the preparation of teachers both the inservice and preservice teachers, who would make a difference in the lives of children. I was now even more determined that my future lay in science teacher education.

Rowhea: Rose, your metaphor equating your Masters degree experience to the opening of "a whole new world" is very powerful. In your narration, the "new world" is actually the resources that became accessible to you during your degree program. Whereas, it is common for the construct of a resource to be understood as material or physical in nature, here you point out, similar to Sewell (1992), that resources span both the human and material realms. For example, as you indicate, the opportunity to work with top science educators in the field and to accompany a DOE team constituted your access to a variety of human resources. Since resources, like schema, shape and are shaped by agency, as your resources expanded, your capacities for action as a science teacher educator also expanded. You were building a repertoire of skills, knowledge, and human relationships that would influence the ways in which you could interact with future preservice and inservice teachers. Moreover, you were reinforcing a set of schema you held with regard to the teaching profession (e.g., teachers make a difference in the lives of their students) as well as developing new schema (e.g., teachers need support). Since structures are mutually sustaining (Sewell, 1992), the schema you held and were building were dialectically related to the actual resources that you might attempt to gain access to during the new masters program. For instance, your belief that teachers can impact student lives more substantially when provided with useful support during their teacher education programs propelled you further distance upon your quest in graduate education for the development of an appropriate skill set.

FROM SCIENCE TEACHER EDUCATOR TO SCIENCE EDUCATOR

The Thirst for and Restraints of Earning a Doctorate in Science Education

At the end of my program at FSU, I knew I wanted to do the PhD program. The masters had opened up just a slit in the curtains to reveal the possibilities lying behind. I could have petitioned to continue the program but no amount of encouragements would have kept me in the US beyond the 16 months. My son had just received a scholarship to high school and my five year old daughter was beginning to make it known that it was time for me to be back with my family. Additionally, I was not ready to move my family from their comfort zone in Jamaica to facilitate my PhD. My plan was to return home to work as a "lecturer" in a teachers' college and simultaneously complete the PhD program. Unfortunately, this plan was incompatible with the demands of being a lecturer. It would take more than ten years to complete the doctorate, thus I decided not to choose that option. Instead, I accepted a position as a science teacher educator at my alma mater.

My first Position in Academia

My job as a science teacher educator at Mico seemed, at first, to be a dream come true. My head of department, who had also recently completed courses at FSU, gave me the go ahead to explore! I experimented with some of the ideas I had learned, as I taught science education to both secondary and primary teachers. For example, I explored action research to replace the traditional classroom research project, which was an important aspect of the internship program. Coordinating the action research allowed me to work with preservice teachers in a wide range of classroom settings outside of our science program. This was rich research territory, yet I struggled with the thoughts that I lacked the research tools, the expertise and the authority to explore possibilities of publishable work. At the time, teachers' colleges lacked a research culture and so any attempt at conducting such was on your own time. Preparing teachers was the focus and the research was what "others" did! But I wanted to be a part of the "others." I wanted the science education community to know what we were doing in teacher education in a developing country. I wanted to add to the knowledge about science teacher education, not only to consume what others were constructing.

Although my masters degree had prepared me to think and act in certain ways, I felt I lacked the tools and the necessary support to conduct research on my own. I wanted to continue my growth as a scholar, but I had no clout to make that happen in an education system that was tightly controlled by the ministry. I knew I had to leave Jamaica, but I had to consider my family. My husband became supportive under the condition that we would all be together. This would entail much sacrifice but he was willing to support me and he did. His support of my aspiration would prove costly for him because at that time we did not understand the nuances of migration. We thought that being a former high school science teacher with extensive business experiences in an international company, the move would be near seamless. To date he is still not employed.

Rowhea: In your experiences during the Masters program, Rose, you had built a set of schema that valued research, both for yourself as a science teacher educator and for science teachers in their classrooms (e.g., action research). Thus it was through your experiences with the collective at FSU, a research focused institution, that you were able to begin to see dynamic and manifold possibilities for research within educational settings – for multiple types of individuals. With regard to your own identity development, you had easily shifted your conception of 'self as science teacher' to include 'self as science teacher educator'. However, your new experiences in science education and your first academic job in Jamaica emphasized the existence of a subtle distinction between being a science teacher educator and being a science educator. This is clear through the above account in which you separated yourself as a new science teacher educator from the "others" who performed research. Your yearning to develop as a researcher represents another instance in which aspects of your identity would continue to shift. Importantly, your development into a science educator (who both conducted research as well as educated teachers) was contingent upon your experiences with a collective that valued research. Since identity is formed and reformed in the social domain of interacting with others (Roth, 2006), you could better perceive yourself within a researcher capacity if you had actual opportunities to participate as a science education researcher. However, there were structural constraints (both in the form of schema and resources) that limited your ability to interact with a research community. While some of the challenges were connected to family needs and expectations, many of the barriers were also institutional, for instance, with regard to the norms and expectations of "lecturers" in teachers colleges. In addition, other walls loomed high, as you lacked experiences that would have created a refined set of research skills within your toolkit. It seems that your recognition of your need to build additional sets of resources in order to become a "researcher" was pivotal to your future development and for your expanded sense of agency as you pursued your Ph.D. at FSU.

Going Back to Graduate School

Entering graduate school a second time was different. A number of individuals with whom I had planned to work had moved on to other institutions, but I was still determined to make the best of my experiences. I was there to sharpen my tools of research in science education and be empowered to contribute to such a community. I was confident in my skills as a teacher and science teacher educator, and my doctoral program allowed me to further explore and study science teacher preparation and the complexities of teaching science in America. One issue that constantly rose in my program, as a student and a teacher, was assessment. Two courses I took challenged me in their assessment practices and at the same time, as a teaching assistant, I had to deal with assessment with the preservice teachers. Many questions emerged around this issue of assessment and responding to them led to my dissertation. The focus of my dissertation work was specifically on alternative assessment as a tool for continuous improvement among preservice elementary teachers. I remember my major professor's poignant question when I accepted my professorial position if I was going to continue to develop my research around issues of assessment. My answer was a resounding yes, but I was unsure of what that meant beyond graduate studies.

By the time, I graduated with a Ph.D. I was ready for science education which I perceived as three roles combined into one- science teacher, science teacher educator and researcher. I was no longer a high school teacher and had easily adapted into a K-12 persona as I worked with the elementary preservice teachers. I also knew I wanted to be involved in teacher education. After all, this was my main reason for returning to graduate school and the area where I thought I could make the greatest difference. I believed in the concept of 'ripple effect,' thus if I made a difference in the lives of 10 teachers versus 10 high school students ultimately more people would be impacted. Finally, I had developed a level of comfort around my abilities to conduct research and planned to make a difference with a newly found understanding of schooling in America. Equipped with a set of resources that I had developed over many years, I accepted a position at the University of Florida, with a confidence in my abilities to succeed against all odds. I didn't forget that I started from a position with both social and economic deficit in Jamaica, yet had become successful in an American education system that was highly autocratic and competitive. My success was also attributed to the influence of my mother and her constant reminder of the power of hard work to be successful and education as the means for social and economic mobility. After all, I totally embraced these teachings and they worked for me.

Rowhea: Often times, when individuals, particularly those of us coming from economically and/or culturally marginalized backgrounds, experience success, we attribute it to hard work and educational attainment. This is commonly described as the achievement ideology – a dominant schema within mainstream American culture (MacLeod, 1995). Ingrained within the political, social, economical and educational structures in society, the achievement ideology proclaims that individual merit is what makes the difference. If you work hard, the ultimate reward may be financial success. Whereas schema plays an important role in shaping the ways in which we participate in society, the achievement ideology undermines the centrality of both accessing and then appropriating resources. Without paying attention to resources, we may fail to recognize the ways in which they are key to our exercise of agency. In your case, Rose, while hard work is an important thread in your story, you have also beautifully highlighted again and again your agency in finding and securing different forms of resources that would allow you to meet your clearly defined goals. Your story has helped to illuminate that 'hard work' can be better conceptualized as the garnering/accessing and appropriation of resources in the form of knowledge, skills, or relationships, for example.

Finally, as you entered an assistant professor position at the University of Florida, it is very important to point out that you had reached a point in your life where the multiple roles/aspects of your identity (that of science teacher, science teacher educator and researcher) were synthesized into one and formulated your definition of self as a science educator. However, in relation to our theoretical conception of identity, we would expect that this manner of perceiving oneself is fragile and will continue to shift through interactions within the collective, particularly when an individual joins a new context – in this case a new position in a different university.

WORKING IN A RESEARCH INSTITUTION

While my desire was to function as a science educator, I was very unsure of what that would specifically entail in a research-focused environment. I needed to become familiar many territories if I was going to succeed as a science educator. However, I was without a mentor. I was employed in a teacher education program and my role was to ensure that the preservice teachers were effectively prepared to teach science in the inclusive classroom. The undergraduate program had approximately 150 students organized into five cohorts in the fall semester, and with three teaching assistants I set out to make the science program "work." Interestingly over a period of three years, I worked with six teaching assistants with experiences ranging from science laboratory instructor to teaching middle school science. Thus, my focus became the development of the TA's pedagogical skills to better facilitate the preservice teachers learning to teach science. At the same time, the program was piloting mathematics, science and technology integration. So I involved with the teaching assistants in implementing the science education and working with a team of educators to integrate the courses the science.

Upon reflection, I had traded my teachers' college lecturer position for a more demanding position in a university and had less support to effectively carryout the assignment. With time, I began to recognize that I was in a culture for which I had not fully developed the tools to become successful. While I had confidence in my teaching and my research skills and was soon heavily involved in service to college, university and community, I lacked the real knowledge needed to succeed in the highly political, research focused, science education culture. I still believed hard work led to success. So I worked hard - in the areas of teaching, research and service. However, hard work could not alleviate issues that I had in understanding my position as a science educator in this context. First of all, my context did not foster collaboration on issues in science education. The department had a secondary program and that was usually referred to as "the science education program." However, it was made clear to me that I was not allowed to interact with the students nor the program; moreover, there were a very limited number of graduate students whose program of studies contained an emphasis on science education. Without my involvement in the 'main' science education activities, I began to seriously question: Was I a science educator? Immediately after graduation, it had been so easy for me to define myself as a science educator. However, as semesters rolled on, I began to wonder to what the extent I was maintaining that identity.

Rowhea: Rose, you experienced what many beginning assistant professors face, that is, maintaining the definition of self as a science educator within your new employment context. While the completion of a doctoral degree in science education assumes the development of a particular set of skills and knowledge, the ways in which you can and do participate in the university impacts whether others in the department see you as a science educator. Most problematic in my mind as I read your account, is the way in which you were ostracized from the main science education activities. These structural arrangements created a situation where you would have to find and claim new space for science education activities. Being a female from an unrepresented group and having to operate along the periphery rather than in a central location made your job doubly difficult as well as rigorously unsettled the ways in which you had come to perceive yourself. For instance, the fact that you were unable to work with secondary teachers limited the wealth of resources you could offer the department from those years you had spent teaching in secondary classrooms in Jamaica. That is, your identity as 'high school science teacher' was hidden instead of highlighted. Although these structural restraints were present, your sense of agency did not have to wither away. You would need to find new ways to access and appropriate the resources you had built over the years to meet newly formed goals.

STARTING AND MAINTAINING A RESEARCH AGENDA

As I began to consider how to conduct research, I believed that asking questions about science teacher education and what goes on in science methods courses would be of interest to the science education community. Hence, I looked toward connecting my teaching and research activities so that there would be an opportunity to gain the necessary publications expected of tenure track faculty at a research focused institution. After all, in my classes, I was learning from and with real preservice teachers and preparing them for an environment in which science was of utmost importance, evident in the calls for the reform emphasizing the development of a scientifically literate society. I partially rejected the notion of an "objective researcher" and fully accepted my role as a researcher making the "familiar strange and the strange familiar." My goal was to contribute to the knowledge of the process of learning to teach science. I therefore set out to develop my research agenda around the phenomenon of learning to teach science, within the context of my teaching science and science education to elementary education majors.

To build and maintain a presence in science education, each year, I would submit conference proposals to a number of science education organizations. At times, depending on the nature of my project, I would also send submissions to other organizations concerned with general teacher education or with technology. My observations at these conferences revealed that many colleagues were involved in collaborative activities. They worked on issues inter and intra universities and also with school districts. Further observation revealed that many of these links were formed with major professors during graduate school programs and continued beyond. Thus, it seemed that establishing an identity in science education was more than presenting at science education conferences. What was I missing? For one, I was missing collaboration and collegiality with others in the field. Secondly, the curt responses from journal reviewers inferred that I was not asking the kinds of questions that were publishable in national and international journals – my findings regarding my methods classes were not adding enough new knowledge, or the issues had already been extensively researched. Thus, while I was very interested in my research on how preservice teachers make sense of teaching science, I believed that the real evidence of their learning was in studying how such practices were translated into the classroom. Accordingly, I tentatively ventured to make connections in public school classrooms in an effort to investigate how the preservice teachers translated their learning into practice. Yet even as I attempted to develop a research agenda around these opportunities, I lacked the support to maintain prolonged involvement.

GRANT WRITING AS A RESOURCE

Support for research, what did that look like? I learned from some of my colleagues that procuring grants could allow for prolonged involvement in schools to facilitate my research interests. I was beginning to recognize the signs and symbols of such support to be reduced teaching loads (devoid of supervision of adjuncts and teaching assistants), research assistants and classes with low enrolments. My heavy teaching responsibilities were completely in opposition to what was ideal. How then could I compete and be successful in such a climate? What could I do or what did I need to do to receive the necessary support? More so, why should this be a competition? I remember reluctantly raising the issue and being told that there were two options, one was to get a job and negotiate these issues in the employment package and the other was to procure grants. I felt abused and really began to observe the inequities that I had worked with all these years and how they had constrained my development as a science educator.

As a high school teacher and later as a science educator in a teachers' college, the process of grant writing and its implication to support practice was not a part of my experience. Alone in my academic growth, I began to explore the process of writing grants and made submissions to the college for funding of classroom projects. I wrote several in-house grants, yet these were to develop curriculum to extend science education to some inservice teachers I had met through placement of my students in field experiences. I was successful on my first attempt and, though it was a small amount of $2000, I was elated. Sadly the money was not used. My project was to develop and implement a unit of study in a 5th grade classroom. I developed the unit, but did not ask request fiscal support. This clearly indicates my need for a mentor. In retrospect, I missed an important opportunity to become situated in a classroom outside of the university's science method course. I also did not know that a grant would mean I could be bought out of the labor-intensive teaching that had enveloped my every waking moment. Thus, I was virtually oblivious to how grants could allow me to focus on research that would be favorable to prestigious journals and top science educators.

Rowhea: Clearly central to the development and maintenance of a science educator identity in an academic position is the role of researcher. "Start your research agenda," new assistant professors are strongly advised. "You need to find the time to write," we are constantly reminded. "You don't have enough publications in the 'right' places," we are warned. Rose, while you and I know that we must conduct research, present at conferences and publish in prestigious journals, in actuality, the development of a research agenda is perhaps the most difficult part of an assistant professor position. There are issues of access both within the department, and outside of the university – moreover, financial support in the form of grants is often the catalyst for pushing forth a solid, productive research agenda. As you point out, Rose, the benefits of grant money are multiple; grants speak both to the research context you are attempting to join as well as to the university and department in terms of course load reduction and prestige. However, in addition to financial resources, collaboration and social networking with others (within your institution as well as with science educators in the field) is additionally powerful. Colleagues who can provide perspectives, advice and share experiences of how they began and built their own research efforts assist young scholars like you and I on our own journeys. Moreover, collaboration with senior professors invites new opportunities to join and/or contribute to existing research initiatives in ways that align with your own interests. In summary, Rose, your experiences illuminate that both human and fiscal resources are necessary for the development of a research program, and emphasize grant attainment as a symbol of status that opens other doors of opportunity.

FINALLY, BUILDING A RESEARCH PRESENCE

At times, what had been communicated, especially recently, was that teaching at my institution was third in line in terms of importance. For example, you could be a poorly rated teacher and still be acknowledged as contributing to the university's mission. Teaching fell behind research and attaining grants so when I was selected teacher of the year for a second time, it was hard for me to conceive of this as an actual achievement because teaching lacked currency and this was not communicated silently. I desperately tried and was able to maintain a publication rate of two to three per year, however, as I struggled with receiving reviews that viewed my research as simply classroom reports, and as a result I sought to become involved in other projects, situated in schools so that I ask research questions related to teaching and learning science and preparing teachers for the ever changing science classrooms.

I engaged principals and classroom teachers with whom I came in contact and some of my past students introduced me to their cooperating teachers and to their principals. However, in most cases, they all perceived their needs to be one or two workshops. These I gladly did, but I had my eyes set on more long time relationships. These were not forthcoming until fall 2003 when I was introduced to a principal in the county who said, "Welcome." I started out by observing one teacher, worked with her on developing her science curriculum and then volunteered to teach her three classes one day of the week. So I taught two days on campus and went into the 5th grade classrooms on Thursdays. The relationship blossomed with the 5th grade teacher who then introduced me to other colleagues; currently, I am comfortably placed in three classrooms. I used this opportunity to develop a five-week practicum for my preservice teachers. These classrooms provided the environment for the preservice teachers specializing in mathematics and science to translate their knowledge into action while allowing for discussion and reflection toward continuous improvement. My research agenda was taking shape. I was still able to explore the impact of science methods on preservice teachers' learning to teach science but could now track over time what happens as they move from the university classroom to the public school classroom.

Rowhea: The tensions you have delineated between teaching and research are very real and experienced by many in academia, particularly by beginning faculty members. It is not unusual that assistant professors may be given heavier teaching loads and courses that are not precisely aligned with her/his area of expertise. In your case Rose, you were given the elementary education courses with large class enrolments and teaching assistants to supervise. Time became a lacking resource that truncated your agency as a researcher. Regardless, the expectations of high quality research and publications for tenure remain high.

CODA

I do not doubt that I worked to my full potential with the resources and support provided by my institution. However, I feel sure that while I began with academic knowledge, I lacked the practical knowledge and skills to navigate the terrains of academia in a tenure track position. More so, I now realize that I started from an even further deficit as a female, Black, foreigner in a predominantly White middle class male dominant field. It has taken me six years to understand my position and to realize that the resources and rules I amassed over time were deficient for achieving full measure of success as a science educator. I also learned that hard work is not a precursor for success in academia. Moreover, I needed a mentor to help me learn the rules of academia – to be able to understand the university's expectations, and the implicit rules of becoming and establishing myself as a science educator while fulfilling the requirements to become tenured.

Rowhea: Rose, through your autobiographical account of your journey to academia and within the first six years of a tenure track assistant professor position, you have shared a window into the countless moments of success and strife that individuals may face, and made transparent the fragile and shifting nature of some aspects of identity. You have in many ways become conscious of what previously has been within the unconscious realm, as you interacted in academic life on this journey. That is, through cycles of becoming "aware," you have recognized what was "missing" and actively sought to obtain those resources. This access and subsequent utilization of the resources you had acquired constitutes your strong sense of agency, and despite the challenges you faced, you exercised empowering practices time and time again. In addition, you continuously found new ways to look at the context you are within so as to meet both personal goals and university expectations (e.g., increasing publication opportunities by linking your research agenda to your courses – since your teaching load was so heavy); this also reveals your agency as a science educator.

In conclusion, while your story often refers back to your commitments to an achievement ideology, you have clearly indicated that successful navigation of academic waters requires more than "hard work." Rather it requires the creative ingenuity and insight into the structural arrangements of the social realms in which one participates, and engaging in purposeful actions to ensure the garnering and acquisition of those tools that will allow one to move strategically towards tenure. This awareness is especially central for female women from underrepresented ethnic and racial groups. Rose, thank you for sharing the "rites of passage" that you have encountered in becoming a tenured associate professor so that I and other women in marginalized positions can learn, grow and continually become as science educators.

REFERENCES

MacLeod, J. (1995). *Ain't no makin' it: Aspirations and attainment in a low-income neighborhood.* Boulder, CO: Westview Press.

Roth, W.-M. (2006). Identity as dialectic: Re/making of self in urban schooling. In J. L. Kincheloe, k. hayes, K. Rose, & P. M. Anderson (Eds.), *The Praeger handbook of urban education* (pp. 143–153). U.K./Europe: Praeger Publishers.

Sewell, W. H. (1992). A theory of structure: Duality, agency, and transformation. *American Journal of Sociology, 98*, 1–29.

AFFILIATIONS

Rose Pringle
School of Teaching and Learning,
College of Education,
University of Florida

Rowhea Elmesky
Department of Education,
Faculty of Arts and Sciences,
Washington University in St. Louis

GALE SEILER AND SUSAN M. BLUNCK

4. BETWEEN THE EDGES AND SEAMS OF IDENTITY

THE INVITATION

Susan: It started with this invitation: Do you want to write a book chapter with me on women in science education? "What women will we write about?" I asked. "Us," my colleague replied. My first reaction, though I kept it to myself, was who would want to read a chapter about us–two former P-12 teachers turned science educators/researchers? After some reflection, the invitation became more appealing. Gale suggested that we take hold of the opportunity to reflect on our evolving identities and our perspectives on knowledge, authority, and ways of knowing. To be truthful, I was a bit overwhelmed by it all but eager to take on the challenge.

By embracing this invitation, we committed to opening ourselves up to the possibility of getting to know each other and ourselves in deeper and more personal ways. The journey we took in writing this chapter involved thinking, talking, analyzing, and writing about our experiences becoming science educators in different places at different times. We have paused thoughtfully along the way to analyze the transitions and turns we took in arriving at our current destinations as faculty members in science education at the same university.

The edges to our stories may seem ragged and contradictory, but the unraveling of identity is not an even, logical, or obviously connected process. Socio-cultural theorists suggest that each experience we have changes our perspectives on the narratives that comprise our personal histories. We kept the words of Alan Lightman, MIT physicist/essayist/novelist, in mind as we struggled to coherently organize our ideas for this chapter. "If the essayist has all the answers, then he isn't struggling to grasp, and I won't either. When you care about something, you continually grapple with it, because it is alive in you. It thrashes and moves, like all living things...the facts are important but never enough. An essay, for me, must go past the facts, an essay must travel and move" (Lightman & Atwan, 2000, p. xii). We invite our readers to take a look at what stories are alive within us at this time in our lives.

Although these are stories from our lives, they are also stories of academic and science culture, of the ways women's trajectories are dialectically linked with and shaped by aspects of structure. So while the stories are a part of our autobiography (written by each of us), they can also be read as a biography (written by others) within the academic arena. That is not to say that all young women coming into science had experiences such as ours (although many do), but rather that our interests, points of view, and identities are all constituted socially in similar ways.

K. Scantlebury, J. Butler Kahle and S. N. Martin (eds.) Re-visioning Science Education from Feminist Perspectives: Challenges, Choices and Careers, 37–46.

Thus, stories in a narrator's voice, such as ours, tell about culture and the social world just as they tell about individual lives. Women "are in part fashioned and yet also fashion themselves in historically and culturally specific ways." (Holland & Lave, 2001, p. 5).

FINDING WAYS INTO SCIENCE

Access to Science

Though much of science was closed off to us while growing up, to some extent we didn't even know that was case, because the ideas of glass ceilings and gender discrimination were not yet in the public eye. As young girls, of us attended all-girl high schools and found our way into science without much struggle, because everyone took science courses and did the science work; there were no boys to defer to in handling equipment and doing lab activities.

Gale: My familiarity with science grew from my relationship with Aunt Kate who was a nurse. Of my mother and father's 12 siblings, she was the only one who finished high school. Because I appeared to be headed in the direction of academic achievement and college (a first for my family and neighborhood), she became my role model; she was a professional woman–the only one I knew. She paid the tuition, which my parents could not afford, so I could attend a selective girls' high school in a nearby city. Thus, my aunt provided access to a storyline of myself with an education and a career and provided a way into science by helping me study science topics and carry out science fair projects. With her help I excelled in school and in science, but my vision of possibilities of what to do with my education was limited, so pursuing medical school never was considered, and when I chose my first college major, it was nursing.

Susan: I became interested in science in high school during the late 1960s and early 1970s. Every student in my all-girl Catholic high school was expected to take some science, and most of us took 4 years of science as part of the college prep curriculum. Our science courses were part of the 'preparation for life' that the school provided. I remember questioning how science could prepare us for life when, it seemed to me that, very little of the content taught in our science courses connected to the real world. I thought this was absurd as we were living in a society that abounded with advances in science and technology on the upside of the Sputnik era, where every other TV and newspaper ad was focused on better living through science. When I asked my teachers how the science we were learning connected to the real world, they responded, "Just wait, the connections will become clear as you take more science courses." They said it in a mystical, magical, and secretive way that kept me intrigued. So I went on to college, took more science courses, and still failed to find the connections to the real world. I was perplexed and truly thought something was wrong with me. I began to doubt my abilities in science even though my grades were acceptable. How did I miss seeing the science connections that my most respected and knowledgeable high school teachers assured me would be apparent? Maybe they were wrong or just didn't know; or maybe I just needed to take more science classes.

In many ways, we are not authors of our own thoughts, since our perceptions of self and our ways of viewing our place in the world are shaped and constrained by our experiences. These experiences influence the possibilities we envision for thought and action, as our agency and structural forces (both material and human) interact in a dialectic whole (Sewell, 1992). We can begin to understand the agency we have garnered or failed to garner in relation to historical structures of the time brought into the local, situated practice in which we participated. Though we gained initial entry to the world of science with relative ease, by virtue of our schooling, something did not fit for each of us. What things have contributed to our agency, and what constraints have truncated our agency as women in science, in P-12 education and in higher education? How have we re/constituted those structures and ourselves?

WRONG PLACE AT THE WRONG TIME

Gale: The slow methodical voice on the radio rattled me but I could not recall why. As I listened to the NPR report, the story lost it's meaning as I struggled to recognize the voice. "Possible effects of global warming" ... "Plants flowering earlier than ever before" ... "Ranuculus"... "Montana" ... I got it. I knew that voice. It was the voice of my major professor when I attended graduate school long ago with the intention of obtaining a doctorate in plant ecology. At first when I heard his voice, I felt sadness. A sense of loss often returned when I thought of my failed attempt to obtain a doctorate when I was in my 20s. A discouraged feeling arose when I counted all the credits accumulated in courses such as mycology and plant physiology and remembered the hours spent collecting data and identifying grass sprouts and vegetative re-growth in a blackened forest in Montana. But then I chuckled at that little voice that had once scared me to death, and I rejoiced that I had moved on, that I was not still studying the same plants in Montana (not that Montana and its mountains are not spectacularly beautiful). He must be ancient by now, I thought, since he seemed ancient then, when I was fresh out of my undergraduate studies. And he's still in Montana; his office is probably in the same location in the botany building and his workspace is probably still a mess. He is likely doing the same research on post-fire vegetation recovery, I mused. Hadn't he learned everything there is to know about it by now? But what I really wanted to know was how many other female doctoral candidates had this professor discouraged or intimidated into another field? I left the doctoral program after completing all the coursework and collecting all my field data. Instead I became a high school science teacher and many years later obtained my Ph.D. in science education. As I heard his voice I wanted to phone him and say, "See all that I have done, all that I have accomplished, the places I have been, the lives I have shaped ... because you thought women shouldn't be field biologists in Montana!" Perhaps I should actually thank that big man with the small voice that had once bellowed at me, when I was too young to roar back.

Susan: While in college, I came to some profound realizations. Even though teachers/professors alluded to real world connections in science classes very few students could see and understand them, and most were afraid to admit it. Professors often made a statement like, "I am sure all of you see how this concept connects to the production nuclear energy." In response to these comments, usually added at the end of the class, all the heads in lecture hall bobbed in agreement, but they really didn't understand the connections and in many cases neither did the professor. I realized that part of being a talented student was acting like you understood. I could certainly act that way – but why when I didn't understand? My mistake was asking my science professors to help make the connections clearer as I really wanted to try and apply what I was learning. As a result, in my freshman year of college, I was quickly bumped off my physics professor's list of promising students and labeled one of 'those' female students. I realized then that I was asking the professors to help me understand something that they didn't fully understand themselves. It became vividly clear that interacting with female students was a very new experience for science professors at a Big 10, Midwestern university–especially in physics. What was happening here and why was this a different experience than high school? Where were all my girl friends? I called my mother and a few friends, vented to them, and the next day switched my major to nursing. But the thing that I regret most is letting down my high school teachers who really believed that women could do good science. They just did not realize how hard it would be.

What was it about Gale's advisor that scared her away? It is impossible to know for sure, except to say that it was the way the relations developed. Holland and Lave (2001) remind us that relations are not static or fixed, nor can they be pre-determined or planned. Often they cannot be accomplished without tension. What was it about Susan that led her to question the applicability of the way science was taught and for her professors to label her in a negative way? At this early age, both of us found that we were not equipped for the contentious practice over positions, which often unfolds in male-dominated science communities around gender differences, so we retreated. We now understand that specific events and power relations have different meanings depending on "the ways of interpreting the world" (Weedon, 1987) that are available to a woman at any particular time, but we did not have that awareness then. Instead we felt that some essential part of us did not fit into pure science. It is understandable that our identities unraveled to some extent, because science excellence and interest had been vital parts of our autobiographies and of how we positioned ourselves up to that point in our young lives.

As many science students still do, we sought shelter in a place where a woman's way of knowing and being (Belenky, Clinchy, Goldberger, & Tarule, 1986) were more positively valued and honored. We fell victim to status quo views of women in science that permeated society in the 1960's and into the 70s, as we both ended up as nursing majors and then teachers. But while we both initially followed the most traditional career opportunities open to women in science, we did not stop there. We found our way into these careers but then through them to other opportunities after teaching in elementary and high schools for a number of years.

A woman's "sense of herself and her ways of understanding her relation to the world" (Weedon, 1987, p. 32) are not fixed and coherent. Rather this sense of who we are is precarious, contradictory, and always in process. Although we were in some ways outcasts of pure science, we were able to repair the damage, darn the hole in the sock, and keep moving ahead.

FINDING WAYS THROUGH

Susan: I had to meet with the Dean of Nursing for an exit interview, when I decided to change my major. "You want to become a teacher and you're switching your major to education?" the dean asked me. "Yes, that is what I am going to do," I replied. "Personally, I do not think that you are making a good decision as there is an over abundance of teachers. Do you know how hard it will be to get a teaching job?" the dean challenged. "I am going to have two specialty certifications when I finish the education program—one in elementary science and the other in early childhood education. I'll get a job." I replied confidently. And I did.

Gale: The second time around in a doctoral program, my advisor, Kenneth Tobin at the University of Pennsylvania, was very different from the first one. Ken valued tremendously my experiences of high school teaching, and immediately saw me as one who could work with him in exploring urban classrooms in Philadelphia and help to generate some understanding of what was happening in them. Within my first week in the doctoral program on a walk from the high school back to the Graduate School of Education, Ken asked, "So what are you going to do research on?" He didn't mean when I finished my course work or when I started my Ph.D. research in two or three years; he meant right then. And so I began. Ken lived his belief in 'no master narrative', so he was not encumbered by linear expectations of coursework before research involvement, or by labels of teacher, learner, or researcher. I was all three, as was he. He saw many of the traditional structures within the graduate school and wider academic ideologies as senseless and truncating agency, and he worked to counter them and to create opportunities for agentic experiences for me, the other graduate students, and the high school students and teachers at the nearby school as they were drawn into our research. I say 'our research' because I really felt that, together with Ken, I owned it and shaped it in those early days at City High.

Susan: After teaching science in elementary and middle school, I was nominated by my principal for a special teacher leadership program in Iowa City – The Iowa Chautauqua Program. I had done workshops in the district but had never gone out of town to spend two weeks away from home. I went to the workshop the following summer, and it changed my life forever. There was something very different about the experience. Dr. Robert Yager interacted with us in a way that was new to all of us. He wanted to know our questions and ideas on improving science teaching and wanted us to start studying our teaching practices. He said he needed our help in figuring out the hard questions related to effective science teaching. We all were a bit stunned by the fact that he appeared to not have all the answers. I wondered: Why does he need our help? Is he just pretending?

During my first Chatauqua workshop, Dr. Yager asked me to read a report he had been given to review. I really thought he was just being nice as it related to my background. I took it home, read it, and gathered some thoughts to share if he asked about it. He asked me about the report the next morning. I'll never forget how he responded to my comments. He turned to me and said, "I never would have thought about it that way. Those are really good points for me to consider." I was hooked. I became a lead teacher in the program, and five years later I went back to study with Dr. Yager as a doctoral student and ended up as the co-director of the program.

Why did each of us feel so empowered and welcomed when we ventured back into academia later in our careers as teachers? Both of us agree that our mentors were key in affording us agency and making these transitions productive and transformative, both personally and professionally. And they did it through participation with us; as Lave and Wenger (1991) note, participation dissolves dichotomies. Thus, there was no longer a contradiction between our roles as teacher and learner, teacher and researcher, or novice and expert. Clearly, these knowledgeable men were our mentors, but with them we were also near-peers since we had knowledge and 'ways of knowing' as classroom teachers that they were removed from. Both Tobin and Yager altered the activity structures to provide us with different kinds of resources, such as collaborative projects, coauthoring, and other opportunities to take on new roles. They changed the discourse between professor and student in ways that shaped our learning possibilities and perspectives. In different ways, we each were able to create new identities, different perceptions of self, and ways of viewing ourselves in academia that were not available to us when we had our earlier experiences in botany and physics. Tobin and Yager seemed to understand "...(i)dentities as long-term, living relations between persons and their place and participation in communities of practice. Thus identity, knowing, and social membership entail one another" (Lave & Wenger, 1991, p. 53).

IDENTITY (RE)FORMATION: REPAIR, REINFORCE, AND REPLACE

Identity is commonly thought of in one of two ways–either as a core, inner, self-identity held by each person or as a persona or image that is presented to others. But identity is both of those and more. Identity is shaped by a dialectical relationship between who we are for ourselves and who we are for others, and it entails all the space and motion in between these two parts of the whole. Each autobiography (written by self) is thus also a biography (written by others) because our personal narratives are shaped in interactions as we form and re-form our personal storylines each time we enact parts of them or make them public (Giddens, 1991). As we offer aspects of ourselves in a social realm, we are involved in reflexive work on our identity that is fueled by what happens during social interactions; that is, by what kind of response we get when we 'put ourselves out there' and by how others see us. When these efforts are not responded to positively, our agency is truncated and our identities are often contorted, as happened with Susan in her college physics class and with Gale and her plant ecology advisor. Although it continually occurs, we see more evidence of this reflexive identity (re)formation at transition points, such as, when someone is learning to do something new; that is, learning to be someone new or to participate in a new field. At these transition and contestation points, we often rely on the more robust, previously integrated identity pieces that have been with us to that point.

Gale: The blackboard in the cold damp, cellar of the house where I grew up served as the site where my Aunt Bee repeatedly played the role of student as I played teacher. This was truly an act of love, because my aunt had not finished eighth grade and struggled with the spelling, math, and reading tasks I expected of her. Does this help to understand why it was so much more likely that I would obtain a teaching certificate rather than a Ph.D. in botany during those years immediately following my undergraduate schooling? Prior storylines positioned me as a good student in an all-girls Catholic school but not to emerge successfully from the contentious relations with my botany advisor. Although an excellent student throughout the years, at 25 I was not yet prepared to tackle the negotiation needed in this identity (re)formation that involved gender conflicts. Instead I became a teacher, because school had been my place of success.

Contradictions are inherent in practice and the conflict between Gale's interest in science, her experiences with her first doctoral advisor, and her early practice as a teacher contributed to the development of her identity. As Lave and Wenger describe, "Learning thus implies becoming a different person with respect to the possibilities enabled by the system of relations (1991, p. 53), and this is what we do when we transition from one type of practice to another. Although the Dean of Nursing saw Susan's science ability being wasted if she became a teacher, Susan found a way to resolve this contradiction and to allow it to shape her identity in a positive way and to transform her practice as a teacher.

Susan: My first teaching assignment was in second grade in the elementary school I had attended. The first day of the job, my teaching partner turned to me and said, "I am so glad you are here. Here is how it is going to work. You will teach all the science, and I will teach all the social studies. Very few of us like teaching science, so we're counting on you to help us learn more." I just might be able to make a difference at this school. This was the first time I felt like a real science teacher. We learned a lot together over my 15-year tenure at the school.

UNRAVELING AND MENDING THE FABRIC

In weaving, the warp is the lengthwise threads, under and over which the side-to-side threads–the weft–are woven. If our identities are a fabric, what is that fabric like? We think of it as a patchwork of many pieces like an irregular collection of overlapping fabrics of many colors, patterns, and textures that represent our multiple identities. According to Holland and Lave, "any person or group is likely to have multiple selves, and the 'self' of a person is difficult to distinguish from the 'self' of the group." (2001, p. 128). Envision a woven fabric, in places coarsely woven with thick yarn and fiber and in other places finely woven with thin silken thread. It is not a solid, continuous piece of weaving but rather constructed over time on a loom that is multi-dimensional and complex so that the fabric is made of sections woven at different times, collectively, and in different directions but somehow connected and sharing warp and weft fibers at the intersections and overlapping areas. The fabric is stunning in its colors and textures, but it does not reside in a frame on a wall or in a museum case. It is a functional cloth that is frequently put to use as we move through the social world; and it shows evidence of mending and unraveling, which lend beauty, uniqueness, and even strength to the fabric.

Often to enlarge the cloth or to add a new section, edges must unravel to allow the attachment and intermeshing between the new and the old warp and weft. This situation occurred when Susan seized the opportunity shape the science program of the elementary school. Sometimes we might not remember where a woven patch came from or when it was incorporated into the cloth, but it is there and it may later be connected with another part or be called upon to hold the cloth together. We can see this in Gale's return to the childhood teaching part of her identity, when she felt turned away by science.

At other times, a section is severely damaged or even ripped out by some force. But although it might be traumatic, the cloth is not beyond repair. The cloth was woman-made, and thus it can be re-made. There is no core or essence that, once destroyed, cannot be re-built (Weedon, 1987). This view of identity is perhaps less certain and reassuring than other views, but it captures the transformative power of women's dynamic sense of self.

Gale: Despite growing up in an urban area of northern New Jersey, about a 20-minute train ride from Manhattan, I developed a love of nature and a deep wonder about natural science. I don't remember too many specifics from my high school science classes, but I do remember that I had the opportunity to take an anatomy and physiology class in which we dissected cats. Soon after that, while driving in a more suburban area with my high school boyfriend, we came across a raccoon that had been killed by a car. Something compelled me to put the raccoon in the trunk and take it home to study. My family watched with horror as I carried the dead raccoon through the narrow alley that ran between our house and my uncle's house next door into the small backyard. With a knife that my grandmother refused to ever allow back into the kitchen, I examined and subsequently skinned the raccoon, stretching the hide out on a board and nailing it in place. Relying on something I had learned about how Native Americans preserved animal skins, I salted the skin and day after day scraped off the old salt and added fresh, until the hide was reasonably well preserved. Though lost now, I kept that hide for many years as a reminder that it was all right to pursue unusual interests, to go to unusual lengths to satisfy my curiosity, and, most importantly, to proceed even when I was unsure about exactly how to do something. That same feeling fueled me years later, when I applied to graduate school in botany with the intention of studying plant ecology in Montana. What did this city girl know about plant ecology? And again when I moved from 16 years of high school science teaching to the University of Pennsylvania for a doctorate in education. What did this classroom teacher know about education research and Ivy League schools? I was not at all certain. But I did know that as a 'city girl' with no knowledge of animals and nature, I had figured out to successfully skin a raccoon and to preserve its hide!

Susan: Every teacher should teach kindergarten for at least a day. I spent 5 years of my life building a model all-day kindergarten program with a science focus. Five-year-old people intuitively understand the nature of science. They are experts at asking questions and, once they are hooked on a question, will pursue their interests with great passion. My most rewarding days teaching science were at that level. I began to see the power of curiosity and not knowing, when I taught kindergarten students.

With each step, leap, curve, and detour we have repaired tears, reinforced seams, replaced lost pieces, and picked up new threads and materials to try and incorporate into the fabric of our identities. Two common threads that we have found between us are the curiosity to question things around us (both natural and synthetic, both in science and the social world) and the determination to try to answer our questions, and these attitudes have fueled our identity (re)construction throughout our lives. We can recount this curiosity and drive from our childhoods and recognize it in the students we teach. The re-telling of these life stories has enabled us to re-experience them as we represent them here in text. Through this process, at times overt as in coauthoring this chapter and at other times less conscious as we reflect on our experiences, we have further transformed our identities since the actual quest for self and voice changes us and our ways of knowing (Belenky, et al., 1986).

Susan: Our new research center for STEM Education is having its official opening tomorrow afternoon. For the past ten years, when anyone asked what I was doing, I would say that we were creating a center. Everyone smiled politely and often replied, "We can't see it. Where is it?" "Hang in there, you will," was my reply. Gale always provided encouragement with her grin and 'go for it, girl' nod. The center existed in our minds and spirits long before we had the physical space. We have questions that we are ready to research, projects to implement, grants to write, and the courage to tackle the hard work that this entails. If they could see us now!

REFERENCES

Belenky, M. F., Clinchy, B. M., Goldberger, N. R., & Tarule, J. M. (1986). *Woman's ways of knowing: The development of self, voice, and mind.* New York: Basic Books Inc.

Giddens, A. (1991). *Modernity and self-identity.* Stanford, CA: Stanford University Press.

Holland, D., & Lave, J. (2001). History in person: An introduction. In D. Holland & J. Lave (Eds.), *History in person* (pp. 3–33). Santa Fe, NM: School of American Research Press.

Lave, J., & Wenger, E. (1991). *Situated learning: Legitimate peripheral participation.* Cambridge, UK: Cambridge University Press.

Lightman, A., & Atwan, R. (Eds.). (2000). *The best American essays.* New York: Houghton Mifflin Company.

Sewell, W. H. (1992). A theory of structure: Duality, agency, and transformation. *American Journal of Sociology, 98,* 1–29.

Weedon, C. (1987). *Feminist practice and poststructuralist theory.* Cambridge, MA: Blackwell Publishers.

AFFILIATIONS

Gale Seiler
Department of Integrated Studies in Education,
McGill University

Susan Blunck
Department of Education,
University of Maryland Baltimore County

MOLLY WEINBURGH AND BAMBI BAILEY

5. PARALLEL BUT PERPENDICULAR PATH

INTRODUCTION

As feminists we believe that, when given a 'voice', every woman has important and meaningful things to say about the disjunctures in her life and her personal/public struggle for change. This chapter serves as our voice in the form of an auto/biography in which our experiences represent a continuum within which women may place their experiences. Although our paths intersected in 1990, we have been traveling parallel paths for most of our lives. When you look at us from one perspective we appear to have, and actually DO have, a high position in what Michel Foucault (1980) calls the 'power/knowledge' system. We are White, middle-class, intelligent, U.S. citizens. But, we are also women who have an interest in science and who have seen/felt the lack of 'power/knowledge' in our academic lives.

We are aware that during the journey we describe 'center and margin shifts' (hooks, 1984), bringing us, at times, into the center with its privilege and power and, at other times, pushing us to the margins with its lack of privilege and power. Our story is not unique. You can hear much the same refrain from many of our peers. However, by foregrounding the lack of power we found along the journey, we may begin to reduce its prevalence for those newly embarking on an academic journey in science education.

THE JOURNEY BEGINS – UNDERGRADUATE EXPERIENCES

On the surface we followed very similar paths, especially at the beginning of our careers. We both attended old, southern schools with many old, southern traditions. One had begun as a single sex teacher's college that evolved into a co-ed state university and the other was still a single sex private college. Both institutions were in transition as old rules were revoked, minority students recruited, and young faculty employed. Looking back, we (Bambi and Molly) see a parallel between our institutions and ourselves. Our institutions and we were Southern ladies who were proud of our heritage and our traditions. We loved who we were while realizing that change was in the air and that we wanted to be a part of the change in ways that would help shape a better future.

We are aware that we owe much to the women's movement of the 1960s and 1970s. The personal/public struggles of these women opened doors for us to even consider a major in science. Both of us recall shifting climates in which the

K. Scantlebury, J. Butler Kahle and S. N. Martin (eds.) Re-visioning Science Education from Feminist Perspectives: Challenges, Choices and Careers, 47–55.

extremes were either very chilly (Hall & Sandler, 1986; Morris, 2003; Sandler & Hall, 1982) or nicely warm; times when we were in the center and times when we were on the margin. Interesting conflicts occurred regularly when the extremes collided.

Any undergraduate experience has both a personal and an educational (public) component. Reflecting on these facets of our undergraduate lives, we both experienced practices that could have prevented us from majoring in science. For example, on the personal side, both of us had immediate family who supported our choices and even encouraged us to continue to study in the areas that had captured our love but cultural norms as expressed by extended family, friends and professors gave different messages. We were often asked why we would want to major in science. We remember many occasions when marriage was the topic and the implication was that women, even very smart women, should be working toward marriage. This naturally caused some conflict for each of us as we struggled to reconcile personal needs and desires with social norms.

On the educational side, there appears to be more variance in our experiences but the underlying message still seemed to be that science was not the major of nice, southern ladies. Bambi's experience included more overtly sexist aspects. On the one hand, she had a male mentor who openly encouraged her and other female students. This chemistry professor and his wife became her mentors. In fact, he asked her and three other students to go to Florida State University the summer after her first year to do research with him as he regularly did to provide undergraduate research experiences and to broaden their ideas of what science really was. The professor made appointments for his students with a variety of faculty members in different areas of chemistry so that they could tell the students about their research and what it entailed. By the end of the summer, Bambi was actually considering changing her major to chemistry.

On the other hand, another chemistry professor changed her goal, but not her interest, forever. This organic chemistry professor opened class saying that two things he hated in his class were biology majors and women. He noted that the only thing he hated worse than those were women majoring in science on scholarship because they, "would only graduate, get married and make babies after taking money from a good man." As a female biology major on a National Merit scholarship, Bambi was at the bottom of the barrel although she ended up with a great deal of company there. One day when a female, African-American student missed a question the professor asked her, "What do you think you're going to do, get in medical school because you're a Black woman and then kill someone because you can't answer a question?" This certainly made the climate chilly for a variety of students including Bambi.

Mixed messages such as these appeared in Molly's undergraduate experience. However, her experience was much more covert. Publicly, her single sex college advocated that women could excel but undercurrents of sexism could be observed. A female biology professor was Molly's mentor. The professor's office was always overflowing with books and papers as well as love and encouragement for students. Almost every discussion resulted with her going to the bookshelf, pulling down a book, and saying 'This is one of my favorites' as she used it in some instructional way. The truth is that all of her books were her favorite. While all the other biology majors were thinking of applying to graduate school, Molly was taking electives that would allow her to teach biology at the high school level. The professor did not try to discourage her or change her mind. As Molly's advisor on her senior thesis, the professor continued to influence her intellectual growth while encouraging her to be herself. On the other hand, although this professor had a doctorate and spent her summers at Woods Hole, she was never addressed as "Dr. X". However, all the male professors were addressed as "Dr." At first, Molly did not think that this was strange, perhaps because she did not understand about academic rank. However, as she looks back on those years, she remembers conversations with peers about why their female professors were not given the academic title they had earned. Why were the men, even very young professors, given this open acknowledgment of a terminal degree when the well-established women were not? Both authors still observe this kind of differentiation in naming male and female professors among students today.

Both of us graduated with degrees in biology and became biology teachers. The choice to become teachers moved us from a place in the margins in science to a more central place in the world of teaching. Choosing a more stereotypical profession eased the concerns of extended family and friends although the choice to teach science to high school students still raised questions.

THE JOURNEY CONTINUES – TEACHING HIGH SCHOOL

As with any transition from being a student to being a professional, significant changes occurred in our lives. During this period, the students were the outside force that we most remember. We were aware that they differed from our extended family and college peers regarding our professional and personal choices. Our students did not have a problem with our academic decision to major in biology, but rather, found our personal decisions to be more unsettling. They saw our unmarried status as pushing us to the margins of southern culture. Some examples of these concerns are highlighted in conversations described below. Bambi recalls the day that three senior boys took it upon themselves to explain what they perceived as a problem. They kindly, but purposefully, informed her that she was too confident and straightforward, thereby scaring away any prospective husband. In their opinions, a woman needed a husband to 'center' her and by behaving in an assertive manner, she would never find a proper husband. Molly recalls an on-going conversation with an African-American female who was very concerned about Molly's unmarried state. The young student would often ask, "Who will make sure you get a proper burial if you do not have children?"

This also played out in the reactions of some of the parents. Molly has a vivid memory of teaching the son of a professor who had emigrated from India. The son was not performing well, and she requested a parent conference. The father refused to come, saying to her, "You are only a woman. My son does not have to listen to any women." Bambi describes several instances when her students tried to introduce her to their recently divorced fathers in a matchmaking scheme and similar fathers who asked their children if she would be a suitable date.

We see these as evidence that students could more easily accept our desire to participate in the scientific community than they could accept our lack of concern for social norms. It is possible that our students were more open to females entering non-traditional fields because the impact of the feminist movement had been a part of their entire lives. In addition, another possible explanation for our students' lack of concern for our chosen field would be that they perceived us as 'teachers' rather than as 'scientists'. For years teaching has been an accepted profession for a woman so it moved us to the center of cultural expectations.

We did not know one another at this point in our lives, but many of the same forces were working on us. As science teachers we had a foot in two worlds. We gained professional power as teachers of science, a field associated with higher status in schools. However, in the world in general, our position as a teacher lessened our personal power due to the gendered nature of the position and the low economic return for our labor. We were single women teaching biology. District wide, female science teachers were still in the minority resulting in a general lack of mentors. However, we did have other women in our science departments. We loved our discipline, adored teaching, and enjoyed our students. For both of us, interactions with others who questioned our abilities, and our decision to stay single, shaped our thoughts about feminist ideas and social responsibilities. Without female mentors each of us found our way toward wanting to teach science and create a classroom culture in which equity was paramount.

THE ROAD LESS TRAVELED – GRADUATE SCHOOL

We were encouraged for different reasons to continue our education beyond the baccalaureate. Bambi entered a masters program to get her initial certification. She can still see her university mentor leaning back in his chair with arms crossed saying, "So, when are you going to think about your doctoral program?" Molly vividly recalls being called into her principal's office and asked for proof that she had enrolled in graduate school. He informed her that without such proof she would not be offered a third year contract. As each of us decided to pursue a doctorate, Bambi did not feel constrained to a geographic location and therefore was open to the suggestion that she look for the doctoral program that best fit her interests. Her mentor recognized that she focused on equity issues in the classrooms in which she observed. He arranged for Bambi to meet Dr. Jane Butler Kahle, one of the most well-known and respected researchers in gender equity and science education. As a result of meeting Dr. Kahle, Bambi applied for and was admitted into Miami University. There she was enculturated into the science education community.

Molly's selection of a doctoral program was based on immediate need. In fact she made inquiry to the public university in Atlanta but had missed the deadline for summer admission. Her inquiries at Emory University were met with more flexibility. Although she had missed their deadline as well, Dr. Richard was able to find a way to meet her needs. The bottom line was that she was accepted into the graduate program and began to take classes that summer. Dr. Richard then recommended that she continue with her doctorate.

Based on our selections we had very different experiences. These experiences at the extremes of the continuum may still resonate with many women and reflect their experiences. In order to enhance the clarity and juxtapose our position, we have chosen to personally describe our stories in the first person.

BAMBI

It was interesting to think back and remember how independent and strong my students thought I was and then remember going to school to get a doctorate. Compared to the very strong women with whom I interacted, I was like the students who came to my room when I was Resident Assistant in college crying because they did not have a boyfriend and that was the only reason their parents sent them to college. I was backward, asked permission too much, apologized too much, missed appropriate opportunities to apologize because I was trying to do it less, and questioned my own judgment. However, I was essentially bathed in a blend of feminism, friendship, intellectual discussions, tough love and hard truths. I met strong women in a variety of fields, most not the traditional purview of women, who acted as role models and clarified my ideas about women in the world. I was in an intellectual, feminist developmental womb where I could propose ideas, argue, agree, disagree, etc. In this world it was perfectly normal for me to be in science and science education and to be outspoken about ideas. Just outside the door to the office suite and down the hall, though, there existed a world that was intolerant of those vehemently against outspoken women.

Two powerful men in the department in question, joined to eliminate a female assistant professor who conducted research in their field from a feminist viewpoint. She lived the personal is the political in a variety of ways. She dressed casually to say the least when teaching. It was not unusual to see her in zebra striped leggings, a hot pink tee shirt with feminist slogans and large colorful earrings hanging almost to her shoulders. She didn't "schedule" her pregnancy as others did but had her baby in the middle of the semester - a baby she breast fed in class if her teaching schedule did not accommodate the baby's feeding schedule. She fought the allegations of uncollegiality; but because of her difference, her lack of power in the field or in the department, and her naiveté about or disregard for the political machinations within a College of Education, she lost. I was amazed, horrified and confused. I mourned the day that she asked me to go shopping with her to look for a "black, navy blue or gray suit for interviews" because she had finally decided that in order to teach the students who needed to be educated about equity issues she had to "play the game" at least until she got tenure. I wondered to myself how she would keep up the pretense long enough to get tenured. I also wondered what the reaction would be once she remembered herself after tenure if she could still remember the person she was. She wasn't hired during the last year of my doctoral work and was considering other avenues when I left.

How could such a thing happen among supposedly intelligent people – people who were trained that multiple viewpoints are desirable? Deep in my heart, in hindsight, while listening to my mentors about the danger she faced and how common such danger was, I think I regarded this as an aberration, something that didn't, couldn't, happen often among university colleagues.

After I graduated, I was lucky enough to continue my personal womb-like existence when a post-doctoral research associate ship opened up with one my friends and mentors from graduate school. Again, I was in what she called "rarified air" and, to use a trite phrase, continued to bloom. I learned more about research and about the questions scientists have about those in science education as I watched my mentor work toward tenure. She met every challenge they put to her, and after I had left, received tenure. The research in which we were involved required significant work with middle and high school science teachers. I was able to meet more strong women in science education at that level and to learn their stories as well as those of university level women. Their stories included widowhood, child raising, loss of a child, and career challenges regarding lack of mentors at the administrative level. This environment of supportive women saw me through medical emergencies and job searching and then it was gone.

MOLLY

Although Emory University was well known and had highly respected graduate programs, the Division of Education was very small. The Ph.D. awarded in education was Educational Leadership with an emphasis in a discipline. I was the only person with an emphasis in science education for the first three years I was at Emory. During my last year, another student declared science as the major emphasis. By the time I entered graduate school, I knew that I was interested in equity issues in science and science education with an emphasis on women's equity issues. My mentor was a man. During his doctoral program he married a fellow doctoral student who was a feminist. They had 'lived' some of the inequities for women in graduate school and in higher education. This history prepared him to work with females in a way that was somewhat unique. When I first began working with him, he did not have tenure. He was generous in showing his graduate students how he was positioning his research and teaching in order to make a case for tenure. The year he submitted his tenure brief, I think that I was more afraid of a negative verdict than was he. As the months passed without word from the committee, I was the one with sleepless nights. I worried for him as well as for myself – what would I do if he was forced to seek a position elsewhere? What would happen to the research that had begun? The day he informed me of a positive review and continued employment at Emory, I cried.

One of my duties as a graduate student was to open the computer lab on Saturday mornings and lock it on Saturday night. Dr. Engelhard liked to work on his scholarship on Saturday so he and I met every week at 10:30. This was our time to discuss research (both his and mine), lay out a plan for the following week, debate the pros and cons of teaching methodologies, and argue the fine points of a book. I took this one-on-one mentoring for granted and did not fully appreciate it until I began to attend professional meetings. At the National Association for Research in Science Teaching (NARST) and the Association of Science Teacher Educators (ASTE), I discovered that all female graduate students did not have the same level of mentoring. I lamented that I was not in a big department with lots of science education research until I saw the lack of guidance some of the students received. I did not have a science education research community but I soon decided that I had something better – a nurturing and caring environment.

Viewed from any vantage point, Bambi was 'privileged' and in the 'center' of equity issues (especially gender issues) in science education whereas Molly was not privileged and was at the margins. This was apparent at the NARST conference in Atlanta where we met. Bambi was one of several graduate students being mentored and systemically introduced to the right people – those researchers who were at the center of gender research from around the world. Molly attended the conference alone. Our research interest led to us to select to attend the same paper sessions dealing with gender and attended by feminist researchers. This convergence of circumstance brought us together as poor graduate students interested in the same research and with similar origins.

APPROACHING THE JOURNEY'S END - FIRST UNIVERSITY POSTION

We both wanted to be at a college/university that was more diverse than the universities in which we were professionally prepared. We thought that if we were going to continue to investigate issues of equity in science education, we should go where the students faced true inequity. Bambi examined the statistics and noted that most teachers get their education and certification through smaller, nonselective universities. She also knew that at such universities education faculty tend to be from similar elementary education programs and get their doctorates as generalists. Therefore, she believed, and continues to believe, that part of the problem with elementary science education in our schools is that most of the teachers are trained by those who do not know science, do not like science, and do not know how to properly teach science because they never had a specific science methods course themselves. Naively, she thought the presence of someone with a science and science education background would be welcomed.

Instead she found that the culture of some of these colleges of education is to be, as one tenure document reads, proud generalists. The assumption is that anyone who has taught can now teach others how to teach anything. Specificity can be a deficit and seen as a challenge or insult to the culture. In addition, the understanding of feminism was primarily that learned from the media, not reading or doing feminist research or using feminist methodologies for teaching (Digiovanni & Liston, 2005). It was a margin for which neither feminist theory nor theories of science and science education had prepared her.

Regarding feminism at the assistant professor level, she learned that there is a breed of woman who uses the label feminism when it will get her support but will leave a fellow woman in the lurch to get/continue support from non-feminist administrators and faculty members. One colleague professed feminism but would denigrate the work of others in the presence of powerful individuals. For example, at one dinner this colleague told the wife of a powerful donor that Bambi had been "sifting through garbage all day." She had actually been helping to pack toner cartridges, cell phones, etc. for recycling as part of a project with a student organization for future science teachers. On the other hand, Bambi found women who would never use the "f" word to describe themselves, yet would fight for other female faculty members and support them in the same ways she experienced among her feminist colleagues in science education. Labels, especially self-chosen labels, do mean so little. Just as Nel Noddings (2002) describes caring as being defined by the career rather than the individual professing to care, the descriptors feminist and mentor may best be bestowed by those around a person, not worn like a coat.

Molly chose an urban university because it had a diverse student population. She found that the men in science education in department of middle/secondary education were truly a part of the 'good ol' boy' movement. Many of their ways of interacting clashed with the feminist ideas that helped shape her. She found that they were 'centered' and had power as men, tenured faculty, and long-time employees whereas she was definitely had little power and was back on the margin. Her research agenda and her service in inner-city schools were not valued.

The only woman in the science education taught only graduate classes which were at night so she and Molly only passed one another in the halls in late afternoon. This woman could have been a mentor (she was a feminist and well respected as an advocate for her female students) but teaching assignments made interactions difficult. Molly would later regret not getting to know this woman.

CLOSING

As feminists we are glad to have the opportunity to share our 'voice' with others. As we reflect on our journey, we find that our movement from the margin to the center was often due to a mentor who believed in us and encouraged us to believe in ourselves. When we found that we were back at the margin, it was due to not having a mentor. In business there is a proverb of sorts about mentoring that says that confident managers advance their promising employees but uncertain managers push themselves forward. As we continue our work at the university, we want to pass to the next generation the wisdom, courage, and determination that were given to us by our various mentors.

REFERENCES

DiGiovanni, L. W., & Liston, D. D. (2005). Feminist pedagogy in the elementary classroom: An agenda for practice. *Feminist Teacher: A Journal of the Practices, Theories, and Scholarship of Feminist Teaching, 15*(2), 123–131.

Foucault, M. (1980). *Power/knowledge: Selected interviews and other writings, 1972–1977* (C. Gordon, Trans.). New York: Pantheon.

Hall, R. M., & Sandler, B. R. (1982). *The classroom climate: A chilly one for women?* Washington, DC: Project on the Status and Education of Women, Association of American Colleges.

hooks, b. (1984). *Feminist theory: From margin to center.* Boston: South End Press.

Morris, L. K. (2003, November 5–7). *The chilly climate for women: A literature review.* Paper presented at the annual meeting of the Mid-South Educational Research Association, Biloxi, MS.

Noddings, N. (2002). *Educating moral people: A caring alternative to character education.* New York: Teachers College Press.

Sandler, B. R., & Hall, R. M. (1986). *The campus climate revisited: Chilly for women faculty, administrators, and graduate students.* Washington, DC: Project on the Status and Education of Women, Association of American Colleges.

AFFILIATIONS

Molly Weinburgh
College of Education,
Texas Christian University

Bambi Bailey
College of Education,
University of Texas at Tyler

NANCY W. BRICKHOUSE

6. SCIENCE AS A WAY OF LEAVING HOME

This autobiography is about the contribution of science in my development and the role my father and other individuals played in enculturating me into science. The story is also about growing up in a time and place where opportunities were limited and tightly circumscribed by rigid gender role expectations. I begin with a brief description of a theoretical framework, followed by narrative autobiographical sections, and concluding with how my particular science identity has influenced my reading of research in science education.

THEORETICAL FRAMEWORK

My recent scholarship in science education uses a situated cognition framework to examine the ways in which girls engage in science (see, for example, Brickhouse, Schultz & Lowery, 2000; Brickhouse & Potter, 2001; Brickhouse, 2001). I have told stories about the ways in which the girls with whom I have worked have successfully (or not) negotiated school science and science/technology identities. It somehow seems only fair that I should do the same for my own story.

What I mean when I use the term "identity" is characteristic ways of acting, valuing, believing, talking, writing, interacting that successfully communicates to others what kind of person you are and aspire to be (Gee, 1999). It is related to self-concept or how you see yourself. However self-concept and identity are not synonymous. To have a scientific identity one must perform in ways that are recognizably scientific to others. As one performs and is recognized as being scientific, the actual competence becomes internalized in a way that it becomes a part of who you are. This is what Wenger (1998) describes as reification.

For example, imagine a confident, 8-year-old basketball player who is generally fast and agile and unafraid of sports. She has a strong self-concept as an athlete and basketball player and joins a mixed sex team. The boys on the team are an overwhelming majority and do not pass to any of the young girls on the team. In other words, this young girl's peers do not seem to recognize her as a good basketball player and do not provide much opportunity for participation in a way that would actually build the young girls' skills. Suppose one of the coaches has a daughter on the team and recognizes that the girls' opportunities are limited by the boys' refusal to play with the girls. The coach introduces some plays for the kids to practice, and assigns positions in a way that basically assures that the girls get the ball. As time passes the girls are better able to participate in the game and their skills improve. This young girl gradually learns

K. Scantlebury, J. Butler Kahle and S. N. Martin (eds.) Re-visioning Science Education from Feminist Perspectives: Challenges, Choices and Careers, 57–63.

to participate in basketball in ways that others recognize as competent. The boys begin to pass to her as they "learn" that she can make the shots she shoots. The young girl no longer just thinks she's a good basketball player, she is recognized by others as such. In other words, she has developed an identity as a basketball player.

What this example illustrates is that self concept is an important piece of identity, but so is recognition by others. In order for others to recognize you as a particular kind of person (in this case, a basketball player) you must have certain skills, abilities, and knowledge. However, bias can influence identity development simply by constraining how it is one sees him/herself, what kinds of practices are made available, as well as what others are willing to recognize and accept as good basketball playing.

My autobiography is about how I acquired a science-related identity. The person who was most influential in my becoming someone who engages in science professionally is my dad. I do not think he ever really intentionally encouraged me in this way, but he literally surrounded my life with science-related projects. I could not help but be a part of them. However, it was also this access to science that eventually led me away from him and the community in which I grew up.

THE MAN

My dad was raised in a poor farming family in Grapevine, TX – where the Dallas-Ft. Worth airport now sits. Daddy always believed strongly in the importance of the farmer and in how science could improve farming practices and solve the problem of human hunger. He obtained college degrees in animal husbandry and nutrition. I was born in College Station, TX while he completed a Ph.D. in biochemistry through the College of Agriculture at Texas A&M. His dissertation research was carried out at the university farm, studying the effect of various diets on the animals raised there.

Daddy always saw science and education in very practical terms. Daddy's science was never intended to bring about basic knowledge; it was always a means to other ends. In our back yard (literally), Daddy built a laboratory. It began as a laboratory that tested agricultural products. For example, we would test hay or chicken feed to determine its protein or fat content. When environmental regulation became law in the 1960s, Daddy's lab developed the capacity to carry out the tests that were now required. For example, we tested wastewater for heavy metals, fecal coliform, biochemical oxygen demand, pH, etc.

Science was not only a way to make a living; it consumed our spare time as well. Outside my bedroom window, my dad and his friends worked late into the night building a portable dental office to be driven to the Rio Grande Valley to provide dental care to the indigent. There were periodic mission trips to Central and South America for which my daddy provided scientific expertise to facilitate farming practices and the acquisition of clean water. Daddy was also very interested in finding ways of generating cheap energy in poor areas. His experiments, again, in our backyard, included a salt-gradient solar pond and a fermentation pond for water hyacinths. The solar pond measured about 100'X40', was lined with a black tarp, and filled with salt water – the densest water on bottom so that the warm water would stay at the bottom of the pond. Water for our home passed through coils underneath the pond, heating it. The water hyacinths pond was about the same size as the solar pond. In it we grew the plants and built a conveyer belt to move mature plants under a black tarp where they were fermented. Theoretically, we were then going to collect the methane gas that the fermentation process produced. Our backyard was not pretty, but it generated a lot of scientific conversation.

My daddy is in some ways very much a part of the culture that surrounds him. He is very religious, politically conservative, and loyal to the community and its people. In other ways, he is atypical. He has a Ph.D., which is a degree that requires an explanation and earned him the nickname "Doc." And perhaps even more shocking in northeast Texas was the fact that he was apathetic about football.

THE PLACE

I grew up in a small town in northeast Texas in the 1960s and 1970s. The town of 10,000 people boomed during the Great Depression when oil was discovered there. Very little industry in this town was not related to working in the oil fields. What mattered here was football and church. Friday nights were sacred because that is when the high schools played football. Everyone went, even my daddy. There were other sports that boys played, but the only sport that really mattered was football. I do not think Title IX made much impact here. The only sport for girls was volleyball. Cheerleading and being on the drill team were preferred to sports for girls. African American girls also participated in cheerleading and drill team, but in relatively small numbers. Girls were typically dancers, not athletes.

I cannot recall any professional working women during the time that I was growing up, except for teachers. I remember some working in the shops downtown, but they did not own them. Women often reached their peak of independence at the age of 18-20 and then married and raised children. This was the fate of my two best friends from high school.

Protestant evangelical religion was hegemonic at that time and is probably even more so now. There were plenty of people who were not very religious but respectability required religiosity – and the only real option was evangelical Christianity.

When I was in the second grade, a federal court order led to the closing of the black school system and led to its integration with the White schools. Since there were no private schools or suburbs, there was no white flight from the public schools. The schools I attended were racially mixed. However, the rest of the community was not. The churches, in particular, were highly segregated. The largest Southern Baptist church in town had as part of its by-laws, the prohibition of African Americans from membership.

MY PLACE IN THIS COMMUNITY

As a girl, I was very much a part of this small-town community. My family was by no means wealthy, but we were considered appropriately religious and unusually well educated. I went to football games and participated in church activities. I chose to spend huge amounts of time at church. Church was one of the few places where serious ideas were discussed and debated. (My family's dinner table was the other.) However, as a youth I rebelled against the racism of the church particularly because I could not reconcile bigotry with the New Testament gospels. I also resented the very limited range of identities available to me as a girl. I occasionally attended religious services at an African American church, where I was welcomed with open arms.

My recollections of school are primarily of overwhelming boredom. With very few exceptions, there was just nothing being taught that was worthy of a conversation. I have very little recollection of science. I concentrated my efforts on my music, which provided both a creative outlet and a challenge. Through music and church I found a social group, but never felt a strong connection to those I called my friends.

By the time I was in high school I was restless and curious about the rest of the world. I left home at 18 for college, rather than attend the local community college with my peers. After college I returned to a small town near home to teach high school. Following a couple of years teaching I left for good.

Each year I return to northeast Texas for a week or two to see my family. It is no longer home. I feel more like an anthropologist than like part of the community. And I feel some guilt for having left.

A SCIENCE IDENTITY

As I have already described, my childhood was quite literally surrounded by science. It was not the kind of intellectual science in which one observes and explains the world around them and achieves a kind of satisfaction with being able to understand why things are as they are. Instead, the kind of science that surrounded me was of a more practical variety. We were trying to do good and worthwhile things with science as a mechanism.

My mother tells me that as a child, no one would have recognized me as being particularly scientific. I was good at science in school, but I was good at all the academic subjects. Others would have said that I was a strong student, very musical, and very religious. When I look at the materials I collected for my scrapbook from my grades 1-12 school years, this is consistent with those artifacts.

Yet, I was performing science, not only in school, but at home as well. When I was about 12 years old I broke a mirror and began working in my daddy's lab to pay for it. Initially, I washed glassware. Gradually, however, I learned to do many of the routine tests. Eventually I worked there after school, on the weekends, and during the summers. While I did not directly participate in Daddy's other science projects, it was nevertheless the case that these rather large holes in our yard prompted quite a lot of questions from guests that I could generally respond to with some facility.

By the time I got to college, I had decided that I wanted to go into one of the health professions. I knew that I needed a science degree to do that. I registered for freshman chemistry. Given my prior laboratory experience, I could accurately complete a chemistry laboratory exercise in a fraction of the time it took my peers to complete it. It was the first time I can recall being recognized as a strong chemistry student. I eventually decided to major in chemistry and was nominated by one of my chemistry professors into Phi Beta Kappa – once again providing me with good evidence that others recognized my performance in chemistry.

As a child I was taking up many of the performances of a science identity. Yet neither I, nor those around me, recognized these performances as particularly scientific. As Wenger (1998) has noted, it is not enough to participate in the practices of a particular community to take on an identity as part of the community. These performances also have to be recognized by relevant others as scientific for one to take on a scientific identity.

So why was I not recognized as scientific as a child/young person? Perhaps being a girl in a community of narrowly defined gender roles, there was simply no performance that could have been recognized by either others or me as scientific. Perhaps part of the difficulty is that there were few opportunities for me to demonstrate scientific competence at school. There were no honors or advanced classes in the sciences. My final science course was as a junior in chemistry. Years after I graduated, my high school chemistry teacher told my mother I was the strongest chemistry student she had ever taught. I was extremely surprised. I never felt like a star.

LEAVING HOME

In college I never fell in love with chemistry, but I did find courses that introduced me to ideas that were worthy of a conversation. I met people who were interested in ideas. I studied very hard because I believed that everyone around me had been better prepared for college than I had been. I wanted to be successful, but was also interested in what I was learning. College changed who I was. I was heartbroken when I had to graduate and wished that the registrar would call and tell me I needed another English course.

After college, I did not know what I wanted to do, so I took a job teaching high school chemistry and physics in a small town (population 2000) in northeast Texas. I found teaching to be very challenging and interesting. However, I also knew I could not stay there. When I read about Purdue University's program in chemistry education in Chemical and Engineering News, I knew that this would be the way out.

Like my daddy, chemistry was always a means to some other end. Initially, it was a way to pay for a broken mirror. Later it was a way into the health professions. Eventually, chemistry provided me with the opportunity to leave a community in which I knew I could not thrive. When my parents unpacked the last of my boxes in graduate student housing at Purdue, we all cried. We knew the move was not temporary, nor was it merely geographic. I no longer belonged to the community that they could never leave.

AUTOBIOGRAPHICAL REFLECTIONS ON SCHOLARSHIP IN
SCIENCE EDUCATION

Much of my recent scholarship has focused on understanding learning as identity construction. One acquires certain skills, values, and knowledge in order to be a certain kind of person and to be a part of particular kinds of communities. However, I worry that at time these "communities" are written about as though membership in them is an unmitigated good. The term connotes a feeling of comfort and sense of belonging. Yet as Noddings (1996) noted, there is a dark side to this notion of community. Communities can be totalizing places that insist on high levels of conformity. The values they promote in individuals may be bad ones. Not every community is worth joining and not everything about every community is worthy of preservation.

Science played a key role in providing me a way out of the community where I grew up. I think of this often, as I read scholarly writing about how education should not do this. Multiculturalists often argue that education should draw on local community resources and provide an education that does not separate a child from his/her community. We should aspire to participate in these communities –empower and change them – and to help our students do the same. I had no desire to change or empower the community I grew up in. I simply wanted to leave.

Scholarly discussions of evolution by natural selection/creationism also provoke a strong autobiographical response from me. Although I now enjoy dispassionate commentary on the science and the theology behind these debates, at times I feel exasperated by those who advocate teaching natural selection in schools in ways that seem to me to miss what the conflict is really about. I do not believe this controversy will ever be solved with evidence and better teaching. I think the intensity of this controversy has to be understood in terms of relationships and communities. A student who rejects a Biblically-based version of creationism and embraces evolution by natural selection is not simply changing his/her mind based on reason and evidence. They are changing who they are, and the relationships established with significant others. I was not taught evolution by natural selection in high school. I doubt that I would have been receptive to it. My first exposure was in college, at a time when my identity had already shifted significantly so that I could easily accommodate evolution by natural selection.

I read scholarship on knowledge versus belief in teaching about evolution. Generally speaking, most science educators seem to take the view that we should not aim to change any students' beliefs about evolution by natural selection if it appears to conflict with the religious views of their home communities. We should only care about knowledge. In other words, we should not care what our students actually believe to be true, so long as they can pass a test to show that they understand evolution by natural selection.

While it is, of course, impossible to coerce belief, I worry when we no longer even consider it a goal of science education. If science education is not to impact belief in any way, then it is at risk of becoming merely a credentialing system.

The knowledge students learn has no real impact on identity. I believe that education rather fundamentally changed who I was, and that this is a proper, if at times risky, aim for science education.

My autobiography almost certainly affects the way in which I "read" research about role models and mentoring. While I understand the desire to provide young girls with images of women engaged in science or to institutionalize mentoring relationships, this seems to me to be an incredibly weak "treatment" relative to my own experience with my dad and his science projects. I find it rather amazing that special programs for girls that provide this kind of support have any detectable impact at all.

Finally, my own autobiography draws my attention to girls' experiences with science at home. Ruby's story in Brickhouse and Potter (2001) describes a girl whose father surrounded her with the material and cultural resources of computer technology. It was perhaps a story I found compelling because there were ways in which it overlapped with my own. We were both enculturated into science by our fathers. Ruby's scientific trajectory has thus far not lead her into a science-related profession as mine did. While as an educator I have always encouraged students to take a critical stance toward science, I also recognize that the science my dad taught me has profoundly shaped my adult identity.

REFERENCES

Brickhouse, N. W., & Potter, J. T. (2001). Young women's scientific identity formation in an urban context. *Journal of Research in Science Teaching, 38*, 965–980.

Brickhouse, N. W. (2001). Embodying science: A feminist perspective on learning. *Journal of Research in Science Teaching, 38*, 282–295.

Brickhouse, N. W., Schultz, K., & Lowery, P. (2000). What kind of a girl does science? The construction of school science identities. *Journal of Research in Science Teaching, 37*, 441–458.

Gee, J. P. (1999). *An introduction to discourse analysis: Theory and method.* New York: Routledge.

Noddings, N. (1996). On community. *Educational Theory, 46*, 245–268.

Wenger, E. (1998). *Communities of practice: Learning, meaning and identity.* Cambridge: Cambridge University Press.

AFFILIATION

Nancy W. Brickhouse
School of Education,
University of Delaware

SECTION III: CONTEXTUALIZING WOMEN'S CAREERS AND EXPERIENCES FROM SCIENCE TO SCIENCE EDUCATION

The third section offers five chapters authored by individual women who share their experience transitioning from women research scientists to women who have in some form or another become science educators. We offer this collection of stories to provide a realistic account of the experiences of several women, who over the last forty years, have struggled to be successful as researcher scientists in academia. As such, this section offers readers both a historical and social context from which to examine women's experiences in science, as the authors represent women who have studied science in different parts of the world spanning over five decades. A commonality that is readily evident is that each story describes a young woman with insatiable curiosity about the world around her, even while this curiosity did not always translate into academic success in K-12 science courses and college. Each contribution describes shared challenges, including teachers and colleagues who were at best unsupportive and at worst, actively malicious in their attempts to thwart these women from progressing in a career in science. There are five chapters in this section in which the contributors each employ a variety of writing styles within the genre of auto/biography and auto/ethnography. The authors utilize a variety of methods to share their individual accounts, including using episodic stories, short vignettes, and autobiographical accounts interwoven with analytical responses from the perspective of the co-author, none of which conform to conventional writing formats. The first four chapters are each co-authored such that the contributors blend their voices to share and analyze their experiences as women in science from perspectives that range across generations, race, class, and geographical location. The final chapter is a solo contribution examining the ways in which science can serve to both liberate women from social constraints and alienate them from others as a result of their liberation.

Fortunately, these experiences, coupled with the support of several key mentors in the lives of these women, have served as catalysts to spark their desire to act as change agents in science by becoming science educators! Thus, the contributors in this section have not only garnered impressive achievements in science, but they have also become science educators who, through their research and progressive teaching practices, are transforming science education for new generations of students – both male and female. We offer their stories as a tribute to the challenges that many women have overcome in their careers and as inspiration for the men and women who seek to eradicate inequities in science education through transformative research and teaching practices.

The first two chapters in this section began as a co-authored project, but Penny Gilmer (Chapter 7) and Jennifer Lewis (Chapter 8) found they needed space to tell their individual stories and so the chapters remain paired, but offer two important accounts of becoming women chemists in the United States in two different eras.

Gilmer and Lewis invoke the same theme in each of their chapters, using the wind as a metaphor as either a deterrent or an aid in their academic journeys in chemistry. In Gilmer's chapter, she characterizes her struggles to become a full professor in chemistry at a large university in the South as being a journey going "upwind", symbolizing the many challenges she has faced and overcome during a career spanning more than three decades. Gilmer's contributions as a biochemist have been rivaled only by her successful endeavors in educational research and in her extraordinary service to the science education community. Earning a second doctorate in science education near the end of her academic career, Gilmer works tirelessly to inform her scientist colleagues about alternative research methods, the significance of educational research, and serves as a role model for young women scientist and science educators as a leader in several national and international science education organizations. Gilmer credits her accomplishments to the "winds" which she feels served to energize and empower her to continually move forward with a goal of changing the culture of science and research to be not only accessible to young women, but to also reflect the interests and values of women scientists.

Jennifer Lewis's autobiographical narrative (Chapter 8) provides an interesting contrast to Penny Gilmer's work, offering a contrasting account of her journey into academia as a research chemist who characterizes the wind as a force propelling her forward into her career. Indeed, Lewis describes a force that has at times pushed her into science even when she did not consciously see a career in research science as a possibility for her future. Chronicling her journey into academia, Lewis offers the reader a more positive account of both the challenges and supports that young women are apt to find in academia today. However, as a chemistry educator in a chemistry department, Lewis points to several inequities with regards to expectations for research and teaching that continue to place women in precarious positions in university science departments. Read as a twin text, Gilmer and Lewis's chapters provide the reader with the sense that while "we've come a long way, baby!", we have many miles to go before women and men are treated equitably in academic science departments. However, these two authors leave the reader with a sense that they are on the path and are cognizant that others must also join them.

The next three chapters in this section enable the reader to explore the experiences of women in science in three different countries and cultures, including Jamaica, Austria, and Northern Ireland. In each instance, the authors describe their early educational experiences, the routes they have taken into academia, and how their experiences have influenced their current-day research and teaching as science educators. Karen Phillips (Chapter 9) explores the socio-historical influence of race, ethnicity, and gender on the development of a young girl's identity as a scientist and racial minority. Phillips' description of her educational experiences in Jamaica, including a variety of informal learning opportunities provided by occasions she assisted her grandmother, an experienced mid-wife and holistic healer, as well as her family's desire to provide her with both the freedom and support to pursue her own educational interests, presents the reader with important insights into the early development of Phillips' identity as a science learner. Phillips experiences as an immigrant student in the United States, where she is racialized as "Other" by her peers and teachers, enables her to recognize the role race and ethnicity play in shaping educational and career opportunities for many minorities in the United States. As a chemistry graduate student at a top research university, Phillips began to notice the ways in which certain administrative structures and teaching practices limited access to resources for some students, many of whom were immigrants and/or racial minorities. Phillips concludes her chapter describing the ways in which these experiences have inspired her to enact different teaching practices in her university level organic chemistry courses, utilizing pedagogical strategies and participatory research methodologies, such as cogenerative dialogues, to engage with her students on a personal level so as to meet their individual needs as science learners.

Helga Stadler (Chapter 10) provides the reader with what she describes as "an interpretation" of her professional life as a physics educator and gender studies researcher and an account of how the "facts in her life might influence the way she thinks and what she does". As such, Stadler describes her educational experiences growing up and living in Austria. Specifically, Stadler describes her career trajectory moving from studying physics to becoming a physics teacher to becoming a physics educator and researcher as "living the cultural clash" between "hard" and "soft" sciences. Introducing the concept of a dualism between the sciences, between the 'hard' (natural) and 'soft' (cultural) sciences, Stadler asserts that this dualism is a reflection of the social construction of the dualism between males and females. As Stadler recounts her experiences in learning physics, navigating the world of academia, including defining her interests conducting research into physics teaching, she found herself trying to bridge a cultural gap between being engaged in 'hard' science as a physicist and 'soft' science as a physics educator and researcher. Stadler argues that this partition of the sciences into 'hard' and 'soft' strengthens the dualism that divides the world into a male and a female one, forcing men and women to decide between the two. Citing numerous studies from her own research, Stadler asserts that if we are to attract more women to the 'hard sciences', women and men need to change the image of science through science education research and by enacting transformative teaching practices.

The title of Colette Murphy's contribution (Chapter 11), describes her journey from science to science teacher educator as that of a "reluctant scientist". Murphy cautions the reader that her story is different from that of many other science educators as she relates that she had very little encouragement to do science either as a young girl growing up in northern Ireland, or even as an adult while pursuing her doctorate in botany. Research on women in science, however, indicates that Murphy's experience, as a reluctant scientist is not an uncommon one. Many of our female readers may find their own life mirrored in Murphy's narrative account of her transition from a career in research science to that of a science education researcher. Murphy's chapter provides the reader with an analysis of the events and decisions in her life that she feels most influenced her career first towards, and then away from science, and how these experiences have impacted her teaching of science, as well as her scholarship as a science teacher educator.

Finally, this section offers readers several representative experiences of women in who have begun their career in the academic sciences and have transitioned into science education research based on a desire to expand not only their own opportunities for learning, but also their students by implementing pedagogical practices that provide students with greater access to resources and by engaging in on-going, critical self-reflection on their own teaching and research practices.

PENNY J. GILMER

7. GOING UPWIND IN BIOCHEMISTRY

I am both a biochemist and science educator professor in a Department of Chemistry and Biochemistry at Florida State University. My original doctoral training was in biochemistry at the University of California, Berkeley. My research was fast reaction kinetics of the binding of a vitamin B6 analog to a transaminase enzyme. I determined the pH dependence of the overall equilibrium constant and the on and off rate constants for the enzymatic aldimine formation.

As a faculty member, I conducted my biochemical research for 15 years at which time I started to become interested in understanding learning and in particular, science education. Eventually, this new interest led to my earning a second doctorate in Science Education through Curtin University of Technology in Western Australia. I just finished my 31st year as a faculty member in the same department. I focus my research now on science education, mainly at the undergraduate and graduate levels.

Originally, I wrote this chapter in conjunction with a chemist, Jennifer Lewis, but we decided to keep our chapters separate, as we wrote enough to comprise two chapters. Therefore, you may want to read her chapter in this same book in conjunction with mine. We compared our experiences and agreed on using the wind as a metaphor, either a deterrent or an aid in our academic journeys in chemistry or biochemistry. In my case, I saw the wind more as an obstacle in my movement through the academic ladder while she saw the wind as something that helped propel her forward—she could feel the wind at her back. Although I felt energized with the wind in my face, stimulating me, I felt the struggle, trying to move forward in my career against the force of the wind.

Jennifer Lewis and I became scientists and academicians at quite different times (Penny in the 1970s and Jennifer in the 1990s). I feel gratified to see that the climate for women becoming chemistry faculty has improved since I started on my quest to become an academic scientist. There are elements in common to both journeys, but there are enough differences that I feel an optimistic note for the future.

In 1993, there were 80 women who composed just 8% of the full professors in chemistry departments in the entire United States (Long, 2000). I was not in that group but became a full professor two years later. Women full professors were a rare breed at the time. Women faculty members in chemistry departments are still rare, and full professors are rarer still.

This chapter outlines the struggles and joys I have experienced as a budding chemist, becoming a biochemist, and now a science educator. I always felt I was going upwind against the current of males forming the wind in my face (Figure 1).

K. Scantlebury, J. Butler Kahle and S. N. Martin (eds.) Re-visioning Science Education from Feminist Perspectives: Challenges, Choices and Careers, 69–78.

Figure 1. In this sculpture of a woman in an undulating dress by artist, Candy Ryan (from Oldmar, FL), I feel the energy from "going upwind" while becoming an academic biochemist and science educator.

The struggle may have been doubly hard, considering that I chose to move to the southern part of the US, a conservative region of my country. Even though finding my own pathway was difficult, I feel I gained energy and confidence in myself from the struggle.

VENTURING INTO CHEMISTRY

Mine is a journey of being a female who, to become a scientist, had to be serious about her learning of mathematics and science and now is just as earnest about learning science education. I have been on this upwind journey for all my life. I knew in 6th grade that I loved science. Mr. Dudley Bragg, my 7th and 8th grade teacher at a small rural elementary school, taught me a love for learning, and I realized my talent and interest in mathematics and science. From my interest and love of chemistry and mathematics while still in high school, I knew that the pathway would be difficult for me being a young woman and that I would meet great resistance. I dared to go where few women had attempted to tread.

However, I experienced a window of opportunity to enter in the sciences. I was 14 at the time that the Soviets sent Sputnik into space, circling the globe. This call to Americans, much as there is now in the US, pushed for more young people to go into science, mathematics, and engineering. I felt patriotic for entering into a field in which my country needed me. Here was one time when the wind of change was with me—the launching of Sputnik helped propel me into a science track in high school and later in college and graduate school.

In my freshman year of high school, my homeroom happened to be the chemistry room. I remember getting to school early and sitting there, becoming fascinated with the periodic table and how the size of the covalent radii gets smaller as you move across the periodic table elements, so the elements in the same period became denser as they have more mass and less volume (see chart of elements on Purdue University Web site, 2006). I asked my high school principal if I could take the chemistry course in my sophomore year. Through that course, I learned that the answer to my question about the density of elements lies in understanding the inner structure of atoms and their electron arrangements. How fascinating I thought!

In high school I struggled at first with chemistry but persisted as science captivated me, and I did well. I remember during my junior year of high school we used the brand new physics curriculum developed by MIT physicists through the Physical Study Science Committee (PSSC). I fell in love with learning about waves and how they worked, and what waves meant about the nature of light. As I graduated from my high school, I listed myself in the "class will" in the yearbook as leaving the answers to all the mathematics problems. All my peers knew I had figured out all the problems. However, in those times, a young woman who was interested and excelled in science and mathematics was still very strange.

What propelled me to become an academic scientist against so many social odds, despite the Sputnik opportunity? Upon reflection, what I liked most about science is I could make sense of the world. There was so much in those times, especially when I was in college with the civil rights strife and the cold war that did not make sense to me. At least in science, there were theories that made sense to me, that added some order to my life. I could predict the physical and chemical behavior of materials. I felt that there were things knowable in the universe. I felt that at least there was a part of the world that made sense. For me, the world was full of chemistry.

At the time I felt that attending a coeducational institution would have been harder socially for women to excel in the sciences, so I chose to attend a women's college. Half of my college professors at Douglass College (the women's college at Rutgers University) were women. I did have the opportunity to do organic chemistry research, even before I took the course in organic chemistry with a male professor, Dr. Bean. I got to synthesize new molecules that no one had ever seen or characterized beforehand, so I felt enabled and empowered. During another summer I participated in biochemical research with a woman faculty member, Dr. Lillian Ellis. However, I do remember there was one male physical chemistry professor who said to all five of the women chemistry majors in my senior year, "I wonder why I spend my energy teaching you when you'll just become mothers." That really bothered me, and in a way, his saying that motivated me further, to go to graduate school. I wanted to prove him wrong.

FOCUSING MY INTERESTS IN BIOCHEMISTRY

When I got to graduate school, I really started to push myself academically, especially after I got my master's degree in organic chemistry at Bryn Mawr College and went for the doctorate in biochemistry at University of California, Berkeley. Berkeley was the first place where I was no longer at the top of my peer group.

I found myself more in the middle of a group of motivated and talented young biochemists. Being at Berkeley gave me room to grow and pushed me. However, I remember there was a negative incident with one of the members of my doctoral committee, which reminded me of when my undergraduate professor thought the women chemistry majors would just have babies when we graduated. This second incident reignited my drive to excel in my chosen career.

The doctoral research was not a bed of roses. When I started at University of California, Berkeley, I was suddenly in a program in which most of my peers knew a lot of biology. I had only taken one high school biology course and none in college (although I did take biochemistry in my master's program). In my first semester at Berkeley, I took a course in protein synthesis offered by world-renown geneticist, Bruce Ames. Rather than a textbook, we read recent journal articles as the news was breaking on protein synthesis. Without any in depth background in biology, I had to figure out what the genetics must be for these articles to make sense, an unusual way to learn genetics. The challenge stimulated me. Meanwhile I switched my emphasis from organic chemistry to bioorganic chemistry to biochemistry.

My research mentor, Dr. Jack Kirsch, was on sabbatical in West Germany during the third year of my four-year doctorate at Berkeley. I collected most of the experimental data—temperature-jump and stopped-flow kinetics as well as equilibrium data during the year Jack was away. In the early 1970s there was no way to communicate electronically, not even by facsimile. Instead, I would type (on a manual typewriter) a 5-page, single-spaced letter once a week on what I had discovered, what problems I had, and where I was headed in my research. By the time I received Jack's response by airmail two weeks later, I had solved those problems and was on to new ones. What I realized is I could solve my own problems.

Jack Kirsch told me that I was his first woman graduate student who wanted to become a university professor. He was surprised but did encourage me. In fact, Jack called me during my postdoctoral research at Stanford University to say, "Penny, they're looking for you at Florida State University—they advertised for an assistant professor in one of three fields—immunochemistry, fast reaction kinetics, or membrane-mediated phenomenon—all three are your specialties."

BECOMING A CHEMISTRY FACULTY MEMBER IN THE DEEP SOUTH

Indeed the interview at FSU went well, and I was offered and accepted the job. However, moving to Florida was a big change for me, not only because I had a tenure track faculty line, but also I had just separated from my first husband after seven years of marriage. Also I moved into the Deep South of the US, in which I had never lived. The culture in Tallahassee, Florida was very different from the Bay Area in California.

I was the first woman to be hired in my department on a faculty line equivalent to my male colleagues, to do research, teaching and service. However, I knew my primary mission as an assistant professor was to conduct research, attain grants, and publish! Again, I felt like I was going upwind, as there were so very few women faculty in the sciences within my university, and only one other in chemistry.

My one female colleague, Katherine Hoffman, in chemistry did an elegant job with her teaching and service, but she was not hired or expected to conduct research. I felt that my male colleagues were uncomfortable with me, not only that I was their first female colleague who did research like they did, but also because I was a single woman. For many of my chemistry colleagues' their wives stayed at home and never had careers. I did not fit into the nice little box in their minds for women. Therefore, I was obviously different and felt isolated.

I was also different in terms of my research. At that time I focused on immunochemistry, studying cell-cell interactions between an immune cytotoxic T cell and the tumor target cell towards which the T cell had been primed. I wanted to understand the chemical and physical factors that modulated that immune T-cell-mediated recognition event. There was no one else in my department who studied membranes or anything to do with immunology. Therefore, I had to make my own impact. My graduate students and I published how the cell-surface density of major his to compatibility class I antigens on the tumor cell surface influenced their recognition by the immune T-cells. In addition, we purified these same transmembrane antigens by affinity chromatography and inserted the transmembrane antigens into model membranes with defined lipid composition and containing cytoskeletal proteins. We demonstrated that they were immunologically specific.

However, earning tenure and promotion to associate professor was a tough road. My second husband (also a chemist and a colleague) and I had chosen to have our first child while I was still an untenured assistant professor. One female colleague from another department told me later in my quest for promotion and tenure that my male colleagues did not like that I got pregnant and had a child before my tenure decision. To my colleagues, bearing a child was a signal that I was not committed to my career in biochemistry.

I chose to become pregnant because I wanted to have a child and felt there was a time crunch, and were I to wait, I might never become pregnant. In retrospect, I think having my two children (the second was after I was tenured) was one of the important things I have done in my life. Therefore, I do not regret it, and I learned how to survive in academia despite (and maybe) because of those hard times.

One of the important things that I learned in those tenure-earning years and the fight for tenure was that everything is political. Beforehand I had thought I was above politics, but I learned through that fight, that I must pay attention to politics, and I have ever since.

REDIRECTING MY RESEARCH TOWARDS EDUCATION

Once I was tenured and promoted to associate professor I started to branch from traditional biochemical research and teaching. I applied for university funding to offer an innovative interdisciplinary science course in which ethics in science was a prominent theme. In retrospect, I realize that I became well known nationally initially through my innovations in teaching. At that time there were very few scientists that were teaching science ethics (Gilmer & Rashotte, 1989;90). A US congressional committee invited me to become a witness in 1989 hearing on "Maintaining the Integrity of Scientific Research" (Gilmer, 1989). The committee wanted to hear what I had to say about bringing ethics education to practicing scientists. The National Institutes of Health (NIH) had not yet started to include ethical training in programs for graduate assistants and postdoctoral fellows. In fact in 1990, the NIH invited Dr. Ruth Bulger and me to help shape what has become the training program required for Public Health Service trainees.

While I was still an associate professor, I had a fast-growing tumor with which I had to contend. I chose to be as aggressive as I could be in the medical treatment to increase my chances of surviving. My two children were 10 and 12 years old at the time, so I had great motivation to survive. I utilized radical surgery plus seven long months of chemotherapy, and then still had to recover from the insult to my body. I lost all confidence that I had in myself during my illness and initial recovery, because my body had forsaken me. I struggled to put myself up for promotion to full professor, but I did not want to die as an associate professor, so I proceeded. Therefore, having cancer was another critical point in my personal and academic life. I have written about this time in my life (Gilmer, 2002), but after my full recovery I found myself and have lived a richer life, both professionally and personally, since then, now 14 years.

Through my efforts in ethics education within the sciences plus other innovative educational projects in teacher preparation and teacher enhancement, I decided to prepare my binder for promotion. I knew my department chair in chemistry was behind me, and the full professors in the department were too when I put forth my folder for promotion to full professor. However, at that point, I was still going upwind in a College of Arts & Sciences that was not ready to accept educational research, even when my research was nationally recognized, even with a national award (Spiegel, Collins & Gilmer, 1995). With persistence, I gathered forth the energy to challenge the negative vote from the college (Gilmer, 2002). Fortunately, I made a convincing enough case that my colleagues on the university committee recommended my promotion to professor. At that point only 7% of the full professors in the sciences at my university were women, so I was isolated from the other women professors and felt lonely. There was only one other woman full professor in my own department at that time, and we had about 35 "brothers" as colleagues (the number varies depending on how you count, as some were half retired, etc.).

Long (2000) compiled statistics for the 2000–2001 academic year of women faculty at the three professorial ranks for the 50 universities who have spent the most money on chemical research. Since my promotion to full professor, we have added four more women faculty, three of whom are now promoted to associate professors and one newer assistant professor. For a while we had one other full professor but she was hired to be a provost at another institution. One of my former women colleagues, an associate professor, moved to another university, so we have five women faculty members in our department. However,

FSU was one of the top universities listed in the 2000–2001 year, with 14% of its full professors and 38% of its assistant professors as women. The average for the women chemistry faculty for these 50 institutions was just 10%. FSU's chemistry average for women at all ranks was 17%, and the highest ranked was Rutgers (the institution where I got my undergraduate degree) with 26% women at all ranks. I was one of the pioneers at FSU that started the change towards more women.

Although I knew I had "made it" as one of the few women full Professors of Chemistry, I chose to go upwind again. Becoming full professor in chemistry gave me the freedom to explore and learn education more deeply. Learning the field of education, critically reading the literature, presenting research papers at educational conferences, publishing research papers, editing books, and directing graduate students in education have pushed me to expand my expertise. I have read different styles of research (Ellis, 1997; Lincoln, 1997; Richardson, 1994) and have learned to express myself in writing using alternative forms of representation (Gilmer, 2002; 2004).

DIRECTING SELF TOWARDS A SECOND DOCTORATE

In order to keep learning I decided in 1997 to work towards a second doctorate in science education through Curtin University of Technology in Perth, Western Australia. I had taken graduate courses at FSU as a special student for two years at that point, and decided to go forth and learn more. I thought this effort would help me focus and survive the cancer. I traveled with my 15-year daughter, Helena to Perth, so I could enroll in the graduate program at Curtin. That one semester counted as my semester in residence. Helena attended high school for a semester while I edited a book (Taylor, Gilmer & Tobin, 2002) and took a graduate course in constructivism with Peter Taylor at Curtin. During this time I thrust myself into science education.

Peter Taylor and Kenneth Tobin became my co-major professors, with Peter more in the beginning and Ken more in the end of my program. I chose to use a qualitative methodology (which was very different than my very quantitative research for my doctorate in biochemistry) and to conduct action research in my own biochemistry classroom. By action research, I mean that I did research on my own actions (in this case in my own classroom), and how others (my students and colleagues) interpreted them. Instead of teaching using traditional lectures, I taught the first semester course in biochemistry utilizing technology (especially the Internet) with students working together in collaborative groups to develop topics in biochemistry, and then presenting some of the biochemistry content in their Web sites to each other. Students peer reviewed other group's presentations and self assessed their own presentations.

My method of teaching was radically different than what my colleagues used at my university. I chose this, as I wanted students actively constructing their knowledge, using the language of science, while working collaboratively as they struggled to understand and learn biochemistry. I still presented each week an overview of each assigned chapter. However, during the other two days of class per week the students learned how to use the technology and presented their Web sites to each other.

I chose to write up my doctoral research rather unconventionally, especially the fictionalized short story about my classroom and the metalogue that I had with one of my biochemistry colleagues on the problematic issues of bringing reform to higher education. I also had more traditional ethnographic data as part of the doctoral thesis (Gilmer, 2004). I have a book contract with Springer to make my dissertation study into a book, which I am finalizing.

Since finishing the doctorate I put my energy into a grant called GK-12 funded by the National Science Foundation (NSF). I was the internal evaluator of the program and followed the progress of our GK-12 Fellows (who are science graduate students and work about 20 hours per week in the schools and are paid $30,000 per year plus tuition). I also developed a comparison group of graduate students who were not part of the GK-12 program, so we would have some sort of a comparison to the GK-12 Fellows. I was the senior editor of a monograph on this research, with chapters by seven of the nine original fellows (Gilmer, Granger, and Butler, 2005). I accepted an award for FSU from the NSF in GK-12 Dissemination for this monograph in 2006. As a result of this program, I have become interested in the progress of graduate students in the sciences.

Currently, I have a subcontract with the Panhandle Area Education Consortium (PAEC) to offer scientific research experiences to 80 K-12 teachers in rural northern Florida. To prepare my teachers for these opportunities to conduct research I taught them an on-line, distance, graduate class called Nature of Scientific Inquiry. This summer while the students take more science graduate credit from me, I travel to 15 research sites to interact with the teachers and their scientists at state parks, wildlife refuges, estuarine reserves, coastal research laboratories, fish and wildlife services, and state of Florida research sites.

GIVING BACK TO MY PROFESSION

Almost four years ago I accepted the nomination of becoming President of the Tallahassee Scientific Society. I wanted to provide avenues for the general public to become involved in and knowledgeable about science and technology. I served in this position for two years.

In 2005, I decided to run for some national and international positions in professional groups. I ran for four elections, hoping to win one or two of them, and I won all four! The most prominent includes being elected President-elect of the National Association for Research in Science Teaching and Board member of the Association for Science Teacher Education (and Co-chair of the Awards Committee). I also became Member-at-large of the Education section of the American Association for the Advancement of Science and Area 4 Director of District 11 of Zonta International. As you might guess, I am extremely busy but thrilled at the opportunity to lead science education. As a woman who is both a science educator and a scientist, I have a unique perspective. I have the opportunity to make a difference.

REFLECTING ON THE METAPHOR OF "GOING UPWIND"

This metaphor of "going upwind" gives me energy and empowers me to find my way. The power enables me as I move against the winds of the culture. Originally for me, I went upwind against the culture in chemistry and biochemistry as a woman in a male dominated field, and more recently I went upwind as a scientist using qualitative methodologies in my educational research. By doing what I do, I am helping to change the culture within science and change the direction of the wind, which helps other young women chemists and biochemists utilize their talents and achieve their dreams.

IN CLOSING...

For science educators to work within academic science departments, there needs to be a recognition that research in the discipline of education needs to be part of the academic science department. I am trying to convince my colleagues that doctoral students in our department of chemistry and biochemistry should be able to examine chemical or biochemical education for their doctoral research. To date, I have been a major professor to four doctoral students in biochemistry, analytical chemistry or molecular biophysics and eight doctoral students in science education. All students in science education are enrolled in the College of Education. Currently, I now also have two doctoral students in science education. My chemistry faculty colleagues are slow to move from their position of research needing to be in chemistry or biochemistry, but I have convinced at least some of them that this research in chemistry and biochemistry education is worthy of a doctorate in chemistry or biochemistry. Time will tell if this type of research continues after my retirement in a year.

REFERENCES

Ellis, C. (1997). Evocative autoethnography: Writing emotionally about our lives. In W. G. Tierney & Y. S. Lincoln (Eds.), *Representation and the text: Re-framing the narrative voice* (pp. 115–139). Albany, NY: State University of New York Press.

Gilmer, P. J. (1989, June 28). Education and the research environment, committee on science, space and technology, subcommittee on investigations and oversight. *US Congressional Record*, 76–91, 382–384.

Gilmer, P. J. (2002). Opalescence at the triple point: Research, teaching and service. In P. C. Taylor, P. J. Gilmer, & K. Tobin (Eds.), *Transforming undergraduate science teaching: Social constructivist perspectives* (pp. 423–462). New York: Peter Lang Publishing, Inc.

Gilmer, P. J. (2004). *Transforming biochemistry teaching through action research: Utilizing collaborative learning and technology.* Doctoral thesis at Curtin University of Technology, Western Australia. Retrieved from faculty Web site under Publications-2004: http://www.chem.fsu.edu/editors/gilmer index.html

Gilmer, P. J., Granger, D. E., & Butler, W. (Eds.). (2005). *Science graduate students in K-8 classrooms: Experiences and reflections.* Tallahassee, FL: SERC@SERVE. Retrieved from http://www.serve.org/Curriculum/products.php

Gilmer, P. J., & Rashotte, M. E. (1989, December/1990, January). Marshalling the resources of a large state university for an interdisciplinary 'Science, technology and society' course. *Journal of College Science Teaching*, 150–156.

Lincoln, Y. S. (1997). Self, subject, audience, and text: Living at the edge, writing in the margins. In W. G. Tierney & Y. S. Lincoln (Eds.), *Representation and the text: Re-framing the narrative voice* (pp. 37–55). Albany, NY: State University of New York Press.

Long, J. R. (2000, September 25). Women chemists still rare in academia. *Chemical & Engineering News*, 56–57.

Purdue University. (2006). Retrieved July 19, 2006, from http://chemed.chem.purdue.edu/genchem/topicreview/bp/ch7/size.html

Richardson, L. (1994). Writing as a method of inquiry. In N. Denzin & Y. Lincoln (Eds.), *Handbook of qualitative research* (pp. 516–529). Thousand Oaks, CA: Sage.

Spiegel, S. A., Collins, A., & Gilmer, P. J. (1995). Science for early adolescence teachers (Science FEAT): A program for research and learning. *Journal of Science Teacher Education, 6*, 165–174.

Taylor, P. C., Gilmer, P. J., & Tobin, K. (Eds.). (2002). *Transforming undergraduate science education: Social constructivist perspectives.* New York: Peter Lang Publishing, Inc.

AFFILIATION

Penny J. Gilmer
Department of Chemistry & Biochemistry,
Florida State University

JENNIFER E. LEWIS

8. WHISTLING FOR A WIND

INTRODUCTION

When I was initially asked if I could contribute a chapter to this volume, it was in conjunction with Penny Gilmer, a fellow Floridian and extremely well known Chemist, but someone whom I had never met. I confess I was intimidated, nervous, and very conscious of my junior status, but when she called me to discuss the chapter, she was so warm and friendly that my insecurities dissipated. As we explained to each other how we made sense of the events in our lives that had informed our career paths, we hit upon the theme of the wind as a narrative thread that could tie both of our stories together. Penny had utilized autoethnography as part of her dissertation in science education, so she suggested a few references that could help me understand the form. From reading these references and a few others I understood that I did not know how to do autoethnography! What I committed to, however, was to narrate a story from my real life with relevance to the situation of women in science education, to use my authorial voice to expose rather than to obscure my vulnerabilities (as much as possible for a reserved Midwesterner), and to avoid the analytic impulse – i.e. to let the story speak for itself. When Penny and I put our stories back together, each of us had enough story to tell that the narratives could stand on their own. However, in reading our two chapters, remember that they were conceived of together, and notice that we have treated the wind in different ways, reflective of our different experiences with the larger culture. What follows is a story about how I came to claim the identity of chemical education researcher.

COMING TO CHEMISTRY

In high school, I would not have been chosen as the student most likely to go on in science. I participated in band, debate, speech and theater, and I wrote a humor column for the school newspaper, eventually serving as editor. I really liked interviewing people, and I also liked to write, so I thought of journalism as my most likely future career. As a college-bound student, however, I took the standard college preparatory courses in biology, chemistry, and physics. Since I generally enjoyed school, I enjoyed these courses as well, but still did not envision myself as a potential scientist. I had friends, who participated in science fairs, but I never felt an urge to join them – it seemed boring! From my perspective, they spent a lot of time alone, repeating experiments until finally something worked, and I couldn't

K. Scantlebury, J. Butler Kahle and S. N. Martin (eds.). Re-visioning Science Education from Feminist Perspectives: Challenges, Choices and Careers, 79–87.

understand why they found that rewarding. I knew what I enjoyed was working with lots of people to pull a big project – like a newspaper or a play – together, and that had nothing to do with science as far as I could tell. In science classes, it was fun to see patterns and be able to use them, but I could do that in English classes, too (e.g. diagramming sentences or analyzing poetry), and a discussion-based English class was always a better match for my enjoyment of social interaction than a lecture-based science class.

The turning point for me was when my high school chemistry teacher got permission to offer an advanced chemistry course my senior year. Several things fell into place: (1) it was a small class with a focus on qualitative laboratory analysis, so the teacher had an adequate budget for chemicals and we played with them often; (2) we shared lab benches and the teacher encouraged a team atmosphere, so I was surrounded by laughing, talking people while doing chemistry; and (3) I got the highest score in the class on a standardized exam we were given at the beginning of the course as a benchmark. I know now that these three factors – hands-on learning, collaborative learning, and external validation – have long been important in the discussion of how to bring girls into science, but at the time, I was just enjoying myself (Rosser, 1990; Rosser, 1995). After that class, I decided I would major in chemistry in college, still with an eye toward journalism in case things didn't work out.

COMMITTING TO CHEMISTRY IN COLLEGE

For financial reasons, I chose to go to a state institution (essentially for free) rather than the prestigious liberal arts college that was my other option. Unlike at the liberal arts college, where several female faculty had spoken during my visit of their support for young women in science, there were no female faculty members in the chemistry department at the state institution. I didn't think of this situation as a problem – after all, there had been no female science teachers at my high school, and I had done fine there.

My first year in college went well, but when I hit my second year, I began to have difficulty in both organic chemistry and advanced calculus. Annoyingly, my calculus professor routinely referred to the "pretty girls" in his class, thinking he was paying the handful of us who were female a compliment, but I'm sure that was not the issue. In truth, I had finally hit material that I couldn't pick up quickly and easily. I had been accustomed to getting A's and B's with very little effort, but this term wasn't shaping up that way. I also just couldn't seem to get interested in organic chemistry, finding it difficult even to go to class. As soon as I could predict what my grades were going to be, I went to the registrar to add English as a second major. I thought my upcoming "failures" – I was getting at least one C for sure, possibly two – and my lack of interest in organic chemistry meant that I wasn't cut out to be a scientist, and so I wanted to get the process of switching majors started. In fact, when I later read "Talking About Leaving," which was published when I was in graduate school, the voices of the "female switchers" captured my feelings from that time so exactly I was shocked (Seymour & Hewitt, 1997).

As I was deciding whether to leave chemistry entirely, one of the chemistry faculty members invited me to join his research group, and when I declined, he asked me why. He was known for being very supportive of women in science, and I suspect he knew I was considering switching out of chemistry, as a friend of mine worked with him. When I finally admitted I needed to focus on classes because I wasn't doing as well as I had hoped, he arranged for me to be tutored in calculus by a female post-doctoral associate. She was my first female role model in science, and I owe her a great deal. As a physical chemist herself, she informed me that there were different areas of study within chemistry, and that very few chemists enjoyed all of them. After working with her, I found calculus much easier, even if organic chemistry didn't get any more interesting.

After that term, I had the opportunity to take time off for a six-month internship at the state laboratory, running routine analytical tests. Again I was immersed in an environment of playing with chemicals (actually, sewage), with people who enjoyed each other and their jobs. My supervisor was a woman who had graduated from the same university I was attending, and her funny stories about various organic professors made them seem much more human to me. When I returned to campus after the internship, I found that my tutor had been right – the final quarter of organic chemistry, taught by a newly hired physical organic chemist, was much better. (And my physical chemistry courses the following year were fascinating!) So, I stayed with chemistry, and learned soon thereafter that the university was among 14 nationwide that had just been awarded a pilot grant under the Ronald E. McNair Post-Baccalaureate Achievement Program (North Dakota State University, 2002), and I could be qualified to receive some funding for undergraduate research as a McNair Scholar. The purpose of the pilot program was to interest under-represented students in graduate school in science, encouraging them to make a commitment to pursue faculty positions and serve as role models for others. The program's goal made complete sense to me, since I knew that my interactions with female chemists had helped me stay in chemistry, and I wanted, in turn, to help those coming after me to succeed. As it turns out, I can honestly say that if it weren't for the McNair Program, I would not be a faculty member in chemistry, but not for the usual reasons!

Undergraduate research, which typically attracts students into graduate school, is the centerpiece of the McNair Program; however, my undergraduate research experience had the opposite effect. It was completely demoralizing. The same newly hired physical organic faculty member who had made organic chemistry interesting was my research mentor. I would have worked with him even without the support of the McNair Program, since I found his organic lectures truly engaging and his research focus, solvent effects in supercritical fluids, intriguing. The experiments I conducted involved simple absorbance measurements of beta-carotene, but everything had to be scrupulously clean to avoid spurious results. I understood the need for cleanliness and tried many different solvents and cleaning methods, but my research mentor consistently saw evidence of impurities in the spectra. Finally, after rejecting yet another set of spectra it had taken me all night to collect, he fired me, telling me I would never be a scientist. I still believe he was trying to be helpful by preventing me from wasting time pursuing a career in which he felt I would not succeed, but it was devastating. Even all these years later, my primary feeling about that time is that I should have figured out how to get better data! At the time, I was crushed, and decided that he was right and I should use my remaining term to finish my English major rather than my chemistry major. Accordingly, I made an appointment with the McNair Program director to inform her that I had let the program down and would not be going on to graduate school.

In the interim, I received my GRE score report, and once again, the external validation provided by a high-test score played a major role in my career path. After telling me that I would have no problem with graduate school in chemistry if that was what I wanted to do, the McNair Program director assigned me to another research mentor from a different department. I spent only one term in his laboratory, playing with starch and learning how to interpret EPR spectra, but I was having fun with chemistry again. Since I was still feeling shaky about graduate school, this new mentor actually scheduled time for me to come to his office and work on graduate school applications.

Looking back, I recognize that if there had not been a strong wind pushing for the cause of women in science all through my college years, I would not be in chemistry today. Informal support networks and the McNair Program were critical in providing me with a safety net, convincing me to stay in chemistry regardless of setbacks. In addition, McNair's focus on supporting students from under-represented groups, which at that time included women in science, enabled me to begin to construct an identity specifically as a woman in science. I also owe some of that identity construction to the faculty members in the English department in whose courses I had a safe space to discuss gender and power, and who brought Dale Spender to campus for a riveting presentation during my senior year. I recall vividly my amazement that anyone would dare write a book called *Women of Ideas and What Men Have Done to Them* (Spender, 1982)! This openly feminist intellectual stance, which was available to me as an undergraduate only outside of science, became a stronger and stronger part of how I saw myself in graduate school.

SUPPORTED BY THE WIND: GRADUATE SCHOOL IN THE 1990S

I had learned from my undergraduate experience that the "fit" between research advisor and student would be a critical part of success in graduate school. I was still intrigued by the idea of solvent effects, and I used the American Chemical Society (ACS) Directory of Graduate Research to locate seven physical chemists at seven different schools doing research on solvation. With the encouragement of the McNair Program director, I asked for funding from all seven schools to visit in person so that I could meet each prospective graduate research mentor and his (they were all male) current students. In some cases, I was invited to join regular recruiting events, and in others, a special separate trip was arranged for me, but I had no problem getting travel support, which I attribute to the fact that it was the early 1990s and I was a prospective female graduate student with high GRE scores. Recruiting and retaining women in science had been firmly established as important by that time (Dresselhaus, 1991).

With my eyes fully opened to the idea that there might be barriers facing women wanting to go into science, I also made a point to find female graduate students and ask a few questions about overall climate. At several schools, their candid responses immediately removed that institution from consideration. When I was finished with my round of visits, there were only two real choices left from the original seven, and I decided to work with Mark Maroncelli at Penn State University. It was an excellent decision: he provided support, patience, and encouragement throughout my graduate research career, even though I'm sure my full roster of outside activities (addressed below) based on interests in women and science and later in science education made it very difficult at times. He was a true mentor, always checking to make sure I understood what I was getting into, but supporting my decisions even when they weren't in his best interest. For example, when I was offered a summer teaching position as a visiting lecturer the year before I graduated, which is usually the time a graduate student is extremely productive and the research advisor finally reaps the benefits of several years of training, I remember him sighing, looking at me, and saying, "I know you really want to do this, so ok, go ahead." Sure enough, I got no research at all done that summer ... but I had a fabulous time learning how to teach in a large lecture setting.

While I enjoyed my chemistry graduate courses and laboratory research, Penn State in the 1990s was an excellent environment for a female graduate student in science, and I set out to enjoy that larger experience as well. Why do I say the atmosphere was so positive? Well, for one thing, finally I was surrounded by a "critical mass" of women in science. In the chemistry graduate program alone there were sufficient numbers of women that I didn't even know all of them, and a few were actually pursuing the physical chemistry track. The three female professors in the department, including the chair for several years, were very different from one another both in personality and in research interests, so there was a certain freedom from stereotyping. I met even more women in science through organized programs and events outside the department. The Women in Science and Engineering (WISE) organization staged several major events annually, and I also had opportunities to develop and deliver hands-on science workshops for middle school girls through a program called Expanding Your Horizons, fulfilling my McNair-inspired desire to serve as a role model for young girls interested in science. In general, anytime there was an event for which female graduate students in science were invited as role models for younger students, I was there, and I felt good about it.

Another positive aspect of the atmosphere was support for the development of a truly feminist perspective on women and science. Throughout my graduate career, I had the privilege of hearing many invited lectures by current scholars working on issues around women and science, and often was part of the small group invited to meet with them for in-depth discussions. Mildred Dresselhaus, Sheila Tobias, and Margaret Wertheim are just three that I recall, each of whom spoke on women in physics with different critical lens (Dresselhaus, 1991; Tobias, 1990; Wertheim, 1995). My research advisor also gave me permission – with the proviso that it not interfere with my lab work – to sit in on a graduate seminar on Women and

Science offered by Londa Schiebinger, who at that time was a faculty member in History and Women's Studies at Pennsylvania State University. In addition to work by other scholars, she included several chapters from her yet-to-be published book, *Nature's Body: Gender in the Making of Modern Science* (Schiebinger, 1993). Access to such current scholarship was exciting and contributed to my sense that this was a rare opportunity. The class included a handful of students from history and women's studies and another handful from various science disciplines, and my memories include thought-provoking discussions about the values encoded within different disciplinary frameworks. Finally, during my last few years in graduate school, a female faculty member in the physics department ran a "Women in Physics" group for graduate students, which attracted those female students from chemistry, math, meteorology, and physics who believed that there was value in discussing issues faced by women in science. We used this safe space to share research ideas and give practice presentations, and a few of us ultimately developed the habit of meeting for breakfast regularly. Not everything was rosy, but the wind was definitely with me, and I developed a stronger and stronger identity as a feminist woman in science.

With all of this outside activity, where did I find time for research? When I look back, I remember a few signature moments in the lab, but the brightest spots of my life were elsewhere. I did develop solid research skills and produced the useable data on supercritical fluid solvation that had eluded me as an undergraduate, but gradually I began to realize that I was just as interested in hearing about my fellow research group members' experiments, as I was in conducting my own. In other words, as long as I got to improve my own understanding of solvation, which continues to fascinate me, it didn't matter to me whether I was the one making the discoveries. At the same time, I had become involved as a Teaching Assistant (TA) in the development of a new collaborative-learning-based course for at-risk students, and in that case, just hearing about it wasn't enough – I wanted to try everything myself. The instructor in charge of the course, Mary Jo Bojan, gave the TAs a great deal of freedom as long as we used group work in class, and I would wake up in the morning having dreamed a new strategy for forming groups, or a new way to ask for a student presentation, and be able to give it a whirl the next time I met with my students. I found that I really loved teaching chemistry to these at-risk students, and that my own early difficulties with organic chemistry gave me empathy for their struggles. I did, however, want to figure out what was known about how best to teach, so that I could really make a difference in the classroom. Little did I know at the time that this innocent desire to be a better teacher would become the sort of consuming research passion that informs a career trajectory.

As a senior graduate student, I knew that my first stop for information on a new topic should be relevant research literature, but where to start? Rick Moog, whom I had met when he brought undergraduate research students to work in my advisor's lab one summer, had developed materials for guided inquiry in chemistry at Franklin and Marshall College (Moog & Farrell, 1996), so I began with some of the resources he said he had found useful. I soon found that there was enough research literature on cooperative learning to drown in, and I knew I would need more direction. So that I wouldn't drive my research advisor completely crazy, I stopped asking formally for permission and just began sitting in on interesting graduate courses offered by the College of Education. The one-night-a-week seminar format of many of the courses, designed to be accessible to working teachers, was also perfect for a graduate student stealing time from research. My two favorite courses were one on science methods, in which the professor insisted we had to construct our own definition of constructivism based on various texts and our own life experiences, and one on feminist pedagogy, which felt deliciously radical to me. Ultimately, by my last year in graduate school, I had become completely entranced by science education as a discipline ... but I was still on target to graduate with a Ph.D. in physical chemistry. What to do?

During that last year of graduate school, I also won a travel award from the American Chemical Society (ACS) Women Chemists' Committee to present some of my graduate research at the 1998 Spring ACS national meeting in Dallas. Rick Moog was planning to present a talk in a symposium sponsored by the Committee on Chemical Education Research at that meeting, and he casually told me that I should try to catch the symposium because I would enjoy it. I jumped on what I saw as a great opportunity to meet people who would know how a doctorate in physical chemistry could be turned into a chance to pursue a newfound interest in science education. Whatever his own agenda had been for that day, poor Rick wound up introducing me to at least 30 different people, all of whom were welcoming and supportive. My postdoctoral position teaching chemistry at Beloit College and helping with faculty development workshops as part of the ChemConnections Systemic Change Initiative was a direct result of those contacts. To this day, Don Wink reminds me that he was the one who wrote down my e-mail address and forwarded the job ad that led to my post-doc position. After two years at Beloit, still learning about chemical education as fast as I could, I went on the job market and obtained a faculty position.

DID THE WIND SHIFT, OR DID I?

The closer in time events are, the harder it is find the emotional distance necessary to frame them. For the past five years, I have been an Assistant Professor of Chemistry at the University of South Florida (USF) with the defined research area of chemical education. Chemical education, which views itself as a sub-discipline of chemistry on par with biochemistry, analytical chemistry, etc, is typically housed (in the United States) within chemistry departments rather than in schools of education. The field has grown substantially in these few years. For example, when I began accepting chemical education doctoral students at USF in 2001, the Committee on Chemical Education Research reported only twelve other doctoral programs in chemical education in the United States. There are now 21 such programs (Committee on Chemical Education Research, 2006) and my first two doctoral students, both of whom graduated in 2006, had no difficulty finding academic positions within chemistry departments.

My research focuses on chemistry instruction at the college level, with particular concern for students who are at-risk. I have implemented and evaluated a major curricular change in general chemistry at USF (Lewis & Lewis, 2005), and as of this coming semester my colleagues have given me permission to expand it from 200 students per semester to over 1000. I have received NSF funding in conjunction with this project and several others, all in support of improving undergraduate science instruction.

Since I am in a chemistry department and I teach college-level chemistry courses, my identity is still that of a feminist woman in science. However, now that I collect data from people rather than from molecules, the invitations to serve as a role model for young scientists have disappeared. It feels as though the wind that helped to propel me as a woman in science has shifted now that I trust social science research methods and call for curricular reform, but I am grateful that the shelter created by the field of chemical education research has allowed me to find a home in chemistry.

Recently, one of my graduate students defended a research report before a committee composed of an analytical chemist, a chemical educator, a science education researcher, and myself. As I watched him struggle with the challenge of finding language that would be compelling for each of those different perspectives, I recognized again that being in a chemistry department affords me with daily opportunities to talk with faculty who would not ordinarily read educational research results, and I was very proud that my student was up to the challenge. Although I am the only education researcher in a science department at USF, with a network of chemical education research colleagues across the U.S., a department that supports a graduate program, and a group of graduate students who will argue with me about theory on a daily basis if I so desire, I cannot imagine a better position.

As I write this chapter, I am preparing my tenure file. I remember all the people I knew along the way who were not awarded tenure, and take a deep breath as I just keep going, whistling for a wind.

POSTSCRIPT

Nine months after I submitted the first draft of this chapter, I am happy to report that my tenure case has been successful at all levels of the university and I fully expect to change my business cards to read "Associate Professor" very soon. In retrospect, the simultaneous experiences of writing this chapter and compiling a tenure dossier left me braver, more able to take risks regarding less traditional forms of scholarship. I would note that I was not quite brave enough, however, to have included this chapter in my tenure dossier.

REFERENCES

Committee on Chemical Education Research. (2006). *Masters & doctoral programs in chemistry education*. Retrieved August 18, 2006, from http://www.users.muohio.edu/bretzsl/cer/programs.htm

Dresselhaus, M. S. (1991). *Women in science and engineering: Increasing their numbers in the 1990s: A statement on policy and strategy*. Washington, DC: National Academy Press.

Lewis, S. E., & Lewis, J. E. (2005). Departing from lectures: An evaluation of a peer-led guided inquiry alternative. *Journal of Chemical Education, 82*(1), 135–139.

Moog, R. S., & Farrell, J. J. (1996). *Chemistry: A guided inquiry.* New York: John Wiley & Sons.

North Dakota State University. (2002). *The McNair scholars program.* Retrieved August 16, 2006, from http://www.ndsu.edu/trio/msp/msp.html

Rosser, S. V. (1990). *Female-friendly science: Applying women's studies methods and theories to attract students.* Elmsford, NY: Pergamon Press.

Rosser, S. V. (Ed.). (1995). *Teaching the majority: Breaking the gender barrier in science, mathematics, and engineering.* New York: Teachers College Press.

Schiebinger, L. (1993). *Nature's body: Gender in the making of modern science.* Boston: Beacon Press.

Seymour, E., & Hewitt, N. M. (1997). *Talking about leaving: Why undergraduates leave the sciences.* Boulder, CO: Westview Press.

Spender, D. (1982). Women of ideas - and what men have done to them. London: Pandora Press.

Tobias, S. (1990). *They're not dumb, they're different: Stalking the second tier.* Tucson, AZ: Research Corporation.

Wertheim, M. (1995). *Pythagoras' trousers: God, physics, and the gender wars.* New York: Random House.

AFFILIATION

Jennifer E. Lewis
Department of Chemistry,
University of South Florida

KAREN E. S. PHILLIPS

9. IT'S MY LIFE

Straddling the Science, Education and Culture of Different Worlds

I'll never forget the first time someone called me a Black girl. I was about 25 at the time, had been in the United States (US) for two years or so, and was enrolled in a community college - one of a handful of students under 65 in my painting class. Most of my classmates were fixtures - as firmly entrenched in their ways as they were in their artistic styles. Life-long south Floridians melded with snowbirds from up north who stopped making the return trip years before. One day during class, a young man whom I didn't know was sent to find me. Harry, one of my older classmates, had his easel set up closest to the door and responded to the query while packing up his palette box. Harry always made sure that everyone heard him and this time was no exception. His exaggerated drawl burst through the monotone as he shuffled across to his easel. "She's the Black girl sitting over there." He made a broad theatrical stroke with his arm and wagged an index finger in my direction. Without even the slightest pause for thought, I turned and looked over my opposite shoulder to see whom he was talking about. It would take several moments before it hit home that Harry was talking about me.

I am still learning how my views on race and ethnicity, and my upbringing, factor into my identity as scientist, chemistry educator and researcher. I always perceived myself as Jamaican – West Indian to be inclusive of others from English-speaking islands and Caribbean Islander whenever I needed to get fancy. For me, that came with images of widely ranging skin colors, facial features, body types and hair textures. Pictures of our national heroes – Paul Bogle, Alexander Bustamante, Marcus Garvey, George William Gordon, Norman Washington Manley, Nanny of the Maroons and Sam Sharpe – illustrate the visual variety in mythical role models I had as a child, whose looks were not unlike people I saw around me daily.

Women and men of diverse ancestry have occupied positions of political and economic power in Jamaica since before I was born. Portia Simpson Miller, a woman who in the US would belong to a minority group still underrepresented in science and government, holds the highest political office in my native country as its current Prime Minister. Even if they aren't involved in politics, women are primary breadwinners and decision makers in many Jamaican families. This was certainly true in my family, which continually reinforced my impression that Jamaica was matriarchal in several aspects of its socioeconomic structure. These influences made me believe that there were no limits to what I could do or be. As I study the

K. Scantlebury, J. Butler Kahle and S. N. Martin (eds.). Re-visioning Science Education from Feminist Perspectives: Challenges, Choices and Careers, 89–102.

influence of socio-cultural issues on teaching and learning, I see that there is a lot to be learned from a look back at things that shaped my identity, both before and since my arrival in the US.

THIRTY-TWO FLAVORS

I loved to hear stories of my maternal ancestors, the Rowes and the Bothams, from Scotland, who left a trail through the United Kingdom and Europe before heading for Jamaica. My mother spent many years tracing the origins of the distinct eye shape that some of her sisters' share, which seems to derive from a stop that her forefathers made in China en route to the New World. They arrived in my homeland as the Robothams and although I never knew my grandfather, David, pictures of him remind me of suntanned British sailors I saw on television. My grandmother, Maude Beatrice Robotham, was of English, Native American and Jewish stock, and I was always fascinated by the size of her nose. The forebears of her family, the Steers, migrated from the Middle East to England before making their way to the Caribbean. On the Phillips side, my grandfather Jacob's dark skin made him appear more African than anyone else in my family, although he too had English blood. My other grandmother, born Agnes Constantine, bore genes from yet another complex mixture including Greek and African roots with a noticeable South Asian influence. Family pictures looked like posters for our national motto, Out of Many - One People, and we always had great appreciation for all components of our ancestry.

Grandma Maude was an important figure in her community. An accomplished musician, nurse, and midwife, she developed a reputation as the Florence Nightingale of Kingston. My mother, Leila, the bellywash[1] would often go with grandma on rounds throughout the city. She witnessed many being brought back from the brink of death, observed all sorts of complicated deliveries, and absorbed everything she could about making poultices or concocting herb mixtures and pharmaceutical remedies. Most people didn't bother to call a doctor since Nurse Robotham would dash out in the middle of the night and knew as much as any qualified physician. She lived with my family until shortly before her death at ninety-six, when I was about six, and it was she and my mother who first taught me to read. I have been embarrassed by all too frequently repeated stories of my earliest childhood learning experiences, which involved sitting on someone's knee reading a newspaper or hanging out at the back fence being taught to swear by construction workers on site behind our home. From the moment I could talk, I provided hours of family entertainment by reeling off endless strings of obscenities. Ironically, it became impossible for me to utter anything more colorful than damn or crap as soon as I understood why what I said was so amusing to everyone else.

I had my turn helping my mother to monitor her special brew that simmered for three days on an open fire in the back yard. Many strange things were tossed into the cauldron - a white enamel tub with navy-blue trim in which I once bathed. Pimento seeds, Chainey Root, Strong Back, Briar Whiss, Nerve Whiss and other secret ingredients steeped with Sarsaparilla, which we pronounced as the far more ominous Saucy-Periler. The thick, blackish-brown extract that emerged was sweetened with honey and molasses and laced with bottles and bottles of Wray and Nephew White, Overproof Rum.[2] This transformed it into the finished Roots Tonic, reputed to cure anything and make everyone feel really good in the process of being healed.

My mother still brews a batch of tonic on the stovetop every few years, and I keep it, along with some White Rum, nutmeg, fresh garlic, and ginger, on hand at all times as potent remedies for common ailments ranging from colds, chest congestion and influenza, to toothaches, nausea or diarrhea. At a recent, home-cooked dinner, Mummy told friends about a preparation made from young turnips to treat asthma and, on her recommendation, I once prescribed a mixture of coconut palm roots and water from a young coconut to relieve migraine headaches. These proven practices, integral to our culture, were passed across generations and communities through our oral history. Although they weren't printed in scientific or medical texts, they were followed in equally systematic ways and widely accepted for their effectiveness.

DON'T FENCE ME IN

My mother and grandmother decided not to send me to school as a child. My older brother and sister started their formal education at a very young age but the reputation of the school they attended, where my aunt Thelma taught, was waning. I would be taught at home until things improved and everyone in the family took turns guiding me in my directions of interest. I gravitated toward science. My constant companions were a dictionary and a thick, green textbook called Everyday Problems in Science. I memorized a new word each day, learned about chemistry and physics theories and devised experiments based on my reading. I formulated lotions, dismantled and reassembled whatever electronic equipment I could get my hands on and made new gizmos with bits and pieces of broken appliances. I even opened the chest and abdominal cavities of lizards after anesthetizing them with rum, observed their pulsating hearts and drew pictures of their internal organs before stitching them up again. I kept these lizards under observation in a storage room and set them free once they could resume their crawl up the walls.

The year I turned eight stands out as pivotal in my life. I was a prodigious little artist, and I remember standing back from a drawing that I just completed of the singer Barry White and saying, "You know...this is really good for an eight-year-old!" I had trained myself to represent the human form in photorealistic detail and could recognize a big difference between what I did and what I saw in the sketches of playmates. That same year, aunt Thelma started teaching at another school close to where we lived. My mother decided to take that opportunity to send me off for the first time in my neatly pressed and pleated blue uniform.

Once in school, I was teased by other students who pulled my long pigtails and joked about my knock-kneed legs. Sister Mary Grace, a Catholic nun whose family emigrated from China, was a great help in my transition since I was completely unaccustomed to the type of peer-to-peer social life that I encountered. I decided to show my appreciation by giving her a drawing I had done of Norman Manley, one of our national heroes. I approached her on my way to class one day and very shyly handed her the rolled up pencil sketch. She opened it up, raised her eyebrows and asked me repeatedly, "Who really did the drawing?" When I insisted that I did, she gave me a condescending pat on the shoulder and gentle but pious admonishment for not telling the truth. I was absolutely infuriated and decided that I had enough. When school bullies pushed me down a few days later and bruised my knees, I knew I had the ammunition to convince my mother not to send me back. I had only been there for a few months but could feel the constraints of not being free to explore the fullest extent of my scientific and artistic curiosity. Once I was again ensconced in my limitless home environment, I began perfecting my techniques for representing hair with pencil on paper, had my own tresses lopped off in my first visit to a barbershop, and started writing my detailed, scientifically theorized treatise on time travel.

ONE WAY OR ANOTHER

I didn't go back to school until two years later. I was ten, which was much younger than most of the students in the grade five class I joined in the middle of the school year.[3] I had a hard time making friends since everyone else had gone through years of learning and socializing together. The school principal, Mr. Edwards, lived at my aunt Carmen's home and that offered me a feeling of safety. He came into classes at random to administer speed drills on various mathematical operations. We had to memorize multiplication tables up to 16 x 16 and if you missed the product when your turn came, you might get a stinging slap on the hand. He would write a list of one- and two-digit numbers from the top of the chalkboard to the bottom and, by the time he drew the line under the last number, you had to have the entire sum computed in your head. The first person to finish got his most valued praise and I won several challenges. This brought respect from some quarters… antagonism from others.

These drills were a part of our preparation for the Common Entrance Examination,[4] for which Mr. Edwards had a reputation of grooming several Government Scholars every year.[5] He led extra lessons before classes each morning and after classes in the afternoons. The school was on church property and these lessons were held outside next to a graveyard, which doubled as our playground - tombstones serving as obstacles for games. Once or twice, when I answered questions that none of my classmates could, Mr. Edwards called me a genius. This was nice for the ego but escalated my feeling that some of the students might like to hurt me if they could. Mr. Edwards was a tough disciplinarian though, and I knew that I was protected by the fact that anyone who stepped out of line did so in fear of the thick leather strap he kept dangling from his back pocket.

Once extra lessons were over, my cousin and I had little time to play among the graves before piling into Mr. Edwards' Volkswagen Beetle for the ride home. After dinner with the family, our own private lessons began. By the time my parents came to pick me up, I was utterly exhausted. I had gone from no structured schooling to being in class from 7:30 each morning until 9 o'clock every night. I took some comfort in knowing that I only had to do this for a limited time since the Common Entrance Exam was coming up in a short while.

One night, about three months before the exam, Mr. Edwards called my parents in to discuss my progress. He told them that I had tremendous potential – that I could earn a Government Scholarship, but might need an extra year to prepare adequately and mature. My cousin, who is a year older than I am, had actually taken the exam the year before but only earned a Free Place.[6] Mr. Edwards believed that she could get a scholarship too, so she was made to repeat her grade six year with me as her classmate. That evening, he urged my parents to let me do the same. As soon as we were out of earshot, I told them that there was no way in hell I would go through that again!

I still marvel at that moment, not because I could say what I said to my parents, who always made us feel that we were part of the process of making decisions about our lives but because, at eleven, I had the agency to ensure that what happened to my cousin wouldn't happen to me. I felt insulted that Mr. Edwards assumed I wasn't already capable of getting a scholarship and I was determined to prove him wrong. I worked my butt off over the next months, focused every ounce of energy I could muster preparing for that exam, and visualized the only result that I felt could keep me from certain death. When the day came, I remember having a great sense of power over my academic destiny. I knew that I had done well.

We gathered around the Daily Gleaner[7] to search for my name on the day the results were posted. We found it in the upper part of a full-page spread with about fifteen others that had titles of various scholarships written in italics next to them. Karen E. S. Phillips was emblazoned in the top, far-left corner and J. A. G. Smith was inscribed next to it.[8] I searched for my cousin's name and finally saw it in the blocks of small type that filled the lower part of the page. This was the same section where her name had appeared the year before. My heart sank on her behalf. What I felt in response to my own performance was great triumph. I knew that I could do it, but it took a while for it to sink in that what I had done was score the highest point total in my entire country.[9]

UNISON

When I look at these experiences against the backdrop of my research interests, I recognize that the influences of my childhood allowed me to become a self-directed learner. I was motivated intrinsically, assumed responsibility for my education and destiny and could apply my knowledge across a wide range of situations (Hartman, 1990). Once I started school, it was clear that I was ahead of many students in my class. Evidently, I had mastered the essentials of self-directed learning: cognition, involving my ability to encode, memorize and recall information encountered through reading or makeshift experiments; metacognition, enabling me to monitor and understand what was going on in my cognitive processing by assessing what I was learning and how well I knew it; and motivation, which was clearly evident in my strong drive and beliefs about my academic skills (Schraw et al., 2006). My thoughts about drawing Barry White, my paper on time travel, and my assessment of my performance on the Common Entrance Exam were evidence of a strong metacognitive component to this self-directed learning. I was constantly assessing what I knew and how well I knew it. I wanted to dissect everything in my mind and in my reach, armed with the knowledge that I could reconstruct it or make it into something else if I wanted to.

With my J. A. G. Smith scholarship in hand, I entered The Queen's School, an all-girls high school in Kingston that my sister Judy attended before me.[10] As its name might suggest, many of my teachers at Queens were from England or had been educated there. The atmosphere in school could sometimes be quite formal and rather British. The teacher who stood out most in terms of my learning was Mrs. Carlene Ramprashad, my general science and chemistry instructor. The ability to explore scientific concepts had been symbolic of educational freedom for me and I can see how a highly regimented form of instruction might have lessened or even destroyed the relationship that I had cultivated with the subject. My love for science would remain secure in Mrs. Ramprashad's hands as her style of teaching fit perfectly with my way of learning.

Mrs. Ramprashad actively discouraged rote memorization, pushing us to think about questions in relation to the basic principles that we were taught. Now I can recognize that what she encouraged was metacognitive thinking. We were always asked to explain what happened and why things happened the way that they did. My recollection is that she kept asking why until there was nothing left to say. This armed me with the ability to reason things through and check myself for accuracy. If the answer that I arrived at fit the pattern of reasoning that I was taught, I knew that I was right without needing her to tell me I was. This was extremely empowering, allowing me to develop self-efficacy in the sciences, especially chemistry. Many years later, when I finished my Ph.D., I would dedicate my thesis to my mother and Mrs. Ramprashad. I credit them both with being powerful influences on my learning that continue to inspire the way that I teach chemistry today.

FLIPSIDE

I visited America for the first time while still in high school, coming on a brief shopping trip to Florida with my mother and sister. One day, the three of us were milling around the clothing racks in a department store when we sensed that we were being watched. The cashier gestured in our direction to a security guard and another sales clerk, who immediately came closer toward us. We were triangulated. Since the sales clerk made no attempt to ask what we were looking for, it was clear that the intent was not to be helpful. After a brief consultation, we decided that talking to our apparent accusers might belie their negative assumptions. We turned to the sales clerk and asked if she had a certain garment in a particular size. We expected to have to talk for a while, but the response was immediate and visibly obvious. In the instant that they heard our Jamaican accents, the body language and attitudes of all three of our observers changed dramatically. The security guard turned and walked back to his post by the door to gaze outside at passers by; the cashier allowed a little smile to escape from her face and resumed fixing the display behind the counter; and the sales clerk broke into a wide grin as she swooped over to bring us piles of things to try on. They chatted with us, asked questions about our trip, and pleaded with us to come back again. We chatted and smiled in return but walked out of the store in dismay, taken aback by what had likely been our first encounter with racism in the US.

It wasn't an easy decision to leave my homeland for America. For one thing, it was difficult to move away from my mother, especially since my sister already lived in Florida by then. The three of us depended on each other for all kinds of support and I worried about how Mummy would cope with us both gone. It was also difficult to leave the burgeoning sideline I had established as one of the first female disc jockeys in the country. I was becoming quite well known as Lady K, and had just been offered a contract as the featured purveyor of dance music at a new nightclub in Kingston. As a DJ, I was able to exercise skills that I picked up in my childhood. I would often fix my own stereo equipment, built my own speaker boxes, and knew how to use capacitors and resistors to tune the sounds going to different speakers. My reputation had grown as much for these technical skills as it had for my song selection and beat-matching ability. I also took as much pride in helping younger DJs to optimize the power and sound quality of their equipment as I did in keeping a New Year's Eve dance floor packed until 2 p.m. the next day. I knew that I didn't want to do this forever though, and could sense that a move to a different country might provide the fresh start that my academic career needed.

I had experienced failure for the first time while attending the University of the West Indies after high school, and this was crushing to me. It was also difficult to separate this from struggles going on within my family. I had fallen into a pattern of connecting academic success to the approval of others, including my father. I recognize now that my failure was also a form of rebellion or enactment of power against things that I couldn't control. Although it was impossible to return to times when I was free to learn things simply because I wanted to, I needed to figure out how to internalize the desire for my own accomplishment. This seemed impossible in surroundings where I had practiced pleasing others for so long, so I hoped that a different environment would give me both courage and opportunity to change that.[11]

INVISIBLE WAR

My only B during my US college years came in a Sociology class that I took during my first semester at Miami-Dade Community College. The teacher, who identified as African-American, came to class in African garb, and presented the material from the perspective of the African-American experience of racism. I did not have a full appreciation of race in America at the time and couldn't anticipate how difficult it would be to discuss my life. When I tried to, I felt shut down. Once, when I asked this teacher a question in private, I was met with a derogatory remark about the fact that I sat next to a White girl during class. It was difficult for me to believe that someone could be so blatantly separatist, especially in a freshman-level required course. However, another uncomfortable encounter would make me skeptical about this man's sense of fairness.

This came after the final exam, when I noticed that points were deducted for a question that I answered consistently with the answer key. Again, I went to the professor outside of class to ask about it. Without looking at my paper, he said, "Well, if you're that desperate, I can give you the points."[12] I was blindsided by this experience. What I understood of racism at the time led me to think that, if I saw it, it would come from the direction of the White majority. I had many instructors of many an ethnic ilk, but I did not have a similar experience with another teacher or administrator. If anything, I suspected that I was the "victim" of favoritism. I won two scholarships while at Miami-Dade, one for overall academic excellence and another for fine art, and I received Departmental Awards for Outstanding Achievement in Chemistry, Biology, History and Foreign Languages, as well as a Divisional Award for Outstanding Academic Achievement in Natural Sciences.

LITTLE EARTHQUAKES

I remained at Miami-Dade much longer than the two years required for an Associate's degree, mainly because I couldn't afford to go anywhere else. During those years, I also made a conscious effort to overcome my social awkwardness. I started a chemistry club with a few of my classmates and served as its president. I knew that this would force me to address relatively large audiences, which I was terrified to do, but I recognized that pretending that I was someone else and plunging headlong into it my fear was the only way to overcome it. I also became a tutor in the chemistry department, which gave me great confidence in that subject and provided a unique and life-altering opportunity.

As a chemistry tutor, I developed an excellent reputation as well as an excellent rapport with the department chair and faculty. One fateful fall semester, two instructors fell ill and died within the first weeks of classes. All of the usual adjuncts had already taken up their assignments and students were enrolled with no one to teach them. The department chair called me into his office one day and said, "You're our only hope." So, there I was, still a student, but called upon to teach my favorite subject[13] It was scary, but I felt excited by the prospect and honored by the trust that was being placed in me. Once I stepped into the classroom, I was hooked! I fell completely in love with teaching and knew from that moment that this is what I was meant to do.

In the meantime, my mother had joined us in Florida. My sister filed for her to become a permanent resident of the US and then my mother filed for me. A few days before my application for a green card was approved, she was diagnosed as having a tumor resting against her left temporal lobe. She opted to have it surgically removed, and was operated on two days after I was granted US residency. I dropped out of school again, this time to help care for and support my mother.[14] I returned to Miami-Dade's chemistry department, where I taught, tested experiments and developed a manual for the organic chemistry laboratory. By then, I was gravitating toward organic, perhaps because it allowed me to tap into the strong visual and spatial sense that I had developed through art. I remained in that position for two years, until I became a Florida resident for tuition purposes and could accept a fellowship with the Minority Access to Research Careers (MARC) Program at Barry University.

SHADOW BOXING

The MARC Program is an initiative of the National Institutes of Health, designed to encourage students from ethnic groups underrepresented in science to earn doctoral degrees.[15] To qualify for a MARC fellowship, I felt compelled to check a box next to Black/African-American, Hispanic, Asian/Pacific Islander, or Native American[16] There was also the option to check "Other," but I worried that I would risk not getting the scholarship if I didn't identify as one of the targeted groups. At the same time, I didn't feel like I belonged to any of them. I was torn. I am surprised at how much anxiety I still feel as I try to remember what I put down. The point is that this was a dilemma for me. To compound my uneasiness, a few White/Caucasian students on campus were protesting their exclusion from these fellowship programs, declaring it unfair that students get preferential treatment because of race. I wanted to prove that I could win a scholarship against anyone, regardless of race, ethnicity or gender. I didn't want anyone to feel I was given an advantage that I didn't deserve but, realistically, the only way I could afford to finish my Bachelor's degree was with that scholarship.

I graduated from Barry University summa cum laude, opting for graduate studies at Columbia University. Columbia's high ranking among institutions offering a Ph.D. in organic chemistry was definitely significant to my decision, but I had also heard its name mentioned in one of my favorite movies and wanted to see what it was like to live in New York City. The campus left an impression of great formality and tradition in comparison to most other universities that I visited. I found this comforting since it reminded me of my rather British high school experience and other cultural influences left behind in Jamaica. To be perfectly honest, I still knew very little about what it meant to get a Ph.D. Although the MARC Program had done well to prepare me, not having family or friends who went through the experience made it difficult to know what to expect.

RUNNING UP THAT HILL

Earning my Ph.D. was one of the most difficult things that I have ever done. There were only about sixteen of us accepted in the chemistry department at Columbia that year, and I am surprised that I was one of the few who made it through. I worked harder than I ever had to in my academic life, but always felt I was just getting by. Although I'm sure everyone found it difficult, it was not easy to talk about the struggle. It was also not easy to talk about the fact that I really wanted to teach, since, I was told, this might give the impression that I was not serious about research. My classmates would often joke with each other saying, "Research is my life!" knowing full well that this was the impression we had to convey to succeed at the graduate level in the Ivy League.

There were many mechanisms in place at Columbia to inform students about career opportunities in the pharmaceutical industry, and we were constantly bombarded with examples of individuals who earned acclaim through laboratory research in academia. In addition, students whose interests bordered on physics or biology would often take classes in those disciplines, but when I suggested that I sit in on classes at Teachers College,[17] I was actively discouraged with the addendum that what they did at TC was "Mickey Mouse stuff." It soon became clear that if my primary interests were in teaching and learning, I would have to find out about this for myself. I co-founded the Columbia Chemistry Careers Committee (C^4) in order to get the resources and information that I needed.

Our biggest event while I shared leadership of C^4 was a forum titled The Value and Future of the Chemistry Ph.D. Panelists included the director of the Chemistry Division of the National Science Foundation, the editor-in-chief of Chemical & Engineering News, current and past presidents of the American Chemical Society (ACS), the chair of the ACS Committee on Professional Training, and Columbia's dean of the Graduate School of Arts and Sciences. This event garnered much attention in the broader academic community and secured an invitation for me to address the National Academy of Sciences (NAS) in Washington, DC, at a Chemical Sciences Roundtable that was part of a workshop on Graduate Education in the Chemical Sciences: Issues for the 21st Century. Here, I spoke about my experiences as a graduate student, the work being done by C^4, and the difficulty faced by chemistry Ph.D. candidates who intended to focus on teaching and learning.

AN ECHO, A STAIN

In forming C^4 and using that organization to get more of what I needed from my chemistry degree, I transformed certain aspects of the culture at Columbia University. I recognize that my unique set of experiences afforded me the agency to make this happen and must acknowledge yet again that I came to this country with no inner sense of being restricted by gender or ethnicity. It is ironic that I became embroiled in a discussion about race and ethnicity after speaking at the NAS. An African-American woman insisted that my frustrations about a lack of support at Columbia for my interest in teaching and learning were the result of racial discrimination. When I suggested that race was not significant in what I saw as the devaluation of teaching and its related research, and that something about my experience growing up in Jamaica made me look at race differently, she remarked that I did not know what I was talking about. I tried to remind her that what I was talking about was my own life.

I knew that there was something about my formative cultural experience that made me think as I did. I sensed that there was something about the history of people from the West Indies and their emergence from slavery that made them view race differently from Americans. Who would have thought that I would find validation for my feelings about life as a Jamaican living in America in the work of a woman from a White Irish Catholic background who grew up in Brooklyn, New York? I could barely contain my delight when I first read the inside cover of Black Identities: West Indian Immigrant Dreams and American Realities by Mary C. Waters (1999). In it, Waters traces dissimilarities in the histories of the West Indies and the US that translate into significantly different perceptions of race relations and assimilation, especially by first-generation West Indian immigrants. The book also shows how these perceptions can change over time, with greater exposure to discriminatory practices in the US and an awareness of the obvious correlations in this country between race and poverty. I certainly appreciate this now but it still seems wrong that my own experiences were being dismissed as unreal, untrue or unimportant.

MOUNTAIN OF SENSE

I worked in the chemistry department at Columbia University for a year after graduation, before being offered a position at Hunter College. The first time I stepped into a classroom at Hunter, I was struck by the fact that many students looked and sounded like me. I could recognize accents from Jamaica, Trinidad and Tobago, Barbados and Guyana in addition to a host of other countries. I also saw students who were working to support their own education as I had. It was only with this contrast that I recognized how different my experience teaching at Columbia had been. It was also hard not to notice that there was only one woman on the chemistry department faculty when I arrived at Columbia, two at the time when I left, and no one from any group considered underrepresented in science. I know how important that is to my comfort as a teacher and can appreciate even more the plight of students who are unaccustomed to seeing anyone like them at the helm of their science classes. One woman from Barbados even confessed to thinking at first that I was a janitor, because she never before had a woman of color as her professor.

I felt unexpected kinship with fellow West Indians, but my relationships with all students from the myriad ethnic groups in my class were strengthened by the fact that our first day together came only two weeks before the fall of the World Trade Center on September 11, 2001. There's nothing like the feeling of your world being destroyed or not knowing if the other was alive or dead to pull a group of strangers closer together. That experience would color the way I approach all my classes, making me more open with students and more emotional about teaching than I might otherwise allow myself to be.

I joined the faculty at Hunter with the understanding that I would do research in chemistry education. Again, I found myself in uncharted territory as the first person to attempt tenure in the chemistry department with that focus. The fact that I am doing this without formal training in education certainly complicates matters, but I am now beginning to see how to relate my life experiences to my research in a way that I can enjoy. Another person who has validated my feelings about race and ethnicity and helps me to frame my views in socio-cultural theories of science education is Kenneth Tobin, whose research group I have been interacting with for some time. A self-proclaimed White guy from Australia, Ken not only listens to my immigrant's views on race and ethnicity, but also encourages his squad to pursue research that teases out rather than glosses over the ethnic nuances between students, teachers and researchers. I have begun to understand the importance of not viewing others through deficit lenses and not ignoring the potentially valuable insights that anyone can bring to a table by virtue of their difference. I have been introduced to scholarship through which I look more deeply into my relationships with students of the Diaspora (Hall, 1990), and can appreciate the value of autobiographical narrative in science education (Connelly & Clandinin, 1990), which is why I sit writing this today.

BOTH SIDES NOW

My views on race and ethnicity, as well as issues of gender, self-directed learning, and metacognition, inform my research in chemistry education. Through the pronouns that I use, comments that I make in class or the wording of problems that I write for exams, I present images of women and minorities as bright stars in the constellation of scientists. I incorporate workshops into my lectures, which helps to encourage students' ownership of their chemistry knowledge and establishes solidarity among them through collaborative learning. I am acutely aware of the number of questions that I ask in class, the length of time that I pause to allow for answers (Tobin, 1987) and the degree to which I require students to assess for themselves whether a given response is correct. Writing about my past makes me relate this to my days in Mrs. Ramprashad's class at Queen's and how her approach to teaching chemistry encouraged my propensity for metacognitive thinking and learning.

As part of my normal teaching practice, I meet periodically with small groups of students to discuss class requirements and activities and co-generate solutions to issues that arise as each semester unfolds. These cogenerative dialogues (Martin, 2006; Roth et al., 2002) increase my understanding of the diverse group in my class and their needs as learners. It also seems to improve their ability to enact agency by demonstrating that their opinions are valued and can influence change. Through one-on-one meetings with all my students in which I discuss their performance on exams, help them identify strategies for future tests, learn about their cultural backgrounds and talk about their feelings related to the course, I learn that there are several common patterns as well as identifiable differences in their perceptions. My conversation with a recent immigrant from Jamaica confirmed that he too experiences the dilemma of fitting himself into one checkbox, but a surprising finding in my discussions around this issue is the sheer extent of the diversity, even within the group usually lumped together as the White/Caucasian majority.

Teaching and research that truly embrace diversity give value to students for all aspects of who they are and how they learn. This sort of self-acceptance has allowed me to traverse boundaries between theory and praxis, formal and informal knowledge, science and art, teaching and research, literary and scientific writing, Jamaica and the US, Black, White and Other. I have always felt that my primary professional identity was that of a teacher, not a scientist or researcher, but now that I can see how my own experiences come to bear on the scholarship of teaching and learning, I am empowered by the fact that these different components of my unique identity are all coming together.

NOTES

1 This is the term used in Jamaica for the youngest child in the family.
2 Which has a 63% alcohol per unit volume
3 In Jamaica, we have six years of primary school before going into first form in high school, which is equivalent to seventh grade in the US.
4 This was a standardized test for entry into high school, similar to the Scholastic Aptitude Test in the US. The Common Entrance Examination has since been replaced by a broader, subject-based Grade Six Achievement Test
5 These were students who received various ranges of scholarship funding for earning the highest fifteen or twenty scores in the Common Entrance Examination.
6 This indicated that she earned a passing grade on the Common Entrance Exam and was eligible to enter high school but did not receive a Government Scholarship.
7 This is the main Jamaican newspaper.
8 *James Alexander George Smith*, a renowned scholar who earned his law degree at Lincoln's Inn in London, was considered to be the most prominent Jamaican barrister of his time.
9 J. A. G. Smith was also a founder of the country's political system, which is why his name was given to the Government Scholarship with the highest honor.
10 Many of the high schools in Kingston were sex-segregated, but each girls' school usually had a brother school with which it joined forces for things like choir practice and theatrical performance.
11 It did. My cumulative GPA went from 0.67 to the 3.81 that I had when I graduated from Miami-Dade Community College, where I first enrolled. My GPA at that college was 3.98 but some of my credits from the University of the West Indies could not be replaced.
12 This was his emphasis on *give*.
13 I taught an organic chemistry laboratory class for nursing students and an introductory general chemistry lecture.
14 As an international student, I had to be enrolled in a college on a full time basis. This meant taking a minimum of twelve credits each fall and spring semester. Once I had my residency, I was finally allowed to break this rule.
15 It pays the full cost of undergraduate tuition for qualifying students, who must be US citizens or permanent residents, and also offers a stipend for doing laboratory research during the academic year. In exchange, each student must maintain a high standard of academic achievement while also doing research, and must apply to several Ph.D. programs after graduation.
16 Although the NIH has since had to change the official wording its policy to be more inclusive, the MARC Program, at the time when I applied, was only open to students from one of the historically underrepresented groups.
17 Teachers College (TC) is Columbia University's Graduate School of Education.

ACKNOWLEDGEMENTS

I would like to thank Sonya Martin and Kathryn Scantlebury for this opportunity, Lucia Russett and John Shelby for lending me their editorial eyes and my dear friend, and honorary Jamaican, Patricia Purtschert, for her insight and the mutual inspiration. No thanks would be complete without acknowledging my Mama and my sister Judy for always being proud of me.

REFERENCES

Connelly, F. M., & Clandinin, D. J. (1990). Stories of experience and narrative inquiry. *Educational Researcher, 19*, 2–14.

Hall, S. (1990). Cultural identity and diaspora. In J. Rutherford (Ed.), *Identity: Community, culture, difference* (pp. 222–237). London: Lawrence & Wishart.

Hartman, H. J. (1990). Factors affecting the tutoring process. *Journal of Educational Development, 14*, 2–6.

Martin, S. N. (2006). Where practice and theory intersect in the chemistry classroom: Using cogenerative dialogue to identify the critical point in science education. *Cultural Studies of Science Education, 1*, 693–720.

Roth, W.-M., Tobin, K., & Zimmerman, A. (2002). Coteaching/cogenerative dialoguing: Learning environments research as classroom praxis. *Learning Environments Research, 5*, 1–28.

Schraw, G., Crippen, K. J., & Hartley, K. (2006). Promoting self-regulation in science education: Metacognition as part of a broader perspective on learning. *Research in Science Education, 36*, 111–139.

Tobin, K. (1987). The role of wait time in higher cognitive level learning. *Review of Educational Research, 57*, 69–95.

Waters, M. C. (1999). *Black identities: West Indian immigrant dreams and American realities.* New York: Russell Sage Foundation and Harvard University Press.

AFFILIATION

Karen E. S. Phillips
Department of Chemistry,
Hunter College of the City University of New York

HELGA STADLER

10. LIVING THE CULTURAL CLASH

My Professional Life as a Feminist Science Educator

INTRODUCTION

C.P. Snow (1959) described in his book "The Two Cultures", differences between the natural sciences and the cultural sciences. Feyerabend (1975) explained how the gap between the two sciences emerged in the history of science and how the consequences influence science and culture. Scientists themselves construct gender by the ways they communicate with the public and within the scientific community (Bem, 1993; Brickhouse, 1998). For instance, physicists like to distinguish between 'soft' and 'hard' sciences. 'Soft' means that scientists use interpretative methods, whilst in the so called 'hard' sciences supposedly only mathematics and nature decide whether a result is correct or not. Individuals construct their identity along those images (Wenger, 1998); sociologically the dualism constructs a hierarchy (Hirschauer, 1994).

Since Feyerabend (1975), we know that such a simple interpretation of the scientific method is wrong. Sociology, historical background, and cultural background implicate the questions scientists put forward, the tools that are used to solve those questions, and the answers and theories that are accepted by the community. Nevertheless, the gap between the sciences exists in the mind of many scientists; and what is even more problematic, it determines the image of the sciences. The picture most people have in mind when talking about physics, chemistry, or genetics is that of an 'objective', 'hard' and male science.

Feminists state that the culture of science and technology is gendered (Wajcman, 1991). Nancy Brickhouse explains that the image of science girls and boys have in their minds is male and that this image is the reason why girls develop a distance when confronted with science (Brickhouse, 1998, 2001). That conclusion is confirmed by many empirical studies, in which girls and boys are asked about science (Hoffmann, Häußler & Lehrke, 1998; Osborne & Collins, 2001). Very young people distinguish between sciences that are male and those that are female, and girls develop attitudes that show more distance than closeness to the so called 'hard' sciences (Koballa, 1995).

Science educators can contribute to closing the gap between the sciences. We are experts in the 'hard' sciences, but in our research many of us work in the field of the interpretative sciences. As teachers we have to work with young people, continuously interpreting interactions and behaviors, when we want to understand the ways students think and feel. Otherwise we cannot support them.

K. Scantlebury, J. Butler Kahle and S. N. Martin (eds.). Re-visioning Science Education from Feminist Perspectives: Challenges, Choices and Careers, 103–113.

Thinking of my own biography as an educator of physics, the problems and the chances in my professional life emerged out of the gap just described. I had to live the gap, first during my studies, later as a teacher and researcher. But it was not only the gap between the sciences. Out of the cultural gap between the two sciences emerged the gender gap. In addition to being a woman like my female colleagues, I also had to find my way in a male society. Trying to bridge this gap was quite natural for my professional life.

WRITING AN AUTOBIOGRAPHY

Mark Twain (1959) states that autobiography always is a lie. It is true, that history is an interpretation of the data we have from the past and that when looking at one's own history we usually do not use 'objective' data. We get the data from our own memory and, as we know, our memory changes not only the facts but also what happened in our lives. Every time we talk about an event of the past we interpret it, and every interpretation changes our memory. Using artifacts like pictures does not change much: it happens that artifacts slowly extinguish our memory.

Talking about one's own history, therefore, is an interpretation we give of what we have in mind, not of what actually happened. The interpretation of one's own life is situative, given from the intellectual position the person has now. So if one tells you his or her own history, we learn more about how this man or women thinks now than we learn about the historical facts of his or her life. This situation does not change if she or he uses artifacts, because the way the person chooses an artifact and the way she or he uses them is part of the person and the way she or he thinks and lives at this moment.

Considering my own biography as a female science educator I am not going to use any artifacts. I have not written any reflective papers or diaries. So what you will read is an interpretation of my professional life, how facts in my life might have influenced the way I am thinking and what I am doing now. I will write in a chronological order, starting at the fifties of the last century with my childhood.

WHY SCHOOL WAS IMPORTANT IN MY LIFE

I live in Austria, and I have always lived here. I did not have a very intellectual family. I was not what one thinks of a typical Viennese girl. I did not learn an instrument and I heard my first concert at the age of 12, when I visited the concert hall with my school. But I knew there was something that I could not get at home, and so I absorbed everything I could get from outside. Besides books (my mother took me to the public library at the age of six), school was important in my life. There I learned about all the treasures the human mind created in the past, and there I got to know other girls and boys who were as curious about poems, music, and science as I was. In my later life as a teacher I always was conscious about the role of school for children, who do not get much intellectual support from their own home.

My parents supported me as best they could. My father liked math, though he did not know much about it. We used to count long chains of multiplications, when we were walking on Sunday. He was interested in politics, so at breakfast and dinners we had intensive discussions about political questions. When I started to read my mother took me to the library, maybe the most important thing that happened in my childhood.

At the age of thirteen I discovered that I was good in science. I did not know much about it; but when a teacher asked questions such as "Why do you think does this happen?" I just knew the answer. I liked to think in a certain way, and I liked to be the only one in class who could give explanations. So at the age of 14 I decided to study chemistry or physics.

My decision, concerning my future studies did not influence my private life: There, as I had done since I was a small child, I liked to read literature. Later I liked to listen to classical music, and I discussed philosophical questions with my girlfriends. If there had not been my school experience in science, I would not have known anything about physics. Being a science educator I know that girls do not have much chance to connect what they learn at school in science with their private lives. One reason is, that they usually do not know people to talk with about science.

Attending an only girls school, I had only female teachers. I never got the idea, that physics might have a male endeavor. I did not connect physics with technology. At that time I considered physics an intellectual game, in which there were puzzles that had to fit. I remember only very few experiments; the spectrum of light and its beauty is perhaps the only one.

Looking back on my life, I learned how important school is for girls whose families cannot provide an intellectual background. My family gave me the freedom to do what I liked and supported me in that way. But school opened the world and provided opportunities to recognize my strengths.

At the end of my school time, I knew what I was interested in, but I did not know what I should study. Considering professions, the only academic job I knew about was that of a teacher – the job I saw daily. In my family nobody had studied at a university, so there was none to support me but also there was none to try to influence me in any particular way.

At the age of eighteen, the subjects I was interested in were physics and chemistry on the one hand and philosophy and literature on the other. It was not easy to decide what direction to take for my future studies.

What I learned from that period of my life was that school is important for young people if their homes do not provide many opportunities. Not only because girls and boys can learn what they need to know later on in their lives, but also to help them find their own individual identities, by providing different views of life and different aspects that might enrich their future lives. For girls and boys school provides an opportunity to get in contact with physics as one of the big intellectual adventures of humanity, to learn about how it changed the world, and to learn how technology works. For most girls school is the only place where they learn about physics and where they learn whether they are gifted in that field or not. In the best case, school succeeds in encouraging them to enter this field and to be part of it later on.

LIVING THE TWO CULTURES AS A UNIVERSITY STUDENT

I started with chemistry, but staying the whole time in the laboratory did not satisfy my interests. So I changed to physics and philosophy. In the morning I listened to math and physics in the afternoon to philosophy. The two buildings in which the teaching took place were only five minutes away by tram, but what I experienced were two different worlds. In one, things were fixed and clear, every word had a certain meaning. The teachers were the knowing ones, and we students had to try to understand and to learn what they knew.

In philosophy we learned from the beginning we learned, that there existed different systems. We could compare them and build our own meaning and form our own opinions. So, from the beginning, discussion was quite natural. The freedom to think was visible, it made people look and behave differently. While in physics the blackboard was the main medium (because the mathematical formulations were fixed and could be put down), in philosophy it was our own language.

Concerning gender, both communities were male. The teachers were male as well as most of the students. But in philosophy my position was another one. I could contribute to discussions, and others took up what I said. In physics I got the feeling, that only male students really understood the stuff. Nevertheless, although all my colleagues in philosophy made a career at the university, I never thought about that option. It just did not come to my mind.

What I learned from that period of my life is that most scientists live in a split world. They do not know much about the other world, and most of them do not appreciate what the other one does. The cultures the sciences developed are different. This difference concerns not only their content and methodology, but also the way in which students are taught. Later on when students graduate, the differences are not as strong, but in the beginning they are overwhelming. So prospective teachers get a certain image of science, and they transport that image in their teaching and to the public. This problem is the reason that in teacher inservice training my colleagues and I try to show teachers other facets of physics: Physics as a field with many open questions, where young people have the chance to find new ways how to solve these questions.

Later on, I found that most of my female students preferred constructivist teaching and research oriented methods, where they can discuss theories and where they can develop and prove their own ideas. Learning physics in a constructivist way that opens the possibility to discover one's own abilities and confidence. Looking at my own history, I also learned how important it is to encourage young people, mainly women, to follow an academic career.

If you want to work in science, you have first to decide and then to specialize. I did not want to specialize at this very early stage of my life. Today I think that women drop out more often because of the same reasons. Perhaps women are more oriented to the crucial questions of life and those never are too specialized. Many years later, I interviewed female scientists and many of them worked in interdisciplinary projects, such as environmental physics. Today, it becomes clearer that one needs both: the specialized one and the more general thinking one. So, if it is true that women are the more general thinkers, we need them in science.

BEING A TEACHER OF PHYSICS IN A SECONDARY SCHOOL

I started to teach physics and mathematics in a grammar school in the seventies. At the very beginning I did not have much success. I taught what I had learned at the university, and I taught it in the same way I had experienced it. At university, I had learned the theoretical system, but nearly nothing about how it was related to the reality of life. I knew that my students were bored, and I thought about leaving the job. After two years I got the chance to try a new curriculum. What I tried was a historically oriented approach. I liked this approach, because I was able to connect what I had learned in philosophy with what I did in physics. My students got the chance to recognize that their own misunderstandings were not individual ones but part of history.

At that time I started to look at what was going on at university. There were two physicists who influenced my development: Ulrich Sexl and Ina Wagner. Both were interested in science education. The first one was famous for making the ideas of theoretical physics understandable to the public, and his interests were interdisciplinarity, mainly in philosophy and history. It was Ulrich Sexl who asked me to translate the famous book of George Gamow (1980) into the German language. Ina Wagner was an experimental physicist, trying a more student- oriented approach. Together with her and a group of teachers, we developed teaching sequences for topics such as traffic, quite similar to the Nuffield courses in Great Britain.

At that time I taught only girl classes and the girls in my classes liked my new approach. Many of them chose physics for their final exams. At the end of the seventies, our school became coeducational, and in some years there were boys and girls in my classes. I was not prepared for that situation; I just noticed that something was different. I noticed that the girls slowly changed their behavior in physics. The boys took their chance, leaving the girls behind. Now, only a few girls chose physics for their final exams and if I wanted one to do so I had to address her personally. One of the girls told me: "Physics, that's something for boys".

It was in an inservice teacher training where I got first ideas about what might have happened. I got the chance to interview a girl, the best one of her class in math. In the interview she repeatedly explained that those who were "really good" in math were boys. At that time I started to look more closely at what happened in my class, and I tried to foster girls in physics.

Looking at what happens in class now, more than twenty years later I can say, that not much changed. The quality of teaching has improved during the last decade. Teachers use curricula that are more oriented toward the needs and interests of young people; some teachers use constructivist methods; group work is common; and young people have more possibilities to choose subjects and learning environments than they could before. But the gender gap did not close, boys outperformed girls like they did before. Teachers will tell you that in science the really creative and gifted ones are boys. Teachers know that gender issues are a topic, but most of them do not reflect on their own practice or regards to this topic. Trying to close the gender gap changing the curriculum is not enough. Change will only happen if we change attitudes: those of the teachers and those of their students.

Concerning teacher education, it is important that teachers get new inputs at different stages of their professional life. Teacher inservice training and teacher education is only effective, when it is strongly connected with their experiences in class. Being in class a teacher wants to know how to improve, how to change. Learning in advance does not have the impact of combining learning with action. Thus, this experience laid the groundwork for action research. In that sense, my way to action research was clear.

BEING A WOMAN AT A PHYSICS DEPARTMENT: FIRST STEPS IN FEMINIST RESEARCH

My contacts with my colleagues at the university became closer when physics students visited my lessons. I talked with them about methodological questions and supported them in preparing their own lessons. At the age of forty-five, I got a part-time position as an assistant professor at the physics department of the University of Vienna. Some years later, our activities had become so time-intensive that I left school completely. My main activities were teacher training (in- and preservice teacher training) and educational research. In my lectures I introduced methods of self-reflection, mainly videos to initiate reflection and professional discussion. With a colleague I started lectures, in which students had the chance to jointly prepare lessons for school, to teach, and to evaluate their teaching (Stadler 1999a). This part of my work was accepted quite soon. However it was with my research work.

Coming from a school, where it was quite natural to work with female and male colleagues I wondered when I got my university job: 'Where are the women?' My institute had 22 members, only two of them were female, the secretary and one assistant professor. The secretary told me: "Feminism, that's no topic!"

I started to concentrate my studies on gender issues. Together with some female physicists we founded the group "Women in physics", which is now part of the Austrian Physical Society. We looked at statistical data and compared them with international statistics. In order to get more women in higher academia, we founded scholarships for women who wanted to pursue a doctoral program.

Together with my colleague Helmut Kuehnelt, we had a small workgroup within the department of Theoretical Physics. We both were engaged in teacher education. But, what I did in my research work was strange to my colleagues. I used methods used in the social sciences and published in journals they did not know existed. And they were convinced that it is enough to be a good scientist, if you want to be a good teacher. So the gap I was living as a student recurred: the difference between 'hard' sciences and 'soft' sciences. Being a woman engaging in gender issues did not help to bridge the gap.

In a situation like this one, you need somebody who supports you. Reinders Duit, professor at the Institute for Science Education at the University of Kiel, introduced me to an international community. He supported my work and gave me advice.

The Austrian Ministry of Education supported my first research work. It was about female students in higher technical schools (Stadler, 1997). Girls are a minority in these schools. In electrotechnics and mechanical engineering less then ten percent of the students are female. On one hand, the girls appreciate their situation; on the other one, they experience aggressions of their male peers. The girls try to integrate themselves and behave like their mail colleagues. It is a rather neurotic situation, where they do not get much help. At first, the principals of the technical schools were rather offended. Nowadays there are a lot of projects in my country aimed at motivating more women to enter technical schools and to improve the working and learning environment for the girls already working there.

When evaluating a lesson sequence about chaos theory together with Reinders Duit, I discovered that constructivist approaches appeal to girls. I created new ones (Stadler, 1998; Stadler & Duit, 1998) and the results confirmed the hypothesis. They showed how important it is for girls to have time to think, to discuss, and to have the possibility to do some research on their own. Constructivist didactical approaches help girls get a new image of physics. Physics is no longer a hierarchical system, but something where each individual can find her or his own place, according to his or her own interests and gifts.

It was a boy who initiated my cooperation with a linguist. He told me: "If I explain something to a girl, she answers 'I do not understand', even if I know she understands it far better than I do." Gertraud Benke, a linguist with intensive training in education research, and I studied a transcript of the chaos lessons. We found that boys and girls are different in their interaction in class, so the students and their teachers get the impression that the boys are the more talented ones (Stadler, Duit & Benke, 2000). Boys act according to the expectation of teachers, using more technical jargon even when they do not really know the meanings of the words. Girls tend to connect what they learn in physics with their daily experiences; boys stay in the world of physics (Stadler, Benke & Duit, 2001a). For boys it does make sense, because many of them intend to take a science or a technical study. Being somebody who knows something in physics or technology improves boys' status in society. That is not the case for girls, so girls have to find something that makes sense to them when learning physics. Girls act as a sensor of quality in physics education (Stadler, 2000). Gertraud Benke and I used also the transcripts from the chaos lessons to study the interactions in group work, in only girls groups and in mixed groups (Stadler, Benke & Duit, 2001b).

Together with Gertraud Benke we asked boys and girls about their attitudes concerning science (Benke & Stadler, 2003). We found that girls tend to rate the boys' interests in technology higher than their own and the interests of girls lower than it was. Boys tended to have the same bias. In fact the actual interests of girls and boys did not differ much. I learned that if we want to make our teaching and learning environments more gender inclusive we had to change not only the attitudes of teachers but also those of their students.

I think that like me many of my colleagues who work in feminist research and education are rather isolated in their work at their departments. So cooperation between departments and networking is of great importance.

Meanwhile, in my department the situation has changed. We got a centre for research in science education and young researchers are starting to engage in this work. Gender issues have become an important part of science education and research in this field.

FEMINIST RESEARCH IN SCIENCE EDUCATION?

At Austrian schools we find considerable gender differences: Girls get better marks, they finish their final exams and PISA proves their predominance in reading literacy. Boys outperform girls in international science achievement tests like TIMSS (Stadler, 1999b), they are more interested in physics and technology (Hoffmann, Häußler & Lehrke, 1998) and in contrast to girls they tend to choose further education and jobs in this field (Stadler, 1999c). School is the place where we can uncover acts of constructing gender (West & Zimmermann, 1987) and gendered attitudes. Our aim is to liberate us from gender stereotyping in and of our subjects, so girls and boys are not suppressed any more by gendered ideas and can choose what they feel inclined to according to their interests and gifts. In my research and my intervention, I try to reveal 'doing gender' in educational practice, whether it comes from female or male teachers or from female or male students. But I also concentrate on ways to foster girls in physics, because they are those who are excluded from technical studies and physics not only in school but also in society with all its consequences. Not only is the job market widely closed to them, but also their private possibilities are more limited. In that respect I like to call myself a feminist researcher.

TEACHING TEACHERS – EXPERIENCES WITH ACTION RESEARCH

My first experience with action research methods and talks with teachers convinced me of the importance of action research. Teachers usually evaluate their work by testing their students, but they do not know how they can improve the results. For example, how they can make their teaching more interesting, more gender inclusive etc? While teaching they do not have time to reflect upon what happens in class, and they very seldom have the opportunity to talk about it in a professional way. I know how difficult it is to develop a professional language. Action research methods provide different perspectives and initiate professional discourse.

We started an interdisciplinary two-year inservice course for science teachers (Kühnelt & Stadler, 1997). The course is still being offered more than 200 teachers have finished the program with some of their reflective papers dealing with gender topics.

In 2000, a team of Austrian education researchers started another project to foster the quality of teaching and learning in mathematics and science. Teachers documented and evaluated innovations in mathematics and science teaching. Between 2000 and 2004, together with the math educator Helga Jungwirth, I headed the subprojects "Teaching and Learning" and "Gender Mainstreaming and Gender

Sensitivity" (Stadler & Jungwirth, 2005a; 2005b). Each year we supported more than 20 teachers at their respective schools. Action research was an important element. We developed an 'intervention by research'-method, in which research methods and outcomes were used to influence further teaching and learning in class in a very straightforward manner; e.g., by involving students as co-researchers with their teachers. Likewise, we asked students to analyze videos of their own lessons (Stadler, 2005).

Within the part of the project that concentrated on gender issues, we developed a type of personal coaching. For that aspect we used classroom videos. Teachers have "blind spots" (Altrichter, Posch & Somekh, 1993). When teaching and when looking at gender issues the difficulties in changing perspectives is much longer than usual. So we built support groups of teachers, in which the teachers could discuss the videotaped teaching situations (Stadler & Jungwirth, 2005b).

Involving students in the discussion is important when we want to change attitudes. It was not easy for the teachers to do so, but in the end they always appreciated it, because they noticed the changes immediately. Videos are very important, when we talk about gender issues in classroom teaching (Stadler, 2003). Videos make it possible to look at situations again and again with changing perspectives. Gender situations in class are very subtle and usually neither teachers nor students recognize them right away.

Summing up, the most important outcome of this part of my work is that if we want to improve the quality of class we have to start 'cogenerative dialogues' (Roth & Tobin, 2002), that involve teachers, researchers, and students.

FINAL REMARKS

Judging from my experience and my research, I firmly believe that gender issues have to be considered at all levels of education. Gender work has to target different levels: the organizational level, the teaching and learning environments, and the more subtle level of interactions, attitudes etc.

Concerning science, mainly physics and the technical sciences, girls depend on what schools can offer. They do not have a peer group, where they can get input; most do not read scientific journals as some boys do. Only at school do they have opportunities to learn about science, to get to know their own gifts and interests. If school doesn't give them this chance often they will avoid science in their careers and they will tell their children that they never grasped it. So we have to teach teachers how to create an environment, where girls like to learn science. The school system should not make it possible that girls and boys can skip science at an early stage of their school careers (like they can do it in many countries, including Austria). If girls do not learn science in school, most of them will never have the chance to get some knowledge in this field or to start a scientific career (Stadler, 1999b).

Today gender is accepted as a topic of discussion, but very little happens. Discussions do not change class routines and interactions in class. Personal coaching is effective but expensive. And according to many European School Systems girls can skip science at a very early age.

Asking for reasons, we find that the dualism between the sciences has its socially constructed counterpart in the dualism between the males and females. If we partition sciences in natural and cultural sciences, in 'hard' and 'soft' sciences we strengthen the dualism that divides the world in a male and a female one and forces men and women to decide between them. This division limits their options in forming their identities as individual and contributes to a split world.

If we want to attract more women to the so called 'hard sciences' one of the most important tasks is to close the gap between the two sciences. Women and men working in science education as researchers and teachers can contribute by changing the image of the 'hard' sciences.

REFERENCES

Altrichter, H., Posch, P., & Somekh, B. (1993). Teachers investigate their work. An introduction to the methods of action research. New York: Routledge.

Altrichter, H., & Krainer, K. (1996). Wandel von Lehrerarbeit und Lehrerfortbildung [Change of teachers work and teacher education]. In K. Krainer & P. Posch (Eds.), *Lehrerfortbildung zwischen Prozessen und Produkten* (pp. 33–51). Bad Heilbrunn: Klinkhardt.

Bem, S. (1993). *Lenses of gender*. New Haven, CT: Yale University Press.

Benke, G., & Stadler, H. (2003). Students' positions in physics education. A gendered perspective. In D. Psillos (Ed.), *Science education research in the knowledge based society* (pp. 81–87). Dordrecht: Kluwer.

Brickhouse, N. W. (1998). Feminism(s) and science education. In B. J. Fraser & K. G. Tobin (Eds.), *International handbook of science education* (pp. 1067–1081). Dordrecht, The Netherlands: Kluwer.

Brickhouse, N. W. (2001). Embodying science: A feminist perspective on learning. *Journal of Research in Science Teaching, 38*, 282–295.

Feyerabend, P. (1975). Against method.outline of an anarchistic theory of knowledge. London: Verso.

Gammow, G. (1980). Mr. Tompkins' seltsame Reisen durch Kosmos und Mikrokosmos [Mr Tompkins in Paperback]. Vieweg: Braunschweig.

Hirschauer, S. (1994). Die soziale Fortpflanzung der Zweigeschlechtlichkeit. [The social reproduction of sex and gender]. *Zeitschrift für Soziologie, 18*(1989), 100–118.

Hoffmann, L., Häußler, P., & Lehrke, M. (1998). Die IPN-Interessenstudie Physik. [Interest in science. A study made by the IPN Kiel.]. Kiel: IPN.

Koballa, T. R. (1995). Children's attitudes toward learning science. In S. W. Glynn & R. Duit (Eds.), *Learning science in the schools: Research reforming practice* (pp. 59–84). Mahwah, NJ: Lawrence Erlbaum Associates.

Kühnelt, H., & Stadler, H. (1997). Combined updating on science and pedagogy for experienced teachers. *Research in Science Education, 27*(3), 425–444.

LISE. (n.d.). Retrieved from http://lise.univie.ac.at

Osborne, J., & Collins, S. (2001). Pupil's views of the role and value of the science curriculum: A focus-group study. *International Journal of Science Education*, 443–467.

Roth, W. M., & Tobin, K. (2002). *At the elbow of another. Learning to teach by coteaching*. New York: Peter Lang.

Snow, C. P. (1959). *The two cultures*. Cambridge: Cambridge University Press.

Stadler, H. (2005). Intervention durch Forschung. Wege zur Unterstützung der Professionalisierung von Lehrkräften mittels Video. [Intervention by Research. Videos as a tool to foster the professional development of teachers.]. In M. Welzel, H. Stadler (Hrsg.), *Nimm doch mal die Kamera!" Zur Nutzung von Videos in der Lehrerbildung — Beispiele und Empfehlungen aus den Naturwissenschaften. [Take a camera! How to use videos in teacher training. Examples and recommandations.]*. Münster, New York, München, Berlin: Waxmann.

Stadler, H. (2003). *Videos as a tool to foster the professional development of science teachers*. Paper presented at the annual conference of the National Association for Research in Science Teaching (NARST), Philadelphia, PA.

Stadler, H. (2000). Physik und Technik - kein Thema für Mädchen? Modelle zur schulischen Förderung von Technikkompetenz und Technikinteresse bei Mädchen. [Physics and technology – a topic for girls? How to foster interests and competencies of girls in technology.]. In Ch. Wächter (Hrsg.), *Auf den Spuren der Frauen in der technologischen Zivilisation*. Profil-Verlag München, S75–S87.

Stadler, H. (1997). *Schülerinnen an Höheren Technischen Lehranstalten.Eine Studie im Bereich Elektrotechnik/Elektronik und Maschinenbau*. [Students in higher technical schools]. Austrian Ministry of Education.

Stadler, H. (1998). Die Bewegung der Erde. Ein Einführungsunterricht in die Mechanik. *Unterricht Physik, 9*(46), S24–S34.

Stadler, H. (1999a). Aktionsforschung in der Ausbildung von Physiklehrerinnen [Action research in teacher training]. *Didaktik, 2*(99), 14–15.

Stadler, H. (1999b). *TIMSS 3 in Österreich- geschlechtsspezifische Aspekte [TIMSS 3 in Austria – the aspect gender]*. In Tagungsband der 62.Physikertagung der Deutschen Physikalischen Gesellschaft, Didaktik der Physik, Ludwigsburg.

Stadler, H. (1999c). Physik und Technik - kein Thema für Mädchen? [Physics and technics – a topic for girls]. *Erziehung und Unterricht*, Heft 7(8), 635–651.

Stadler, H., Benke, G., & Duit, R. (2001a). How do boys and girls use language in physics classes.In R. Duit (Ed.), *Research in science education in Europe* (pp. 283–288). Dordrecht: Kluwer Publishers.

Stadler, H., Benke, G., & Duit, R. (2001b). Gemeinsam oder getrennt? Eine Videostudie zum Verhalten von Mädchen und Buben bei Gruppenarbeiten im Physikunterricht. [Coeducation. A videostudy concerning groupwork]. In St. Aufschnaiter, M. Welzel (Hrsg.), *Nutzung von Videodaten zur Untersuchung von Lehr- Lernprozessen* (pp. 203–218). Waxmann Münster/New York/München/Berlin.

Stadler, H., Duit, R., & Benke, G. (2000). Do boys and girls hold different notions of understanding in physics? *Physics Education, 35*, 417–422.

Stadler, H., & Duit, R. (1998). *Teaching and learning chaos theory. Case studies on students' learning pathways*. Paper presented at the National Association of Research in Science Teaching (NARST), annual meeting, San Diego, CA.

Stadler, H., & Jungwirth, H. (2005a). IMST[2] - The subproject "Teaching and Learning Processes" on how to initiate and support changes in teachers' professional work. Paper presented at the ESERA conference, Barcelona, Spain.

Stadler, H., & Jungwirth, H. (2005b). *Towards gender-sensitivity in class: Confronting teachers with external perspectives*. Paper presented at the European Science Education Research Association Conference, Barcelona, Spain.

Twain, M. (1959). *The autobiography of Mark Twain*. London: HarperCollins Publishers.

AFFILIATION

Helga Stadler
Faculty of Physics,
University of Vienna

COLETTE MURPHY

11. THE RELUCTANT SCIENTIST

INTRODUCTION

My story is different from that of many other science educators. I can think of little in my early or later life that encouraged me to do science. Having drifted into it, I would not consider myself a very 'scientific' person. However, I treasure my science learning in that I have now access to both the history of ideas and the science underlying current issues. I have the confidence and knowledge to make informed decisions in relation to genetically modified foods, stem cell research and climate change.

My story as a reluctant scientist helps me relate to learners who are not remotely interested in school science. My research focuses on ways in which we can engage with school science in more active, meaningful, emotional, and human contexts. I will focus on those events and decisions that most influenced my career towards and then away from science, and how such experiences have impacted on my teaching of science at school, as a science teacher educator and as a researcher.

LEARNING SCIENCE

If I thought of a future, I dreamt of one day founding a school in which young people could learn without boredom, and would be stimulated to pose problems and discuss them; a school in which no unwanted answers to unasked questions would have to be listened to; in which one did not study for the sake of passing examinations" (Popper, 1945, p. 40).

My experience of learning science at school was dominated by boredom. I studied science because my school (a convent) had just embraced science and the most able girls were 'selected' for biology, chemistry and physics. There were only five of us in the advanced level class and we saw ourselves as the academic 'elite'. Occasionally a teacher, or something I read, sparked my interest. I had burning questions about Teillhard de Chardin's 'noosphere' (1959) and exactly how a straight line could be represented by a mathematical equation - I was told that the noosphere was irrelevant and just to learn the equation. I succeeded at school science by reading non-school science books about things, which interested me at the time – such as psychology, genetics, science fiction and novels. Just like school students today, I yearned for teachers to engage with me and to make science interesting.

K. Scantlebury, J. Butler Kahle and S. N. Martin (eds). Re-visioning Science Education from Feminist Perspectives: Challenges, Choices and Careers, 115–122.

When I reflect on the reasons for continuing science at school, using the lens of sociocultural theory, the associated increase in symbolic capital stands out. I was part of a small, select group, looked up to by younger students and peers and slightly feared by the teachers.

I drifted into studying botany at University and for the most part of the first three years I did just enough to pass the exams. In the later undergraduate years I developed a strong interest in some of the science I was studying and this interest led me to start reading about the history and philosophy of science. Toward the end of my third year one event changed my interest and motivation in science and was crucial to my later decision to do a Ph.D. in botany. We had been asked to write an essay on whether phloem transport in plants was an active or passive process. I found too many articles and too much information to make any sense of the issues so I decided to focus on studies that used one species - willow. I discovered that authors of studies using older plants concluded that transport was passive, whilst those using younger plants suggested it was active. When this essay was returned to me I was stunned to find that I had been awarded the highest possible mark. My lecturer came and spoke to me and told me I had the perfect mind and approach to be a scientific researcher of the highest caliber and that I should do a Ph.D. By the beginning of my final year I was really excited by aspects of my learning. I loved the intellectual challenge of being taught Socratically by one of the lecturers, and I became totally hooked on my research project. I used to pretend I understood everything my supervisor tried to explain to me and then go and struggle with the books. The project was outside my area of expertise, so the learning curve was very steep.

Again, symbolic capital was an important element in my decision-making. If I had a Ph.D., more career opportunities would be open to me. The Ph.D. experience, however, opened my eyes into a very different world of science. I became totally disenchanted with a world that was dominated not by the sincere pursuit of 'truth' carried out by selfless, altruistic scientists engaged in a worthy enterprise. Instead I observed episodes of cheating, bickering, self-interest, and shoddy experimentation. I experienced instances of discrimination, sexual harassment, antagonism, and inferior treatment as a female. I began to wonder what was so great about science research. It seemed to be comprised of rushed experiments, researchers jumping to conclusions, and long 'controversies' in which people 'took sides' instead of pursuing the answer. I thought about science as being a human endeavor that was subject to the same frailties as all human interactions. The difference was that science and scientists seemed to be exalted in my view; there was a reverence attached to science that I didn't think it deserved. My reading of Thomas Kuhn at this time helped me rationalize such misgivings. Kuhn argued that the typical scientist was not an objective, free thinker and skeptic. Rather, he or she was a conservative individual who accepted what they were taught and applied their knowledge to solving the problems that came before them (adapted from Kuhn, 1962). I decided that I would complete my course of study but that I would not continue in the field of pure science.

I became very unsettled, despite carrying out some successful lab work that was published. At the end of my first year I came home for a visit and was offered a job teaching biology for a month. The school was a girls' school in a highly disadvantaged and violent area of West Belfast, but I loved it. I felt useful, that I was doing something special, working with these girls, many of whom had what I considered to be awful lives in and outside school. One child came to me with a note to say she had been absent because she had to help her mother who was having a baby. I asked how many children that made and she said: "Thirteen". This child was about 12; her father was in Long Kesh - the terrorist prison. I used to see her and other very young girls on my way home after school, wheeling prams and doing the shopping - little mothers who were not yet teenagers. My short career as a schoolteacher was highly challenging; I had to use resources I didn't know I possessed and some of the girls were almost impossible. But it seemed so much more real to me than sitting in a lab and looking down a microscope. In later years, I identified aspects of my experience with some of those of Rosalind Franklin, as she was depicted in the Life Story, the 1987 BBC film about the discovery of DNA. In one scene, she shouts at James Watson: "Little boys! You're all just little boys. Go and play with your little boys. I am not a little boy, I don't like your game and I won't play."

TEACHING SCIENCE

Initial Teacher Education

The day after completing the first draft of my thesis I returned to Belfast and started the one-year Post-Graduate Certificate in Education (PGCE) course to become a biology and chemistry teacher. The course was enjoyable. I became very interested in aspects of the philosophy and sociology of education, particularly in the work of Paolo Freire. I was not so convinced by the work of Jean Piaget. Being a biological researcher and familiar with the 'messiness' of most biological processes, even in plants, I was under awed by Piaget's neat developmental stages. I would have expected the story to be a lot more complex. Later, in my Master of Education thesis, I explored, critiqued and carried out some of Piaget's empirical studies using a different 'interview' technique (Murphy, 1987). I got entirely different results and, along with many other workers of the time, concluded that cognitive development was more likely to occur gradually than in distinct stages (Murphy, 1987).

Every time I see a student teaching on their first placement in school I relive my own struggle. It was an all-boys Catholic school, set in a socially disadvantaged area. The main form of control was corporal punishment (which was to be totally banned the following year). I was the first female ever to teach science there. Among the school staff, there was only one female teacher. She taught music. One of my peers taught English and asked his first year students (age 11-12) to write an essay on the best teacher. Nearly all boys rated the teachers on how long their hand hurt after being caned. Those whose hits lasted longest were the best teachers. I was never asked to cane a student (I could not have done it anyway), and I was allowed to call them by their first names. I was desperate to make sure they behaved well when I was teaching, because the teachers were in the prep room (adjacent to the lab). If they heard anything untoward, they would pull out a boy or two and I could hear them being beaten - too awful for all concerned. Lots of boys were 'special'. This meant that they had remedial teaching in several aspects of their learning. Many of the boys came from the orphanage close to the school, and a lot of them had severe emotional and behavioral problems. While I was there, a 15 year old boy committed suicide in the school. I worked very, very hard during those times. I was meticulous in my preparation, particularly for practical classes that were planned with military precision. I needed this planning to be able to survive. I needed to ensure that I was not favoring any student, and I needed to minimize 'dead time' in which they could act up.

When one of the supervisors came out to see me teaching, I had all the special boys in my chemistry class because their remedial teacher was ill. We were dehydrating blue copper II sulfate crystals by heating them in boiling tubes to observe the color change to white. I was terrified of an accident happening - my planning had not accounted for an extra six 'special' 11-12 year old boys. I saw my supervisor talking to Patrick, a 'special' child. "What is the point of this experiment?" I nearly died inside; Patrick would hardly have known what day it was. "Dunno, sir", was his respectful response. The supervisor gave me a look and five minutes later asked me to come and discuss the notes he had made on my lesson. I told him I could not leave the boys in case something happened, only to be told that I was insolent. He threw his notes on the desk and stormed out. I was shaking and the boys were as good as gold. I lasted until the end of the lesson; and when the boys left, I burst into tears.

I will never forget the feeling that I had been judged unfairly, and I will never forget the sinking feeling in my stomach when a supervisor walked into my classroom, totally unannounced. My current research is influenced heavily by that experience. We are developing new approaches to school placements in which student teachers are afforded much more agency in the classroom and the role of the supervisor is more supportive (Murphy, Beggs, Carlisle & Greenwood 2004; Murphy & Beggs, 2006).

Being a Science Teacher

In a discussion of 'truth' being an authority in school science education, Karl Popper states:

> I admit that, unfortunately, this is true also of many courses in science, which by some teachers is still treated as if it was a "body of knowledge", as the ancient phrase goes. But this idea will one day, I hope, disappear; for science can be taught as a fascinating part of human history - as a quickly developing growth of bold hypotheses, controlled by experiment and by criticism. Taught in this way, as a part of the history of "natural philosophy", and of the history of problems and of ideas, it could become the basis of a new liberal

university education; of one whose aim, where it cannot produce experts, will be to produce at least men who can distinguish between a charlatan and an expert. (1945, Note 6 to chapter 11, p. 285).

My first full-time permanent job was in a Catholic convent, mixed gender school. We were a young staff and, again, my experience was that of being a minority female. There were seven female teachers in the school (two were nuns) and 30 male teachers. I was, as expected, the only female in the Science Department. My student population was different. I had 22 students for A' level biology, only a handful was male. In the younger classes there was a more even gender mix. I was very happy in the school and teaching science was very challenging but really rewarding. There was no science technician. I had to do everything myself, from growing cell cultures to preparing rats for dissection. My break time was invariably taken up with preparing for my next classes, and my lunch break was usually very short. My students were very well trained in setting up and helping clear away and washing instruments. Their technical skills were ahead of those in more privileged schools, and I became much better at delegating as the year went on.

I wanted to teach science that was accessible for my students. I knew I was going to be judged on the results of their examinations. In chemistry, I was only a page ahead of the students a lot of the time and I was able to warn them of the 'hard' bits. I drew all sorts of funny analogies, and I created very silly stories and illustrations to aid my own understanding. In fits of frustration, I started to pass these pieces on to the students. We talked about moles of bananas and moles of Marys; I set scenes of unrequited love between sodium and chloride ions until they bonded. My teaching became very popular with the students, but I always felt guilty that I was being 'irreverent' to science. I asked the students not to say that their chemistry lessons were 'a laugh', in case I got into trouble. A few years ago, a priest stopped me in the reception area of the School of Education at the University. By this time, I was running initial teacher education there. He told me I was the best chemistry teacher ever, and how they were so sorry when I left that school. I was shocked on two counts. Firstly, I had never, ever thought of myself as a chemistry teacher, and, secondly, I would never have expected students in the more junior classes to regret the departure of any chemistry teacher.

The first year of teaching was known as the probationary year. During this time, a government inspector observed every new teacher. I was prepared for this visit every day. At Christmas and Easter time, all classes were doing fun things. I tried to create activities that were both biological and chemical but also fun. I designed crazy quizzes; for chemistry the students scored a proton if they were right; neutron if they didn't know; and an electron if they were wrong. The teams were the metals and the non-metals. All of the questions were chemistry-oriented, but some answers needed to be acted, sung, mimed, etc. I dreaded the inspector arriving because there was so much hilarity. At the end of the year I had still had had no visit. The principal, a nun, told me on the last day of term that there had been too many students to be seen that year and that I would not get a visit. She asked me to sign a declaration that I had read and accepted the comments she wrote. The sheet was blank: "Of course, you know I will write nice things about you." I signed the blank.

In my second year my confidence and familiarity with the students had both grown to the extent that I was very comfortable. I loved my work. I really enjoyed teaching advanced biology. I ran a Creationism vs. Darwinism debate for the sixth form (16–18 year olds). The biologists had prepared speakers for each side. A representative from the nuns asked me quietly only to invite science students to the debate. I was disappointed but at least they allowed me to run the debate.

After my second year I was offered a post in the Catholic training college (later referred to as a teacher education college) to teach biology as main degree subject for the Bachelor of Education (B. Ed. degree). I was also to teach subject methods for those intending to teach at secondary level.

TEACHER EDUCATOR

The work of a teacher educator was very different from teaching at school. I could write my own courses and set my own exams. I felt that I was 'educating' in the true sense of the word, as opposed to teaching. I told the students stories about books I had read which I thought were relevant to their learning. During their biology courses, I covered *Brave New World, 1984, The Selfish Gene*, and *The Female Eunuch*, amongst many others. I was free to teach what and how I liked, and I developed many different teaching and learning approaches. Most of these were negotiated with the students, because I was becoming fascinated with what worked for which students. When I became bogged down with some of molecular genetics during my preparation, I would leave it and offer the issue as a problem to the students and see if any of them could work it out. Most of the time they hated me doing this - they didn't like being forced to think. They would prefer that I would just talk or give them notes. Occasionally our 'groupthink' sessions did work though, and they were incredibly successful for all. I learned not to try them too often though. When teaching about science pedagogy, I introduced the students to the works of Paolo Freire, Karl Popper, Thomas Kuhn, and Ludwig Wittgenstein, among others. We struggled with different arguments of scientific method and opposing conceptions of science. We went on field trips all over Ireland. Mycolleague, Jim and I drove minibuses of student teachers all over Ireland. Hewas a keen naturalist, and I learned more biology from listening to him explain the 'lives and loves' of a host of small plants and animals on the roadside, at the beach, and in the woodlands and bogs than I had been taught or read in books. I felt utterly privileged to be a part of this world. But, although I recognized at the time that such intimate knowledge of the local flora and fauna would disappear when Jim retired, I realized that times were changing and my efforts to expand my knowledge base were better served in science education than in natural history.

Some years later I was offered the position of running the new Master's and Certificate in Education programs in the College. By this time the world of higher education had changed dramatically as a result of regulation and accountability. My role expanded from teacher educator to teacher educator and administrator. The latter was principally concerned with developing quality assurance procedures. All of a sudden I was drowned in Government documentation, chairing and attending countless meetings, dressing in power suits, and becoming a bureaucrat. At first it was new and different, and I genuinely thought that such documentation of what we did might improve the experience for our students. As time progressed I observed that whilst it was easy to write things down on paper, effecting change in praxis is very different. I noted colleagues who wrote very good stories about their teaching whist I was dealing with student complaints about these same people for bullying and harassment.

I became skeptical about my role as an administrator. The work seemed endless and did not seem to lead anywhere. Later, I began to question whether there were more sinister explanations for the rise of administration in higher education. David Solway called for a willingness to learn from those in the educational 'trenches' as opposed to the administrators:

> [T]he reference librarian should be questioned about the fate of the book, not the academic dean who has seldom read one; the teacher who has weathered innumerable classes should be heard, not the personnel director who is rarely in the building; the department secretary who is about to lose her job should be heeded while a jaundiced eye is turned on the omnipresent school coordinator (Solway, 2000, p. 16)

As well as the emphasis on quality assurance in higher education, a growing requirement for research was becoming apparent. This was music to my ears. I had just completed a M.Sc. in computer-based learning and had submitted a paper based on my research findings in relation to the uptake of information and communication technology by teacher educators and student teachers. Our Head of Science suggested that we might carry out a research project in the department. He was interested in the question as to whether the inclusion of compulsory science in the school curriculum had improved students' science knowledge. We also decided to look more closely at our student teachers' experience with using constructivist approaches in their science teaching during school placements.

The research carried out in College helped me gain a position in a local university. I was keen to become a serious researcher in science education, and saw this move as pivotal. The post was not as well remunerated, nor as prestigious as the one I left, but I felt I was moving forward in a new direction. I was quite shocked when I realized that I had to obtain money to carry out research. For this I had to write and present proposals to organizations, some of which, to me, had dubious credentials. However, the need to become pragmatic was paramount to my survival in the department.

My first research project was collaborative with my colleagues from the College. We were trying to enhance the teaching of science in primary schools by teaming science specialist student teachers with classroom teachers in school. They shared their expertise in the classroom, and we measured significant increases in children's enjoyment and interest in school science as a result. This work marked the start of several research projects and publications on coteaching. We are now collaborating on coteaching work with colleagues in Australia, Canada, and the USA.

My other research areas also arise from seminal experiences as a scientist, science teacher and science educator: namely, the nature of science, children's ideas and understanding in science, children's attitudes to science, the creationism/ evolution debate, and environmental education.

CONCLUSION

As I reflect on my own experience and on teaching science to reluctant learners, I realize that unless students see a purpose to learning school science, they will not do so. Science as a school subject became compulsory in Northern Ireland schools from the ages of 4-16 in 1991. The reasons for this were never fully explained to the students - nor to the primary (elementary) teachers, many of whom were teaching science for the first time, despite not having studied it at school. We were faced with teachers who were reluctant scientists teaching reluctant pupils. Our new revised curriculum, due to take effect in 2007, mandates that science is compulsory only up to age 14. The science curriculum for 11-14 year olds is to be more flexible, with teachers free to choose more content than previously. If this change results in teachers responding more to their own students' interests and teaching more contemporary science, then we might be able to inch closer to Popper's ideal science education in which children are taught about what they want to learn.

REFERENCES

British Broadcasting Commission. (1987). *Life story* (film directed by Mick Jackson). London: BBC.
Dawkins, R. (1976). *The selfish gene*. Oxford, UK: Oxford University Press.
De Chardin, T. (1959). *The phenomenon of man*. New York: Harper and Brothers.
Freire, P. (1972). *Pedagogy of the oppressed*. Hammondsworth: Penguin.
Greer, G. (1970). *The female eunuch*. Great Britain: McGibbon & Kee.
Huxley, A. (Ed.). (1955). *Brave new world*. Harmondsworth: Penguin.
Kuhn, T. S. (1962). *The structure of scientific revolutions*. Chicago: University of Chicago Press.
Murphy, C. (1987). *Primary science: Concept formation in 5–7 year-olds*. Master's Thesis, Queen's University Belfast.
Murphy, C., & Beggs, J. (2006). Addressing ethical dilemmas in implementing coteaching. *Forum Qualitative Sozialforschung/Forum: Qualitative Social Research*. North America, 730 09 2006.
Murphy, C., Beggs, J., Carlisle, K., & Greenwood, J. (2004). Students as 'catalysts' in the classroom: The impact of co-teaching between science student teachers and primary classroom teachers on children's enjoyment and learning of science. *International Journal of Science Education, 26*(8), 1023–1035.
Orwell, G. (Ed.). (2004). *1984*. Hammondsworth: Penguin.
Piaget, J. (Ed.). (2001). *Language and thought of the child*. London: Routledge.
Popper, K. (1945). *The open society and its enemies*. London: Routledge and Kegan Paul Ltd.
Solway, D. (2000). *The turtle hypodermic of sickenpods*. Montreal: McGill-Queen's University Press.

AFFILIATION

Colette Murphy
School of Education,
Queen's University

SECTION IV: CONSCIOUS AND UNCONSCIOUS FEMINIST PRAXIS, PEDAGOGY AND PRACTICE

In this fourth section, the authors explore the use of feminist theory to transform teaching and research practices. Specifically, these chapters offer the reader examples of the ways in which women in science education are transforming their experiences and the experiences of others in the academy through actions that promote equity, question the status quo, and advance research and pedagogical practices that serve to expand opportunities in science education for both women and men.

The first contribution to this section (Chapter 12), co-authored by Susan Kirch and Sonya Martin, invokes the work of poet Adrienne Rich who, in a classic essay on feminist pedagogy promoted the practice of "taking women students seriously". Writing as science teacher educators in an elementary education department where the majority of students were female, Kirch and Martin share in this chapter a model for approaching science education with pre- and inservice elementary teachers from which teachers gain an appreciation for inclusive science education practices that support all their students, especially females. By focusing their pedagogical practice on strengthening teacher understanding of nature of science, the importance of developing supportive learning communities, cultivating a sense of self-awareness regarding teacher and student-held attitudes towards science, and learning to identify and transform inequitable teaching practices, Kirch and Martin demonstrate several ways in which they both "take women students seriously" and urge the elementary teachers in their courses to take the science learning needs of all of their students seriously.

Following this chapter is a piece by Catherine Milne (Chapter 13) in which Milne invites the reader to consider the implications of conceptualizing science as storied, rather than as definitive, objective representations of science a body of knowledge and fact. Specifically Milne puts forth the notion that science exists as a narrative, which is constructed by participants who belong to and are shaped by the socio-historical contexts of their lives. Milne argues that the recognition that the voices of not only women, but also cultural, racial, ethnic, and religious minorities around the world, have been largely absent from the production of these narratives necessitates a more critical examination of representative texts and stories about science discoveries and knowledge. Employing insights gained prominent philosophers on the nature of science, such as Kuhn, Popper, Toulmin, and, Foucalt, Milne analyzes two science discovery stories to demonstrate to the reader the impact the gendered nature of science has had on the ways in which science knowledge has been represented over time. Ending with pedagogical implications for science teachers and science educators, Milne asks readers to critically consider the relationship between events, text, representation and interpretation in an effort to consciously recognize that science can be "thought of as constructed by multiple voices rather than one dominant voice."

The third chapter in this section, co-authored by Mary Spencer and Sherry Nichols, provides a context for examining the profession of elementary science teacher educators framed as a "biomythography." Spencer and Nichols describe their collaborative composition as being viewed through an ecofeminist lens in an effort to highlight what they see as oppressive and alienating practices of science learning and teaching, which they actively resist reproducing in science methods coursework for elementary school teachers. Spencer and Nichols employ ecofeminism as a means to consciously make explicit notions of embodying science, what they refer to as being science, through which these authors situate themselves and their work as among "the intricate interconnections of all living beings and non-living entities". This belief enables them to expand their view of what constitutes science to be inclusive of both cognitive endeavors as well as more holistic, corporeal aspects of knowing and learning science. Placed within the context of their work with elementary school teachers, Spencer and Nichols view ecofeminism as a lens allowing them and their students to re-envision possibilities for "all to engage in creating and being science" as opposed to being "deficient knowers of science".

Janet Bond Robinson (Chapter 15), author of the final chapter in this section, urges those who want to be inclusive science educators to be prepared to take risks and to recognize that it takes a lot of energy retain and develop uniqueness in a culture in which women are the viewed as the "other"! Specifically, Bond Robinson offers the concept of "personal mental models" as having been significant in providing what she refers to as an "emergent power-from-within" which, she states, "empowers me to strive for challenges and choices that go beyond my present capacity." In sharing narrative accounts of experience raising a family, becoming a chemist, and engaging in transformative educational research, Bond Robinson advocates for what she refers to as "the common woman arising" signifying her desire to see women in chemistry as being a common occurrence rather than an exception. Bond Robinson's chapter reveals how she has worked to "diversify normality" through her personal interactions with colleagues and students, by employing pedagogical practices that are inclusive of all learners, and through her research – all of which she attributes to mental models. For Bond Robinson, entertaining mental models about what she wants the world to be like, who she wants to be, and what she can produce offers her possibilities for not only imagining, but creating what she wants college and K-12 educational environments to be like for young women today.

SUSAN A. KIRCH AND SONYA N. MARTIN

12. TAKING WOMEN STUDENTS SERIOUSLY: EMPLOYING INCLUSIVE APPROACHES TO SCIENCE TEACHER EDUCATION IN PRIMARY SCIENCE

As science teacher educators in an elementary education department, the majority of our student population is female, mirroring a National Center for Educational Statistics report (2005) indicating that 91% of all elementary school teachers are also female. This means that the face of school science is female. Sadly, many of our students characterize their experiences in science as being negative at best and traumatizing at worse. In addition, the majority of our students indicate they plan to leave science teaching duties to a science specialist or science cluster teacher. The ramifications of this decision are that young children are often not taught science until upper elementary or middle school. Their exposure to science is reduced to a series of discrete exploratory activities with little grounding in everyday experience. There is also little time for students to take on more complex intellectual challenges at a younger age (such as designing or interpreting a simple experiment). The opportunity is lost to make connections to other areas of the curriculum. We take our students' concerns seriously. The majority of them are conscientious and do not want to teach something they feel they have failed at in the past. By taking a feminist pedagogical perspective in our science education classes, we hope to model how teachers can develop learning communities in science that include themselves as learners as well as mediators. A feminist praxis should model how teachers can structure a more inclusive science educational experience for all of their students, especially their female students.

Due to the plurality of feminist theories (in a recent Wikipedia search on feminism there were 35 distinct "sub-types of feminism" listed) it is not surprising that there are many opinions about what is important in education and what factors should shape pedagogical choices. To reexamine our own teaching practices we have decided to return to the single most often cited work used by the first generation of scholars and educators trying to define feminist pedagogy, an essay by the poet Adrienne Rich, *Taking Women Students Seriously* (1984). The title of this chapter alludes to Adrienne Rich's now classic essay on feminist pedagogy. She wrote:

> In teaching women, we have two choices: to lend our weight to the forces that indoctrinate women to passivity, self-depreciation, and a sense of powerlessness, in which case the issue of "taking women students seriously" is a moot one; or to consider what we have to work against, as well as with, in ourselves, in our students, in the content of the curriculum, in the structure of the institution, in the society at large (p. 258).

K. Scantlebury, J. Butler Kahle and S. N. Martin (eds). Re-visioning Science Education from Feminist Perspectives: Challenges, Choices and Careers, 125–134.

In this writing, Rich offers us a theoretical/methodological framework that asks that we pay particular attention to the experiences of our female students. While our students are mostly females, their students will not be, therefore we have considered carefully a feminist pedagogical approach to teaching and learning science that will prepare our students to offer an inclusive science education to all of their students. We believe that thinking about their teaching praxis in relation to feminist pedagogy has many advantages.

GENDER ISSUES INSPIRE A CRITIQUE OF OUR PRAXIS

We teach a variety of science curriculum and instruction courses to both preservice and inservice elementary teachers at the undergraduate and graduate level. Together, we have identified several over-arching goals that we hope to accomplish in these courses (Table 1).

The science education community has discussed many of these goals and research is ongoing to identify effective instructional practices to help students and educators realize these goals. This list should not be viewed as static or complete

Table 1. Instructional goals used by the authors in science education courses.

General Theme	Selected Instructional Goals
A. Learning about Nature of Science	– Candidates and teachers should understand nature of science. – Candidates and teachers should be familiar with some strategies to teach their own students about nature of science. – Candidates and teachers should be familiar with the structure of the scientific enterprise vs. how it is represented in media (books, movies, TV, newspaper, internet, etc.).
B. Developing Learning Communities to Support Science Learning and Instruction	– Candidates and teachers should have ample opportunities to practice talking science and talking about science. – Candidates and teachers should be motivated to be life-long learners of science. – Candidates and teachers should be comfortable learning science along with their own students.
C. Cultivating Self-Awareness	– Candidates and teachers should be aware of their own attitudes toward science and the roots of these attitudes. – Candidates and teachers should understand how their attitudes could shape a child's experience in science.
D. Teaching Equitably and Recognizing Inequity	– Candidates and teachers should be able to identify inequities in their own classroom and classrooms of others. – Candidates and teachers should be familiar with strategies to teach science equitably. – Candidates and teachers should be familiar with how to critique the image science has in the popular culture.

but as a guide to inform instructional choices that we would like to discuss further here. For each theme (Table 1, A-D), we explain why the selected goals are important. We also reflect on how a feminist praxis in pedagogy might help us realize our goals and ultimately help improve our students' teaching of science.

A. LEARNING ABOUT NATURE OF SCIENCE

It has been nineteen years since the publication of *Science for All Americans* (Rutherford & Ahlgren, 1990). The authors describe three components of nature of science and highlight the importance of teaching them to students concomitantly with science content. The first component describes the scientific worldview, shared beliefs and attitudes held by scientists about what they do and how they view their work. The second component describes scientific inquiry. For this component, they explain that there is no fixed set of steps that scientists always follow, but they do identify principles common to all scientific methodologies. Finally, the third component, the scientific enterprise, describes science as an activity of the contemporary world that distinguishes our times from earlier centuries (Rutherford & Ahlgren, 1990, pp. 1-13).

The message, to teach nature of science, however, does not seem to be trickling down to the public through educational institutions, because the majority of students we encounter in our courses at the university claim to be unfamiliar with the science as worldview, inquiry, or enterprise. Every one of these students, however, can recite the steps of The Scientific Method – "in order" – and provide this list as an answer when asked how scientific knowledge is generated. Interestingly, when challenged on this point with classic examples from the history of science or recent work presented in the science news, our students immediately recognize that there are a variety of methodological approaches used by scientists such as correlative, descriptive, and experimental methods. Although "The Scientific Method" has dominated their explanatory landscape, our students do understand that the intellectual and social process of science is not so simple.

So, it is on this message that we focus much of our teaching efforts. Why do we think it is important for the general public to understand the nature of science? The scientific worldview is a rational view of how the world works and, in combination with content knowledge, is an empowering perspective. Due to course time constraints (45 hours), we typically focus on the second component of nature of science, scientific inquiry. We try to teach science as inquiry through historical and contemporary accounts of scientists. We model how to teach science through inquiry by engaging our students in inquiry activities.

When our students are asked what inquiry means to them they unanimously state that inquiry means doing "hands-on" activities with kids. Many teachers and researchers have assumed that students will come to understand, on their own, specific ways of knowing that characterize science just by doing science; that is, using experiments or other means to try to get an answer to a question (Bell & Lederman, 2003; Crawford, Zembal-Saul, Munford, & Friedrichsen, 2005; Schwartz, Lederman, & Crawford, 2004). Recently Randy Bell and colleagues conducted a study to test this idea (Bell, Blair, Crawford, & Lederman, 2003). They followed high school student volunteers through a summer science apprenticeship program to determine whether they would come to understandings of nature of science simply through their participation in the program. Even though the participating science mentors were confident that their apprentices had learned about the scientific enterprise, Bell, et al. (2003) found that students' views had changed little and that they still held "conceptions about the nature of science and scientific inquiry that were inconsistent with those described in current reforms" (p. 487).

We use this example in our courses to demonstrate to our students that not only is engagement in inquiry (e.g. designing and conducting an experiment) important, but a period of reflection and meta-analysis of what was learned and how is essential. With this pedagogical strategy, we hope that teachers and their students can begin to view the purpose of learning science differently. We would now like to turn to examine how nature of science is typically represented in school curricula and the popular press.

We find it unfortunate that the fact-based literature that young children encounter rarely portrays scientists at work or explain ways scientists contribute new knowledge to the world. The descriptions offered in such books often represent science as final, complete, static, and a body of knowledge to be assimilated but not questioned. There have been published a smattering of books for elementary school students that present a more realistic picture of science and scientists at work. For example, in the *Scientist-in-the-Field* series, forester and preservationist Sue Morse discusses how she became interested in forest ecology and animal tracking; how she contributes new knowledge to her field; and what remains to be understood in her discipline (Swinburne, 2000). Even when students are exposed to reliable sources like this, they always need to be alert to how science and scientists are represented by the source. For example, Swinburne (2000) presents Morse as possessing a fount of knowledge difficult to grasp, "A walk in the forests with Sue Morse is mind-boggling. It's impossible to absorb all of the wood lore that pours from her" (p. 18). This type of statement alludes to science knowledge as complex and difficult to understand, which we do not deny, but unnecessarily presents the scientist in a stereotypical position of being somehow special or omniscient.

If science is taught in primary school (grade K-5 in U.S.), students experience yet another form of misrepresentation. Commercial kits commonly serve as the extent of early childhood and elementary school science programs, and these kits and other popular primary science activities usually portray science as a method or process of exploration. However, the kit activities are essentially demonstration lessons, and inquiry ends with the successful completion of a classroom chart listing the correct results. Modeling in school what a scientist does means following a procedure and getting one right answer from a select few. Again, in the absence of an adult able to contextualize the activities and then mediate the use and discussion of the information in a critical way, the endeavor looses its meaning and becomes a hollow game. Exploration in the absence of talking about how it was done, what was observed, and what was inferred does a disservice to every learner.

Rich (1984) advises us to "consider what we have to work against, as well as with...in the society at large" (p. 258). In developing a feminist praxis her advice means we must not only focus our teaching on the nature of scientific knowledge and inquiry but also examine the third component described by Rutherford and Ahlgren (1990) – the scientific enterprise. We have outlined here the challenges educators face due to the inadequate portrayal of scientists in books, curricula, and media. From a feminist perspective, we must ask who is absent from science texts and who is marginalized during school science activities. We have mentioned that the public is presented with stereotypical images of scientists and the scientific process. We believe young people are particularly vulnerable to adopting these images in the absence of someone to mediate and critique the representation. The teacher's job as mediator is made easier if she or he has confronted these issues during his or her education. Teachers and candidates should learn about scientists as individuals and how the structures of the scientific enterprise make marginalization and exclusion of specific individuals possible. While we do not contend that it is a teacher's responsibility to change societal structures, we believe that she should be prepared to reveal and discuss the nature of those structures. In the next section, we present possible strategies for arranginglearning communities that cope with learning about the social reality of science.

B. DEVELOPING LEARNING COMMUNITIES TO SUPPORT SCIENCE INSTRUCTION AND LEARNING

In order for teachers to teach nature of science, it is essential that they have engaged in inquiry-based activities and practiced talking through their understandings. Talking and practicing prior to entering the classroom may help candidates and teachers meet the other two goals listed for this theme – being comfortable learning science along with their students and continuing or recognizing the benefits of life-long learning (Table 1). If science is taught not only as content, but also as process and as worldview, students can experience a more realistic view of the discipline and, more importantly, they can learn how to critique representations of it.

How do we structure a learning community so that our students have these opportunities to talk and practice? We begin by formulating critical questions and expecting our students to do the same (Kirch, 2007). For example, when we teach science as a body of knowledge we aim to encourage teachers and candidates to practice questioning information presented in books and in the media. We formulate and expect students to ask questions about content such as: "What is my understanding of the information?" "What new questions does it raise?" The content of science (e.g. facts, laws, and theories), however, must be considered in light of the process used to generate it. Therefore, we ask and expect our students to also wonder, "How was this information generated?" "What is the evidence that supports this claim?" and "Do I believe it?" Underlying these basic questions should be questions of a deeper sort, questions related to a scientific worldview. In this realm we hope students will begin asking questions like "What constitutes evidence?" "What evidence is considered unacceptable and why?" "What is the balance of observation and inference in this claim?" and "What potential bias might the discoverer have and how has that influenced her conclusions?"

Rich (1984) suggests we "consider what we have to work against, as well as with, in the...content of the curriculum" (p. 258). We would like our students to learn how to analyze texts and activities that comprise curricula for biases of gender and evidence of discrimination. We also would like our students to teach children to be critical thinkers and to learn science alongside other learning community members, colleagues as well as young students. Rich (1984) would have us work with teachers and candidates to find ways for them to "gain a sense of their selves" (p. 258) in the science education system and plan how they, in turn, can help girls, minorities, and all of their students find a sense of place in the science curriculum.

Engaging in cogenerative dialogues with our students is one way we hope to achieve our goal of helping our students "gain a sense of their selves" in science. Cogenerative dialogue is a form of structured discourse in which teachers and students engage in a collaborative effort to help identify and implement positive changes in classroom teaching and learning practices (Martin, 2006; Martin & Scantlebury, 2009). Roth and Tobin (2001) use cogenerative dialogue to address the role of the community in mediating the construction of a learning environment. Cogenerative dialogue enables us to talk about issues in our classrooms in ways that are both constructive and non-confrontational. By identifying and discussing issues of concern, we can work with our students to resolve contradictions and develop strategies to affect change. In this way, cogenerative dialogue creates social spaces for us to interact with our students and talk about their experiences in science. Involving students in discussions about the classroom encourages teacher participants to build a collective responsibility for the teaching and learning that occurs. This method of discourse provides us with an effective tool for taking seriously our students' concerns about how they experience our courses and how they can prepare to teach their students science.

One criticism we constantly face from our students is that this style of teaching and talking with students is very time-consuming and unrealistic. Early childhood teachers are often pressured by administrators to ignore science and concentrate on reading, writing, and mathematics. Furthermore, elementary teachers have an obligation to see that students succeed on standardized tests. As a result, neither teachers nor administrators can see how it is possible to take the time to participate in inquiry activities and the subsequent classroom discussions we have recommended. An even more serious concern, however, is that many believe young students cannot understand or formulate answers to the questions we raised earlier. We suspect that many teachers have a low opinion of their young students' abilities as a projection of the attitudes they were taught when they were young. This is in accord with Rich's (1984) comment that the majority of teachers, as women, have been indoctrinated to "passivity, self-depreciation and a sense of powerlessness" (p. 258) and this attitude leads to a perpetual cycle of indoctrination. As feminist educators we must look for ways to break the cycle. If we look to empowered teachers for guidance, they explain how they recognize the debilitating side effects of being trapped in a world that expects passivity and powerlessness (Dewey, 1990; hooks, 1994; Horton, 1990; Friere, 1993; Meier, 2002a;b). Empowered teachers teach science from multiple perspectives, consistent with feminist praxis. Empowered teachers typically describe struggles of a problem-solving or puzzle-like nature; struggles to find out what students know and understand or how to help students use and learn new ideas. The key is that they describe struggles, not the frustration of living with a status quo. By using a feminist praxis in pedagogy, we see that we can work to empower our students, and that this endeavor should begin with exercises on self-awareness within the context of teaching science, which brings us to our next theme (C).

C. CULTIVATING SELF-AWARENESS

We routinely encounter women and men who themselves assume/present negative stereotypical gender roles associated with girls in science. These candidates or teachers are typically squeamish of animals and anxious about physics. In classroom situations we witness them squealing, grimacing, and/or demanding that others handle animals at a distance from them. During lessons, small group or whole class discussions, we often hear some of these candidates or teachers claim, "I am no good at science," "I do not get science," or "I do not like science." They assume that science should be left to science teachers and see no need to incorporate science into other daily or weekly activities. Finally, for the candidates or teachers who do consider exploring science in their classrooms, they express anxiety about responding to the "unanswerable" questions they believe their young students will invariably submit. We recognize that these educators have the potential to negatively influence the attitudes of their present or future students. Research indicates that teachers exhibit instructional styles that are consistent with their own beliefs regarding science and science learning (Lederman, 1992; Tobin, Kahle, & Fraser, 1990).

Our theme of self-awareness aligns fairly well with Rich's (1984) charge to consider "what we have to work against, as well as with, in ourselves [and] in our students" (p. 258). Both of us are very familiar with the field of science. Kirch has a doctorate in cellular and developmental biology and was a former laboratory head. Martin has a bachelor's in biology, a master's degree in chemistry education and has four years experience as a laboratory research technician. Thus, we regularly draw from our experiences and make the effort to expose stereotypical opinions and behaviors exhibited by our students. This is only half the formula according to Rich. To further our development of a feminist praxis in teaching, we also need to talk explicitly about our students' past science learning experiences.

Currently, these discussions with students do not happen enough. When they do, they are held as side conversations with only one or two individuals participating. We need to initiate more of these discussions and involve the entire class in similar reflections. If we are to take a feminist perspective, we recognize that our students must examine the origin of their own attitudes towards science and the impact of these attitudes on their teaching. Our experiences from within the system of science will make it easier for us to mediate the system and culture of science and highlight how it as been, and continues to be, an exclusive club. Our experiences from within the system of science education will make it easier for us to mediate the practices of school science and how these practices can alienate students. By cultivating self-awareness around these issues teachers and candidates will have opportunities to identify their own prejudices and find ways to guard their students against them.

D. TEACHING EQUITABLY AND RECOGNIZING INEQUITY

Learning how to teach equitably begins with understanding the meaning of equity and recognizing what it does not mean. Equity is a general condition or a treatment of others characterized by justice, fairness, and impartiality. Equality is to be, or to become, of the same magnitude, quantity, worth, etc. Equal treatment or a condition of equality is not the same as equitable treatment. The importance of recognizing this difference has been best illustrated in terms of the treatment of individuals with disabilities. For example, if an individual with dyslexia or cerebral palsy or difficulty with fine motor coordination is faced with standard materials and equipment during a science lesson it is unlikely that she will be able to participate or perform at the level of her peers. If, however, this same individual is treated equitably, she would have access to appropriately modified and/or adapted equipment and materials that would allow her to participate and her performance should reflect her true understanding and/or abilities (Kirch, Bargerhuff, Turner, & Wheatly, 2005; 2007).

Now imagine a similar scenario but featuring girls. If we recognize the societal indoctrination of young girls "to passivity, self-depreciation, and a sense of powerlessness" (Rich, 1984, p. 258), then creating equitable structures means finding appropriate modifications and adaptations to defeat these forces and include these young girls. Just as educators should make changes to include students with disabilities, they must make changes that do not continue to alienate girls or reinforce a negative social reality. These suggestions are in keeping with a philosophy known as inclusion, the right of every student to access general education classes. Inclusion also can be thought of as a mechanism for recognizing and expanding social, cultural and academic capital of individuals and as a mechanism to deal with the inequities that came to accompany the creation of categories and labels (Lipsky & Gartner, 1997).

That the teaching population is becoming less diverse while the student population is becoming more diverse also speaks to the need for teachers to develop more inclusive teaching practices. This is particularly poignant given that students of color are expected to constitute a majority of all K-12 students in the United States by 2035, yet almost 84% of the current teaching force is White (NCES, 2002). Research has shown that cogenerative dialogue provides teachers with a means of interacting with their students across borders defined by social, economic, cultural, racial, ethnic, gender, and age differences (Martin, 2005; Martin, 2009). It has proven to be a useful tool for achieving more inclusive practices by engaging in conversations with their students, parents, and other teachers to learn best how to incorporate culturally relevant experiences and knowledge within the science curriculum.

CONCLUSIONS

In closing this essay we hope to open discussions with our students about developing a feminist praxis in science, teaching, and learning. We hope that we have conveyed an agenda concerned with educating, not training, teachers. Teachers are professionals, and as teacher educators we must help our students see how questioning texts, engaging in critical discussions about student-led investigations, working with students to create learning communities concerned with meaningful pursuits, and engaging in self-reflection are all means to creating equitable environments. We will continue to work to foster learning environments where we each identify the strengths we have that can help us meet the challenges that we face. We call on our students and science teacher educator colleagues to take all students seriously and to be skeptical of the different representations of science they encounter in their daily journeys.

ACKNOWLEDGEMENTS

We would like to thank Penny Colman for waking us up and reminding us "to be bold" and ask "where are the women and what are they doing?" We owe thanks to Moshe Sadofsky for tireless and scrupulous editorial commentary. Finally, we thank our students, past and present, for talking openly and honestly about their concerns, frustrations, fears, and excitement and for choosing a noble profession.

REFERENCES

Bell, R. L., & Lederman, N. G. (2003). Understandings of the nature of science and decision-making on science and technology based issues. *Science Education, 87*(3), 352–377.

Bell, R. L., Blair, L. M., Crawford, B. A., & Lederman, N. G. (2003). Just do it? Impact of a science apprenticeship program on high school students' understandings of the nature of science and scientific inquiry. *Journal of Research in Science Teaching, 40*(5), 487–509.

Crawford, B. A., Zembal-Saul, C., Munford, D., & Friedrichsen, P. (2005). Confronting prospective teachers' ideas of evolution and scientific inquiry using technology and inquiry-based tasks. *Journal of Research in Science Teaching, 42*(6), 613–637.

Dewey, J. (1990). *The school and society and the child and the curriculum.* Chicago: University of Chicago Press.

Friere, P. (1993). *The pedagogy of the oppressed* (30th Anniversary ed.). New York: Continuum.

hooks, b. (1994). Teaching to transgress: Education as the practice of freedom. New York: Routledge.

Horton, M. (1990). *The long haul: An autobiography.* New York: Doubleday.

Kirch, S. A. (2007). Re/production of science process skills and a scientific ethos in an early childhood classroom. *Cultural Studies of Science Education, 2*(4), 785–815.

Kirch, S. A., Bargerhuff, M., Turner, H., & Wheatly, M. (2005). Inclusive science education: Classroom teacher and science educator experiences in CLASS workshops. *School Science and Mathematics, 105*(4), 175–197.

Kirch, S. A., Bargerhuff, M., Turner, H., & Wheatly, M. (2007). Professional development journeys educators in pursuit of inclusive science in Journal of Science Teacher Education. *Journal of Science Teacher Education, 18*(4), 663–692.

Lederman, N. G. (1992). Students' and teachers' conceptions of the nature of science: A review of the research. *Journal of Research in Science Teaching, 29*, 331–359.

Lipsky, D. K., & Gartner, A. (1997). *Inclusion and school reform: Transforming America's classrooms.* Baltimore: Paul H. Brookes Publishing Co.

Martin, S. (2005). The social and cultural dimensions of successful teaching and learning of science in an urban high school. Unpublished doctoral dissertation, Curtin University, Perth, Australia.

Martin, S. (2006). Where practice and theory intersect in the chemistry classroom: Using cogenerative dialogue to identify the critical point in science education. *Cultural Studies of Science Education, 1*(4), 693–720.

Martin, S. (2009). Learning to teach science. In K. Tobin & W.-M. Roth (Eds.), *World of science education: North America.* The Netherlands: Sense Publishers.

Martin, S., & Scantlebury, K. (2009). More than a conversation: Using cogenerative dialogues in the professional development of high school chemistry teachers. *Educational Assessment, Evaluation and Accountability, 21*(2), 119–1136.

Meier, D. (2002a). *In schools we trust: Creating communities of learning in an era of testing and standardization.* Boston: Beacon Press.

Meier, D. (2002b). *The power of their ideas: Lessons from America from a small school in Harlem.* Boston: Beacon Press.

National Center for Educational Statistics. (NCER). (2002). *Digest of education statistics, 2002: Chapter 2. Elementary and secondary education table 101 - teacher enrollment.* Retrieved February 2004, from http://nces.ed.gov/programs/digest/d02/tables/dt101.asp

Rich, A. (1978). Taking women students seriously. Reprinted. In A. M. Eastman (Gen. Ed.), *The Norton reader: An anthology of expository prose* (6th ed., pp. 256–262). New York: W.W. Norton & Company.

Roth, W.-M., & Tobin, K. (2001). The implications of coteaching/cogenerative dialogue for teacher evaluation: Learning from multiple perspectives of everyday practice. *Journal of Personnel Evaluation in Education, 15*, 7–29.

Rutherford, F. J., & Ahlgren, A. (1990). *Science for all Americans.* New York: Oxford University Press.

Schwartz, R. S., Lederman, N. G., & Crawford, B. A. (2004). Developing views of nature of science in an authentic context: An explicit approach to bridging the gap between nature of science and scientific inquiry. *Science Education, 88*(4), 610–645.

Swinburne, S. R. (2000). *The woods scientist.* Boston: Houghton Mifflin Company.

Tobin, K., Kahle, J. B., & Fraser, B. (1990). Learning science with understanding: In search of the holy grail? In K. Tobin, J. B. Kahle, & B. Fraser (Eds.), *Windows into science classrooms: Problems associated with higher-level cognitive learning* (pp. 1–13). London: The Falmer Press.

AFFILIATIONS

Susan A. Kirch
Steinhardt School of Culture, Education, and Human Development,
New York University

Sonya N. Martin
School of Education,
Drexel University

CATHERINE MILNE

13. CAPTIVES OF THE TEXT?

How Analyzing Discovery Science Stories Set Me Free

WHAT IS SCIENCE FOR ME?

Even as a child I was interested in science. Growing up in rural tropical Australia, my parents tried to ensure that I had access to games and tools that supported my interest. I had a dissection kit, a chemistry set and a microscope. My parents subscribed to Life Nature and Life Science libraries and a magazine called Look and Learn. I vividly remember when I was ten years old trying to build an electric motor I saw in one of the Life Science books. My Dad helped me to get some of the materials but when I tried to get it to work I was unable to do so (It looked pretty good though). I took it to my Grade 6 teacher and asked him if he could help me but he told me he did not know the science needed. Not surprising really when you consider that science was a truly minor part of the Grade 6 curriculum (I cannot remember 'doing' science at all from Grade 1 to Grade 7). When I was younger I had read that ants could be used to clean the flesh from skeletons so I placed a road-killed toad on top of a bull ants nest. They were right!

These early experiences were not based on a lovef of science but on my need to try things out. My knowledge of what I thought of as science came from both reading and doing but reading came first. I always found ideas powerful and at university I was fascinated by the ideas of philosophers such as Plato, Herbert Spenser, Emmanuel Kant and Martin Buber and enjoyed discussing their ideas critically. However, I was never encouraged to think critically about the discipline I was about to teach. I had been invited to continue studying in the botany department but I decided that after being supported at university by the largess of the State (my education had been free) I owed the country something and decided to teach. I had a chance to teach in Canberra, Australia's capital city, or Darwin, capital of Australia's Northern Territory. I chose hot humid Darwin situated about ten degrees below the equator. This was to be my home for more than ten years. It provided an environment in which I would begin to ask the questions that continue to frame my teaching and my research: what is science and how is it represented in the teaching and learning of science.

When I began teaching I enjoyed 'doing' science but science as a set of understandings remained unexamined. I accepted definitions from school science textbooks that represented science as a body of justified true knowledge and scientific method as the way of doing science. I was comfortable with these

K. Scantlebury, J. Butler Kahle and S. N. Martin (eds). Re-visioning Science Education from Feminist Perspectives: Challenges, Choices and Careers, 135–149.

definitions and I taught students that, if they observed carefully, they would uncover facts about the world. I believed that science was a philosophy of Nature and therefore the knowledge that came from this study of Nature had more value than any other form of knowledge. After all, scientific knowledge was justified and therefore true.

However, after I had been teaching science for about five years I had developed confidence in my teaching skills and worried less about curriculum organization, lesson planning, and classroom management, leaving myself some time to reflect on the nature of science and how I might relate that to classroom practice. My reading of science history and the role of science in modern Western culture had led me to realize that perhaps there was more to science than I had originally thought based on my prior experiences when I began to teach science. I began to worry that the interactive introductory science curriculum that I had developed and which was used by all teachers of Grade 8 science at the school might be misrepresenting scientific inquiry. I began to realize that if I wanted to learn more about the nature of science and how it might affect science learning I needed to do more study. Of course, with now ten years away from an institution of higher learning I was required to start with baby steps towards research.

It was as I was taking these steps that I became interested in the philosophy of Thomas Kuhn (1970). At that time, his notion of paradigms and revolutionary change seemed to be attracting devotees like baits attract cockroaches. Kuhn argued that evidence for his theory could be observed in the history of science which was littered with souls who struggled for acceptance of their scientific ideas against the dominant paradigm or who were ignored until a revolution created an environment in which their ideas became an acceptable part of the new paradigm. However, I was uncomfortable with the need for revolutions to overthrow a paradigm and with the need for incommensurability between two different paradigms. Also, I was uncomfortable with the aggressive metaphor of revolution and my search for other explanations of how scientific understanding developed led me to the theory of conceptual evolution proposed by Stephen Toulmin (1972).

At this time, I was also reading Jerome Bruner's Actual minds, possible worlds (1986). His division of the world into paradigmatic and narrative ways of knowing led me to reflect further on my notions of science. I interpreted Bruner as arguing that science was a paradigmatic way of knowing. However, Jean-François Lyotard's (1984) critique of grand narratives and Michel Foucault's (1974) critique of global claims lead me to think of science in alternative ways. It seemed to me that, if science evolved, then it existed as a narrative that was constructed by the participants not as a paradigm as Bruner argued. Alternatively, accepting narrative as a feature of all cultures (Barthes, 1978) led me to identify science and school science as weakly bounded cultures in which narrative was important. I realized that a narrative notion of science could be fruitful in school science because I could encourage thinking of understanding as composed of both, an appreciation of an idea in its context, and the history of that idea. A narrative notion of science encouraged me to think of science as constructed rather than accepting that scientific change was caused by factors outside the immediate influence of the practitioners. I started to consider the implications of conceptualizing science as storied.

The notion of science as a story can be an anathema to science teachers because they often equate stories with fiction and they know that science is about facts, not fiction. I remember vividly talking with elementary teachers about science as storied. One of the teachers was terribly concerned that she might be teaching untruths. Her notion of stories was that they were fictionalized narratives and therefore totally inappropriate for use in science which was about facts. This represents a pervading but constraining view of science. But I wondered if science teachers might find the chance to examine the relationship between science and stories liberating and agentic.

I began to think about science and stories thus! Think of all the knowledge that we have about science, even a tiny area. When we represent this understanding, do we include all the knowledge that we have about that area? Quite clearly we do not. Consider that we might be interested in talking about the life cycle of the flea (See Figure 1). I chose this example because life cycles are often an aspect of science that is taught at the elementary and middle school level.

Some teachers might agree that they can accept that "The life cycle of the flea" is an account in which facts are recounted within a time frame and therefore consistent with the definition of a narrative as a symbolic presentation of a sequence of events connected by subject matter and time (Scholes, 1981). However, this

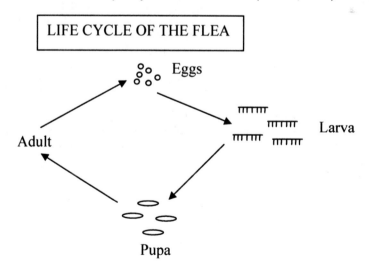

Figure 1. Life Cycle of the Flea

137

'account' raises questions of its own such as, "Which flea is this the life cycle about?" "Have we told all the facts about the life of a flea?" "If not, who decides which facts are included and which are left out?" "What implications does the selection of events have, for the meaning and values that we impose on this account?" It seems to me that once ideas are presented selectively, we are no longer telling 'the facts' we are telling a story. It is in the process of selection that an account becomes imbued with meaning and value and therefore becomes a story (Carter, 1993; Scholes, 1981). I argue that in every account we choose events for the telling and, in the process of that selection, we construct a story. Thus all of science is storied and so the question becomes not how is science storied but whose science stories are being told? Recognizing the storied nature of science allowed me to understand the gendered nature of science and led me to encourage teachers and students to value the discovery aspects of scientific endeavor.

DISCOVERY SCIENCE STORIES

It would have been easy for me to choose to examine stories about women scientists who have been poorly served by history and the culture of science in which they worked which I have done elsewhere (e.g. Milne, 1998; Venville, & Milne, 1999). However, in this chapter I wanted to examine how scientific knowledge is generated and validated in specific stories that are told about scientific discovery. How often have you read a story like this?

Pasteur's Plague

Pasteur's discovery of a vaccine for chicken cholera happened by accident. Firstly, Pasteur wasn't getting anywhere with his attempts to find a cure for anthrax so he decided to study chicken cholera. Secondly, Pasteur and his assistants decided to go on a two-month holiday and accidentally left some cholera germ cultures out on the bench in their laboratory at the Ecole Normale in 1879.

When they arrived back from their holiday no fresh cultures were available for them to continue with their work so Pasteur decided to use the old cultures that had been left out. To their surprise none of the chickens injected with the old culture succumbed to the disease. After this minor set back, they decided to continue their work. However, no fresh hens were available from the markets so they had to use the hens that had already been inoculated with the old culture. To their immense surprise, these hens survived inoculation with fresh cholera germ cultures. Pasteur had discovered vaccination!

Reid, D. & Booth, P. (1974). Biology for the individual Book 7: War against disease, pp. 21-22). London: Heinemann Educational Books.

Figure 2. A discovery science story

I called this type of story a discovery science story because it is based on a particular notion of what it means to discover something in science. You might have read some of these yourself. There is even a section on the web at trivia-library.com that contains stories about 'accidental discoveries'. Generally speaking, these stories portray scientists as finding something in Nature that ultimately is attributed the status of a 'fact' in science. The story of 'Pasteur's Plague' can be read to imply that discovery in science happens by accident. There is no shortage of stories in science that have been presented as 'discovery by accident', for example: Alexander Fleming and lysozyme (Morgan, 1981); Becquerel and radioactivity (Duncan, 1977; Sutton, 1986); Alexander Fleming and penicillin (Macfarlane, 1984); Oskar Minkowski and diabetes and the pancreas (Kohn, 1989); Wilhelm Röentgen and X-rays (Roller, 1957); Jocelyn Bell and pulsars (Ward, 1975); Charles Richet and anaphylaxis (Holmes, 1972); Goodyear and vulcanization (Kauffman, 2001); Salk and polio vaccine (Blackwell, 1969) and viagra (BBC, 2002).

Discovery science stories with their emphasis on accident raise questions about the way discovery in science is represented. Some questions relate to the actual process of discovery and led me to ask if discovery in science really was accidental. Reading such discovery science stories also led me to ask about the relationship between the discovery of new science knowledge and the justification of such knowledge. I wondered why there seemed to be much more emphasis in science on how scientific knowledge was justified rather than on the 'discovery' of new science knowledge.

IS DISCOVERY AN ACCIDENT?

In order to answer my questions I had to go back and look at the writings of philosophers of science. The idea that discoveries happen by accident has led some philosophers of science to distinguish between the 'process of discovery' and the 'process of justification' (Reichenbach, 1951). According to this imposed dichotomy, discovery defies logical analysis. Indeed, in his Philosophy of Natural Science, Carl Hempel (1966) wrote that while the process of discovery can be influenced by "scientifically questionable notions" validation of discoveries was based on scientifically acceptable reasoning processes of induction or deduction. According to philosopher Karl Popper (1980):

> [T]he question of how it happens that a new idea occurs to a man (sic) - [such as] a scientific theory - . . . is irrelevant to the logical analysis of scientific knowledge (Popper, 1980, p. 31).

Thus Popper differentiated between the process of 'having a new idea' and the justification or validation of 'questions of fact'. Philosophical positions such as those of Hempel and Popper imply that, unlike justification, which involves a process of 'scientific method', there is no 'logic' in discovery. The argument goes that anyone can do it. You just have to be in the right place at the right time. Intuition and imagination, which are important to the process of discovery, are to be less valued than is slavish adherence to a scientific method. However, there were other philosophers of science who argued differently. Feminist philosopher of science Sandra Harding claimed that:

> [T]he text of discovery, where problems are identified as appropriate for scientific investigation, hypotheses are formulated, key concepts are defined - this part of the scientific process is thought to be unexaminable within science by rational methods. Thus "real science" is restricted to those processes controllable by methodologic rules (Harding, 1991, p. 40).

According to Harding, this imposition of an artificial dichotomy between discovery and validation occurred because the notion of discovery could not be explained in a logical, methodological way but was tinged with overtones of subjectivity – intuition, imagination, and creativity. Philosophers such as Hempel and Popper largely ignored discovery and instead focused on the methodology of validation. Further reading indicated that an emphasis on methodology was not restricted to the writings of philosophers of science but permeated also how authors wrote about science and scientific discoveries. For example, when describing the role of discovery of anaphylaxis in Charles Richet's physiology research Fredrick Holmes commented that:

> [Richet] had made few discoveries that strayed beyond the normal development of these fields. Most of his investigations were typical of a large, well organised science; that is, they clustered around the fundamental work of other men. . . . [W]hen he had passed his fiftieth year, Richet finally entered the charmed circle of scientists who have discovered major unexpected phenomena (Holmes, 1972, p. 429).

It seemed to me that although Holmes celebrated Richet's discovery he implied that discovery happened by <u>accident</u>. This notion of accidental discovery implied that anyone observing what Fleming or Röentgen or Pasteur observed would come to the same conclusions as did they. However, Emile Roux, Pasteur's collaborator, observed the same results as Pasteur but did not attach significance to the attenuation of the disease causing microbes and William Crookes observed the same phenomena as did Röentgen, that is fogged photographic plates, but did not realize that the cathode ray tubes might have anything to do with the observable phenomena. Nicholas Wade (1975) reported in his article on the discovery of pulsars by Jocelyn Bell that there were rumors of another British astronomer who had noticed pulsar signals on his charts before she had but he had dismissed the phenomena as an artifact of his data collection methods.

THE RICH, MESSY BUSINESS OF DISCOVERY

I recognized the attraction for some writers who found validation easier to explain than the "rich, messy business of discovery" (Root-Bernstein, 1988, p. 28). However, I believed the notion of discovery, messy or otherwise, was fundamental to science and was one of the most exciting aspects of scientific endeavor. It was in the context of a problem that an observation became a 'fact'. Furthermore, science was not just about confirming and building up facts; it was also about turning ideas and hunches into concepts by a process of discovery. The tendency of some philosophers, biographers and textbooks to intimate that scientific discovery happens by accident could be attributed to the perceived messiness of scientific discovery. The reasoning might go something like this, 'If it is difficult to explain, then it must be due to an accident'.

I recognized that if it was possible to dismiss discovery as a happy accident then writers could minimize the importance of subjective notions such intuition, imagination and creativity that are fundamental to the art of discovery in science. I had begun to read feminist philosophers of science such as Helen Weinreich-Haste (1986), Linda Shepherd (1993) and Harding (1991) and found their argument that in Western science these notions are considered feminine and therefore are less valued than a logical, rationalistic and methodologic approach to validation compelling. To make sense of this dichotomy I needed to unpack the definition of science that underpins representations of discovery and justification. In her study of stereotypes in different disciplines, Weinreich-Haste (1981) asked school children and undergraduates to rate disciplines using dichotomous scales such as feminine-masculine, concrete-abstract and feeling-based-intellect-based. She reported that there was a "constellation of beliefs" about science subjects that led the participants in the study to describe science as hard, complex, abstract and fundamentally masculine according to cultural stereotypes of 'masculinity' (Weinreich-Haste, 1986, p. 115). According to Weinreich-Haste (1986), bimodal categories represent a common sense explanation that can be expressed in metaphor, myth, and folk wisdom, for example accidental discoveries. Once presented, these dichotomies have to be justified. Francis Bacon (1620) reinforced the notion of science as masculine, rational, logical and methodological. He differentiated Nature as a 'she' that could be forced to yield her secrets by the application of science. Such a notion of science leads practitioners to differentiate between discovery and justification in science on the grounds that discovery has overtones of feminine characteristics, such as intuition, creativity and imagination, whereas justification can be conceptualized as a scientific activity that is rational, free of emotion, logical and methodological. These dichotomies connate a lack of rationality associated with discovery.

By implication, a logical, rational, methodological scientist would never allow feelings or beliefs or values to interfere with his or her search for justification. This methodological approach to science supports a narrow view of objectivity supported by the myth of 'value-free' science: scientists can and should free themselves from the influences of society and culture in order to examine Nature 'as it really is' (Harding, 1991). Accordingly, discovery is 'infected' by human values and interests which determine the type of problem to be studied and the concepts that are supported in the hypotheses to be investigated. Because of its infected status, proponents of this form of objectivity do not value discovery. However, Londa Schiebinger in her books *Nature's Body* (1993), *The Mind Has No Sex?* (1989), *Plants and Empire* (2004), and Stephen Jay Gould in *The Mismeasure of Man* (1981), clearly demonstrate the social-embeddedness of the verification of scientific knowledge. From this perspective, science cannot be separated from society and, therefore, it always examines Nature through the 'lens' of socio-cultural expectations. Clearly from this perspective, science is not value-free and cannot be explained by a set of methodological rules. It requires an integrated framework that can accommodate values, interests, creativity, and abstract and concrete notions both for discovery and verification.

Another approach to considering the relationship between science, discovery and verification is presented by philosopher of science, Stephen Toulmin. He attempts to redefine rationality so that discovery can be considered a rational process. *In Human Understanding* (1972), Toulmin separates rationality from 'logicality' and, consistent with his notion of 'conceptual evolution', defines rationality as our ability to alter our belief systems in the face of changing circumstances. He claims "the rationality of science is embodied not in the theoretical systems current in it at particular times but in its procedures for discovery and conceptual change through time" (Toulmin, 1972, p. 84). Thus, rationality can be described as 'intellectual adaptability' (Nickles, 1980) that is essential for the innovative reasoning that leads us to new conceptual discoveries.

I was convinced that intuition, imagination and creativity were essential for the evolution of new knowledge in science. According to Toulmin, an understanding of science as an intellectual enterprise can be achieved only by examining its historical evolution. This might seem to be a rather simplistic explanation; however, scientific knowledge often is presented as timeless and universal. For example, when the history of the development of a concept is forgotten there can be a tendency to present models of scientific explanation that emerged at different times as a mixture of timeless facts. This can be quite confusing for science students (May, 1980). Science is not a 'snapshot' that means the same thing to all people, but a 'moving picture' that must be interpreted dynamically.

The gendered nature of science and society also helped me to understand why discovery in science was often presented as a happy accident. My next question was whether the history of discovery might serve to confirm or negate the gendered nature of Western society's understanding of discovery.

RECONSIDERING ACCIDENTS

Based on my understanding of how stories tended to be constructed from the selection of events for the telling, I wondered what the historical evidence told me about Pasteur's discovery of a vaccine for chicken cholera; whether it was possible by looking at the events more thoroughly to decide whether it was a happy accident or a rational process requiring thoughtfulness, intuition and creativity. According to Root-Bernstein (1988), Pasteur's breakthrough with chicken cholera vaccine was anything <u>but</u> an accident. Pasteur's response was the result of his expectations. It was well known by the 19th century that people who survived certain infectious diseases tended to become resistant to the disease, and Pasteur used this knowledge to experiment with chicken cholera. Analysis of his notebooks indicates that he was thoroughly investigating the problem of how to develop an attenuated microbe that led organisms to develop resistance, but did not kill them (Stokes, 1997).

The breakthrough did not come from him leaving flasks out unattended while he went on a holiday as the discovery story implied (see Figure 1). Actually Pasteur left the flasks in the care of M. Roux and on his return in early 1879 he used the material from the flasks to inoculate chickens. As narrated by David Reid and P. Booth (1974), the birds did not become ill. However, when Pasteur infected these chickens with freshly prepared cholera culture they died. They did not survive the "stronger dose" as this story claims. Pasteur did not attempt experiments designed to attenuate the chicken cholera microbe until later in 1879 and it was not until October 1879 that he conducted his first successful experiment with attenuated microbes. He and Roux attempted many different ways of attenuating the microbe including heat, exposure to air, and different growth media, before any of the attempts worked. Pasteur found that he could weaken the microbe, but then it became too weak to initiate an immune response in the chickens. Finally, by March 1880 he had determined that growing the microbes in a mildly acidic medium for a long time produced a weakened microbe that caused the chickens to develop immunity.

Therefore the discovery of a vaccine for chicken cholera was no accident but due to a series of well planned and well executed experiments that were designed to answer a question: Is it possible for organisms to develop immunity by using a weakened version of the infectious agent? Discovery was not a fluke, but the result of carefully planned experimentation.

Next I decided to investigate the discovery of anaphylaxis because I was fascinated by the idea that organisms could develop a lower and lower tolerance for toxins through repeated exposure. Was Charles Richet's discovery of anaphylaxis an accident? Richet was a physiologist. He and his colleague Paul Portier were conducting tests on sea anemone toxin. Richet expected the toxin to cause the immune system of the dogs that he was using for the tests to produce something in the blood that increased the dogs' resistance to the toxin if it was readministered. However, when they injected the dogs, which had recovered from a previous dosage of the sea anemone toxin, they discovered that a much smaller dosage of toxin was needed to kill the dogs. This was the opposite to Richet's expectation based on his earlier work with serums, attenuated bacterial cultures, and other toxins in which the resistance of the animal had been reinforced by sub lethal dosages of toxin. With this toxin, the animals' resistance had been lowered. If Richet's previous research had not sensitized him to the significance of this work he may have thrown away the samples or given up the trials because the results were contrary to expectations. However, he and Portier persisted with their experiments on this effect, which they called 'anaphylaxis', that is, 'against protection'.

They decided to attempt to extract the active ingredient in sea anemone toxin. After numerous tests they extracted a white powder they called 'congestin'. Richet demonstrated anaphylactic effects in substances such as morphine and blood serum. He developed a theory of anaphylaxis which he based on both his own and his colleagues' observations and on the antibody-antigen interaction proposed by Paul Ehrlich and Jules Bordet. He argued that the original injection of toxin caused the formation of a substance in the blood which was not toxic but which reacted with the toxin to produce an extremely toxic substance. Thus, Richet's discovery also was no mere accident. If he had not conducted previous research on immune responses, he would not have been interested in the toxin of the sea anemone and he might not have appreciated the significance of the results that he and Portier obtained.

By presenting these stories of Pasteur and Richet, I am not arguing that I have presented all that is known about their work in these areas of science but I am trying to demonstrate that it is possible to tell other stories about scientific discoveries by selecting other events for the telling. The process of writing different stories emphasized two things for me: firstly, that science is storied and secondly, the importance of careful observation and the need for an appreciation of theoretical frameworks in discovery and validation. Discovery is a complex notion and requires a lot more than a fortuitous accident (Root-Bernstein, 1988). It requires first of all a problem, a paradox, and an inconsistency, which can be identified only if the researcher has a detailed understanding of a specific research field. These problems are more likely to be identified if the researcher is 'in touch' with the organisms or the processes with which she or he is working. The researcher's mind must be prepared to recognize inconsistencies, to relate these inconsistencies to evidence, and to set aside time for reflection so that random thoughts can incubate. The researcher seeks to prepare her or his mind to connect disparate pieces of evidence into a meaningful pattern. Finally, the researcher needs to carry out the tests that provide the verification for the discovery that she proposes. Thus, discovery and verification are interwoven in the complex human endeavor that we call science.

ANOTHER MODEL OF DISCOVERY

My emerging awareness of the complex nature of discovery led me to ask if there was another way we might think about discovery in science. At this stage, I was influenced by Evelyn Fox Keller's biography of Nobel Laureate Barbara McClintock (1983). In her biography, Fox Keller emphasizes McClintock's "feeling for the organism" which was based on an understanding of, and empathy for, the organisms that she studied. McClintock worked at a time during which the "central dogma" for genetics became the notion that DNA was the unidirectional master controller of protein synthesis. Contrary to this dogma, McClintock's work indicated that sections of DNA could move on chromosomes, so called 'jumping genes', in response to signals from other segments of DNA, and that the signals might be influenced by the internal environment of the cell. McClintock conducted her work at a macroscopic level on maize plants when molecular biology was all the rage and so her overwhelmingly male contemporaries did not value her claims. When asked about her ability to see further into genetics than could her colleagues McClintock responded that you needed the patience to "hear what the material has to say to you", a willingness to be surprised by the ingenuity of Nature and an awareness that, although Nature is lawful, reason and experimentation alone is not enough to articulate these laws without intuition (Keller, 1983, p. 201).

Trevor Pinch (1992) described this 'feeling for the organism' as listening to the material as science discoverers worked hard to understand the phenomenon or process with which they were working because discoverers needed an extensive theoretical framework to make meaningful observations. This might help to explain why Minkowski's sharp-eyed assistant who was the first to see flies around the experimental dog's urine was not able to make Minkowski's conceptual connection between observed flies around a dog's urine and the removal of the dog's pancreas. Over time, Pasteur became very knowledgeable about the chicken cholera microbe, its behavior and its effects on its host. In common with all his other investigations of specific problems, Pasteur developed an extensive card system and spent hours meditating on his card entries.

These discoverers did not work to impose order on Nature but, instead, listened to what Nature said to them. Microbiologist Alexander Fleming was another discoverer who knew the bacterial organisms that he was working with very well. He used his knowledge to create bacterial colony 'art work' which required an intimate understanding of both the colors produced by specific bacterial colonies and their incubation periods (Root-Bernstein, 1990). Fleming may not have displayed the intellectual brilliance of Howard Florey and Ernst Chain who proposed the biochemical mechanism for the action of lysozyme on bacteria and who produced the first viable penicillin. He said of himself that he "just played with microbes" (Macfarlane, 1984), but his knowledge of them was deep and intrinsic.

Cecilia Payne-Gaposchkin also demonstrated the ability to listen to the material. As a graduate student, she used M. N. Saha's theory, which combined quantum theory and statistical mechanics with a thermal equilibrium mixture of atoms, ions, and electrons, to propose that stellar atmospheres were composed primarily of hydrogen and helium. This was contrary to the accepted scientific wisdom of the time, which assumed that stars such as the sun were composed of the same elements as the earth, and in similar proportions. Her work formed the basis of the modern theory that heavier elements are synthesized from hydrogen and helium in stars (Brush, 1985).

These accounts suggested that stories such as 'Pasteur's Plague' (See Figure 1) with their emphasis on accidental discovery presented a simplistic view of what it means to discover something in science. As a teacher I felt this was especially worrisome when I found such stories in science textbooks because I felt they did not represent the nature of science in its complexity and humanness. I felt such stories presented a malnourished view of science. Discovery does not occur in a vacuum but in the social and cultural milieu of scientific endeavor.

PERSONAL AND PUBLIC IMPLICATIONS

This analysis of discovery science stories opened my eyes to possible pedagogical implications, acknowledging the sophistication and understanding needed to make discoveries in science and valuing questions for learning about science. I knew I had to emphasize in my interactions with teachers and students that scientific discoveries do not occur by accident but because scientists know very well the phenomenon, process or material with which they are working. Discoverers seem to have empathy for the organisms, material or processes with which they are working and often are excited by the work that engages them. Therefore, for students to travel on their own journey of discovery in the science classroom they need to become familiar with the theory/conceptual framework as they engage in observation and experimentation. Meaningful observations of the natural world require more than an open mind. They also require a theoretically informed mind. As I know from personal experience, students do not observe cells the first time they look down a microscope. Rather, they need to know about the operation of the microscope and the structure of cells before they're 'seeing' becomes 'observing'. In school science, an important curriculum emphasis should be the human construction of theory, discourse and experimentation in science.

I recognized that the lowly status of discovery in scientific text books could be due to the lowly status that science places on intuition, imagination and creativity, characteristics which might be considered subjective and, therefore, rather feminine (Shepherd, 1993). In school science, we need to celebrate discovery. Thomas Nickle's notion of intellectual adaptability and Toulmin's emphasis on the historical development of science has application to the development of curricula in school science. With students we need to highlight the process of discovery and emphasize its communal nature. An individual scientist working in splendid isolation never performs discovery. Perhaps science stories need to emphasize the way scientists seek to understand the processes and organisms with which they work, rather than emphasizing only the search for justification in science. Perhaps our stories should demonstrate how science constructs meaning from Nature rather than discovers the facts that are thought to exist in Nature.

As I analyzed discovery science stories, reflections on the nature of discovery also led me to recognition of the importance of a question rather than an answer focus for students learning science (Milne, 2007). Many of the teachers, experienced and inexperienced, with whom I work know lots of science and feel that it is their responsibility to tell students the answers of science and to ensure that laboratory activities reinforce this focus. Over the past couple of years, I have begun to develop strategies with teachers to help them to focus on developing activities that encourage students to pose questions in science. I have found that one of the challenges is to convince them that science content will emerge during the answering of questions (Milne & Blonstein, 2005). I believe strongly in this strategy because it invites everybody on a voyage of discovery even when they believe they know the answers.

The tendency to dichotomize discovery and justification is based on the 'difference as deficit model' and not on any sophisticated understanding of the practice of science. All teachers should work to present science in all its richness and not as something that has had all the cream removed. Science is not based only on a set of methodologic rules but is a flexible and dynamic aspect of human endeavor. It seems to me that the over-emphasis on method in school science has led to a 'cook–book' style of science presentation and a narrow commitment to verifying laws and facts. Not surprisingly, many students, girls in particular, find such an approach boring and unengaging. It makes science seem like a static form of knowing and obscures the excitement and involvement of discovery. A greater emphasis on the art of discovery might not only attract more girls to science, but might also change the way science is represented in school science texts - books, policy documents, curricula and discourses.

WHY STORIES ARE IMPORTANT

All stories have in common their relation to a culture via codes. We use these codes to make sense of events by ordering events into a narrative and by introducing causality into the interpretation of texts that have been presented as an account of the narrative. If teachers and students of science understand how stories and narratives are structured, if they understand the relationship between events, text and interpretation, and if they appreciate that stories contain explicit or implicit messages about values and meaning, then they can develop an awareness of the possibility of multiple representations of events.

If we wish to improve the quality of teaching and learning in science it may be important to understand the influence of narrative structure on the representation of science because stories are an undeniable feature of the human condition. A critical awareness of the possibility of creating more than one set of meanings and values in a story is important because of the significance of stories in science. Because science stories reveal implicitly something about the nature of science, they serve to legitimate particular philosophical frameworks in science, which may not be consistent with contemporary developments in philosophy of science or educational practice. Stories in school science tend to emphasize the importance of objects of science over both the processes of science and the involvement of scientists in the construction of scientific knowledge. But these values are often presented implicitly. What we tell and how we tell it is a revelation of what we believe about the nature of science just as I am doing in this chapter.

The process of examining science stories has helped me to realize that there are many events available for the telling of a story. Through the process of selecting events for the telling we imbue the story with specific meanings and values just as the authors of discovery stories emphasize "accidental" discoveries. It is possible to re-create these stories as I have tried to do by selecting other events for the telling. Rather than a story about accidents, I want to tell a story about understanding and listening to phenomena. Of course, I believe my "listening to the material" stories represent scientific endeavor and discovery more accurately than "accidental" discovery science stories but what is important about this process is the recognition that science can be thought of as constructed by multiple voices rather than one dominant voice. All science stories are a particular reading of the narrative of science. Perhaps this approach will encourage people as it has encouraged me to ask, "Is this the story I want to tell?" I am not sure how well I have told this story but this is the story I wanted to tell.

REFERENCES

Bacon, F. (1620/1968). Paraceve/Novum organum. In J. Spedding, R. L. Ellis, & D. D. Heath (Eds.), *The works of Francis Bacon*. New York: Garrett Press. (Original publication 1620, facsimile reprint of 1870 publication)

Barthes, R. (1978). *Image-music-text* (S. Heath, Trans.). New York: Hill & Wang.

British Broadcasting Commission. (2002). *Sexual chemistry*. Retrieved April 28, 2006, from http://www.bbc.co.uk/source/horizon/2003/sexchem

Blackwell, R. J. (1969). *Discovery in the physical sciences*. Notre Dame, IN: University of Notre Dame Press.

Bruner, J. (1986). *Actual minds, possible worlds*. Cambridge, MA: Harvard University Press.

Brush, S. G. (1985). Women in science: From drudges to discoverers. *The Physics Teacher, 23*(1), 11–19.

Carter, K. (1993). The place of story in the study of teaching and teacher education. *Educational Researcher, 22*(1), 5–12.

Duncan, T. (1977). *Physics for today and tomorrow*. London: John Murray.

Foucault, M. (1974). *The archaeology of knowledge*. London: Tavistock.

Gould, S. J. (1981). *The mismeasure of man*. New York: Norton.

Harding, S. (1991). *Whose science? Whose knowledge? Thinking from women's lives*. Milton Keynes: Open University Press.

Hempel, C. G. (1966). *Philosophy of natural science*. Englewood Cliffs, NJ: Prentice Hall Inc.

Holmes, F. L. (1972). Richet, Charles Robert. In C. C. Gilispie (Ed.), *Dictionary of scientific biography* (pp. 425–432). New York: Charles Scribner's Sons.

Kauffman, G. B. (2001). Charles Goodyear (1800–1860), American inventor on the bicentennial of his birth. *The Chemical Educator, 6*, 50–54.

Keller, E. F. (1983). *A feeling for the organism: The life and work of Barbara McClintock*. New York: W. H. Freeman.

Kohn, A. (1989). *Fortune or failure: Missed opportunities and chance discoveries*. Oxford: Basil Blackwell.

Kuhn, T. (1970). *The structure of scientific revolutions* (2nd ed.). Chicago: University of Chicago Press.

Lyotard, J.-F. (1984). *The postmodern condition: A report on knowledge* (G. Bennington & B. Massumi, Trans.). Minneapolis, MN: University of Minnesota Press.

Macfarlane, G. (1984). *Alexander Fleming: The man and the myth*. London: Chatto & Windus.

Milne, C. (1998). Philosophically correct science stories? Examining the implications of heroic science stories for school science. *Journal of Research in Science Teaching, 35*, 175–187.

Milne, C. (2007). In praise of questions: Elevating the role of questions for inquiry in secondary school science. In J. Luft (Ed.), *Science as inquiry in secondary schools* (pp. 99–106). Washington, DC: NSF Monograph series.

Milne, C., & Blonstein, J. (2005, January 19–23). *Confidence in questions: Examining the tensions between pedagogy and subject matter knowledge in a science methods course*. Paper presented at the AETS 2005 International Conference, Colorado Spring, CO.

Morgan, D. (Ed.). (1981). *Biological science: The web of life* (3rd ed.). Canberra, Australia: Australian Academy of Sciences.

Nickles, T. (Ed.). (1980). *Scientific discovery, logic and rationality. Boston studies in the philosophy of science* (Vol. 56). Dordrecht, Holland: D. Reidel Publishing Company.

Pinch, T. J. (1992). Opening black boxes: Science, technology and society. *Social Studies of Science, 22*, 487–510.

Popper, K. R. (1980). *The logic of scientific discovery*. London: Hutchinson.

Reichenbach, H. (1951). *The rise of scientific philosophy*. Berkley, CA: University of California Press.

Reid, D., & Booth, P. (1974). *Biology for the individual, Book 7: War against disease*. London: Heinemann Educational Books.

Root-Bernstein, R. S. (1988). Setting the stage for discovery. *The Sciences, 28*(3), 26–34.

Schiebinger, L. (1989). *The mind has no sex? Women in the origins of modern science.* Cambridge, MA: Harvard University Press.

Schiebinger, L. (1993). *Nature's body: Gender in the making of modern science.* Boston: Beacon Press.

Schiebinger, L. (2004). *Plants and empire: Colonial bioprospecting in the Atlantic world.* Cambridge, MA: Harvard University Press.

Scholes, R. (1981). Language, narrative and anti-narrative. In W. J. T. Mitchell (Ed.), *On narrative* (pp. 200–208). Chicago: The University of Chicago Press.

Shepherd, L. J. (1993). *Lifting the veil: The feminine face of science.* Boston: Shambhala Publications.

Stokes, D. E. (1997). *Pasteur's quadrant: Basic science and technological innovation.* Washington, DC: Brookings Institution Press.

Sutton, C. (1986, February 27). Serendipity or sound science? *New Scientist,* 30–32.

Toulmin, S. (1972). *Human understanding* (Vol. 1). Oxford: Clarendon Press.

Venville, G., & Milne, C. (1999). Three women scientists and their role in the history of genetics. *Australian Science Teachers' Journal, 45*(3), 9–15.

Wade, N. (1975). Discovery of pulsars: A graduate student's story. *Science, 189,* 358–364.

Weinreich-Haste, H. (1986). Brother sun, sister moon: Does rationality overcome a dualistic world view? In J. Harding (Ed.), *Perspectives on gender and science* (pp. 113–131). London: The Falmer Press.

AFFILIATION

Catherine Milne
School of Teaching and Learning,
New York University

M. E. SPENCER AND SHERRY NICHOLS

14. SCIENCE EDUCATION: INTERTWINED JOURNEYS, LIVED MYTHS, AND ECOFEMINIST ECHOES

INTRODUCTION

As elementary science teacher educators and researchers, we find it highly troubling that those responsible for teacher preparation and conducting research in this area may be most complicit in perpetuating reasons why many become disenchanted with science in the early years of science in school. Our insights about these situations have come through many discussions–made possible because we live only an hour drive from one another in Alabama. As friends and colleagues, we have shared with each other about our experiences as young backyard explorers, being science teachers of young learners, and our journeys to where we have taken up our present careers as university elementary science teacher educators. In recounting our experiences, we have often noted similar moments of joy, heartbreak, and oppression. When asked to contribute a chapter featuring an auto/biography of feminist science educators' career pathway, we realized that our own narratives could serve as an insightful contribution to this book.

Accordingly, this chapter provides a context for examining the profession of elementary science teacher educators framed as a "biomythography." Our collaborative composition viewed through an ecofeminist lens brings to light oppressive and alienating practices of science learning and teaching, which we resist reproducing through our own practices of teaching future elementary teachers in our science "methods" coursework. Taking this path not often traveled in science teacher education, we consciously make explicit notions of embodying science, what we would refer to as being science.

DANCING IN BOXES

The backdoor screen slams as I jump off the porch and chase Johnny around the side of the big white rambling house and into the garden. He runs through the huge bushes where bees appear to protect him from me. A truce is called and we move on to the next adventure, which he identifies as "bee keeping." Catching and observing live bees is fun! We quietly snatch an old mason jar with a rusty lid out of the root cellar. I catch the first bee as usual because the jar is empty and I don't have to be concerned with escapees. He grabs the jar and quickly has five more

K. Scantlebury, J. Butler Kahle and S. N. Martin (eds.) Re-visioning Science Education from Feminist Perspectives: Challenges, Choices and Careers, 151–163.
© 2010 Sense Publishers. All rights reserved.

prisoners. He wants to keep them...let them make us some honey. What will they eat? How much water should we give them? What kind of houses do they need in the jar so they can make our honey? How big will the lid holes need to be so that they can breathe?

As twilight comes creeping in, the bees and questions are abandoned to the next day. Twilight – a magical time for kids, bugs, and other life forms. Tiny little lights twinkled in the night sky just begging for our attention. We catch them and put them on our hair, clothes, and fingernails, but they would always fly off. His solution for keeping his glowing monster fingernails is to quickly rip off the bugs' abdomens and press them onto his stubby fingers. How horrifying! Screaming I went into the house and told!

The next afternoon we were back building dirt cities for our roly-poly prisoners. Tonka trucks and heavy metal bulldozers pushed the mounds of dirt to make walls. Our roly-poly citizens pushed the mounds too and their many legs set them free. Rolling into perfect little spheres helped increase their speed down the hills and hastened their escape.

That night while lying between cool crisp sheets fresh off of the line, I could smell the sweet mimosa tree blossoms and hear the crickets, cicadas, and tree frogs singing. The chorus became louder, louder, and hauntingly familiar. Two syllables – ee oo, ee, oo. Faster now em, e, em, e...M.E.!

When I was a school-aged child, science was a dance was done in formalized curricular boxes – the boxes of physical, life, and earth/space sciences. Over a long period of my public schooling, these boxes I danced in became ragged, torn, wind whipped, and sweat stained. Tiny holes appeared and I could see out between the boxes. I realized as I danced in one, the others shook. Webs, branches, and light beams connected them. The more I danced the greater the holes became. Vines, rain, and colonies of beetles and ants helped the boxes to decay. Eventually there was only dust — dust and dancing among the interwoven and inextricably linked no-longer boxes of science. They were and are "being" science—part of what I am and I do. It is impossible to put science teaching, learning, and being back into boxes that no longer, nor had ever, existed. Teaching, learning, and being science for me continues as a passion filled, rhythmic dance that I do with other beings and things I encounter.

Over past year the science curricular initiative in our state, the Alabama Mathematics, Science, and Technology Initiative, has been offered as the new and improved way of teaching science to children. The science boxes are back. Lessons learned from the golden era of science education in the 1960s are being reproduced in the new millennium as curriculum reform is promised through the deployment of science kits across the state. Almost literally, from our backyards rocks and minerals are quarried and hauled away and trees are killed and sold for human use. Thankfully the science boxes have mini collections of such materials for eventually we may have no place to collect such. Science kits are moved in and out of elementary classrooms delivering a mythical view of science as if contained in some neatly labeled sturdy box. Elementary teachers trained in the use of boxes follow their utilitarian roles as they instruct the children, further separating them from the natural world of which they are inextricably linked. Ecofeminism helps us to recognize and explore this "new" notion of science pre-packaged for all.

BEING ECOFEMINISTS

M.E.'s early childhood narrative provides an introduction to concepts of ecofeminist thought. Residing at the junction of feminism, science and technology, and native perspectives, ecofeminism embraces the interconnectedness of all living and non-living things and furthermore, recognizes the equal value of knowledge and being given to all forms of life (Merchant, 1980; Warren, 1990; 1993). Rather than focusing on individual beings or individual knowledge as many would do, as ecofeminists we seek to make visual the interwoven tapestry of all living beings and non-living things. Ecofeminism unveils the nexus between women, children, and non-human environment and the ways that male privilege and power are unjustifiably imposed upon them in forms of oppression through the logic of domination (Statham, 2001; Warren, 1993; 1997). We would describe ecofeminism as a holistic cultural theory, which values, accepts, and embraces as its fundamental premise interdependence. Furthermore, we agree with Sanchez (as cited in Adams, 1993) that "most Euro-American or Euro-Western peoples tend to separate themselves from "nature" and to rank humans above animals, plants, and minerals in hierarchical fashion, and so it is not easy for them to perceive or accept a personal relationship with what they describe as the "natural world" (p. 211). In our work, ecofeminism serves as a lens to interpret the vision of being science through holistic perspectives that include more than the mind, but rather promote awakening (Clandinin & Connelly, 2000; Merleau-Ponty, 1962) of the mind, body, emotions, perceptions, and consciousness.

Ecofeminist projects in science education "need to begin with identifying the actual constraints on the present way most of us interpret science education" (Zell, 1998, p. 146). Indeed, the use of ecofeminism as a theoretical foundation or lens in science education research is quite rare. New possibilities for science teaching and learning are opened as ecofeminism "positions the researcher as part of nature, not as master over it" (Zell, 1998, p. 143). Science educators, science teachers and learners are part of nature and, therefore; must come to understand science as action, as being, as opposed to what Harding (1986) identified as a "western, bourgeois, masculine project" (p. 8) –a boxed set of knowledge from which understanding can be extracted as needed.

The narrative accounts composed for this chapter reflects insights based not only on our ecofeminist understandings, but also speaks to our approach writing this chapter. The notion of writing an autobiography or biography would be incompatible from a feminist perspective as the reification—object making—of a person's lived experience possibly positions the individual as separated and ripe for domination. In our view, to write such individualized accounts about life may promote unintended acts of colonization and utilization through our scholarly activities. Listening to each other's experiences, we recognized familiar pathways taken from our different spaces and places. We sensed a similar journey, one that while wondrous, also had shadows of alienation and separation, springing forth from "natural" pathways readily taken.

WRITING OUR CAREERS AS BIOMYTHOGRAPHY

Our collaborative writing of this auto/biography as "biomythography" recognizes the power of seeing personal histories, traditionally written as "I" accounts, instead we recognize the social composition of individuals (Smith, 1998). Biomythographical accounts weave together myth, culture, history, and biography in narrative form. King (cited in Kaplan, 1998) has described biomythography as an outlaw genre that recognizes "layers of meanings, layers of histories, layers of reading and rereading through webs of power-charged codes" (p. 212). Kaplan (1998) characterizes the resistant stance of this literacy approach:

> The homogenizing influence of autobiography genres identifies similarities; reading an autobiography involves assimilating or consenting to the values and worldview of the writer [p. 212]....out-law genres [enable] a deconstruction of the "master" genres, revealing the power dynamics embedded in literary production, distribution, and reception (p.208).

Engaged in composing account spanning across our experiences we began to recognize common myths that had shaped our choices and pathways as science learners and teachers. Roland Barthes (1985) describes myths as codified language that serves to notify us of cultural values, and simultaneously impose on us the sense that we should adopt these as values without question. Catherine Milne (1998) in her analyses of "science stories" demonstrates how mythologies have shaped how science becomes texts to be taught in school. Milne (1998) points out that "[a]ll stories have in common their relation to culture via codes that are agreed-upon sets of rules or social norms or myths" (p. 177). Metacodes deeply embedded in science texts, science curriculum standards, and the like, communicate and structure our interpretations of how and why we teach science. Texts that limit science history to descriptions of how European White males is an example of a metacode that communicates a myth that females and non-Europeans have not contributed to science. Mythologies similarly work toward establishing norms that shape how teachers, such as ourselves, come to make sense of teaching (Britzman, 1991).

These ideas are important to our thinking about the nexus of relationships, identity narratives, and philosophical currents that have influenced our becoming teachers and researchers of elementary science teacher education. In the processes of "becoming a teacher" we recognize that mythologies have worked to censor and unify our emerging images of what it means to be a teacher (Britzman, 1991). Drawing on ecofeminist perspectives, we contest myths associated with being learners of science, and becoming teachers of science teacher education (Nichols & Tippins, 2005; Roychoudhury, Tippins & Nichols, 1991). In the process of composing our biomythographical accounts, we engage in critique of myths that have historically alienated learners and teachers from science as a means to envisioning alternative possibilities for embodied science.

ERODING ENTHUSIASM

The small, rural elementary school where Elizabeth taught second grade was an old building and desperately needed repairs and updating. The driveway to the front was paved, but the bus lanes were not. Buses would bounce up and down in the rutted dirt road to the side of the school jostling the children so that the younger ones would often fly right off of their seats! On the other side of the deeply channeled road was the playground, which was enclosed with a chain link fence and rusted gate.

Elizabeth was in the second year of her career as a teacher; a career she loved. She was so enthusiastic about her children's learning that she would sometimes accompany them to art or physical education just to watch and interact with them in different settings. On the way to physical education, her young charges would often tumble down as they jumped the ruts in the bare naked earth of the bus lanes. They complained about the ugly scars on the earth and also about their own physical wounds. Many times they asked Elizabeth, "Will all of the dirt just fall away? What will happen to our playground and buses? Where will we go?" Elizabeth pondered those questions and asked the students what they could do about the problem. "Pave it over!" and "Scoop it up!" were some of the suggestions.

Elizabeth was shortly going to begin an environmental science unit of study with the children. She was excited as she recognized this problem with erosion as an opportunity to teach her students meaningful real-world science, as opposed to the science of the textbook. She did not know a lot about erosion and this perception caused her to begin to research the topic. Amazingly erosion was a very interesting concept.

Administration at this elementary school, as well as at the system and state level, strongly enforced an academic focus clearly and primarily on reading. Science was not viewed as being very important, but Elizabeth knew that it could and should have been. Every day in her lesson plan book she had to account for the exact time that she spent teaching all of the academic subject areas; however, the largest part of the school time had to be spent on reading skills. Principal Strictman regularly checked all lesson plan books for accuracy of time and measurable behavioral objectives for learning. Elizabeth's classroom was often observed to ensure adherence to the schedule and on task work.

Nevertheless, Elizabeth and the children exuberantly began to learn about the physical processes involved in erosion. Possibilities for preventing further damage and for correcting the ruts were shared among the students and Elizabeth as they gathered ideas and information from printed materials. Most solutions to the erosion problem involved large sums of money for rocks, paving, landscape timbers, and labor. Skeptically she wondered how seven year olds could do anything about this huge environmental "problem". Finally a solution was planned.

Elizabeth, being a non-tenured new teacher, tentatively approached Mrs. Strictman with her class plan for remedying the erosion problem. Principal Strictman was most certainly focused on the state mandated reading initiative, upcoming standardized testing, and the goals of reading achievement set forth for her school. She readily enforced teachers' meeting every objective in the state courses of study, especially the ones related to reading. She interrogated Elizabeth regarding her rationale for spending valuable time on an environmental "problem".

Feeling overwhelmed, under-supported, and less than enthusiastic, Elizabeth returned to her classroom and questioned her decisions as a teacher. "The objectives that we are supposed to meet just seem so...big. They say that they are specific, but I find them to be very broad," she thought. Many of the teachers at her school were not interested in science; "they just went by the book." Being a new teacher, Elizabeth knew that many of her peers, parents, and the principal were watching her. She felt it was going to be very difficult to "break the barrier" and teach science differently when her fellow teachers appeared to have lost their wonder about the world around them and their interest in teaching environmental education, if they had even had it at all. After all, there was not even a course of study for environmental education and it certainly was not mandated or tested. Feeling her own mountain of enthusiasm slowly wearing away, she considered postponing or eliminating the project altogether.

Many days passed and the children continued to ask about the erosion project, as it had become to be known. Having decided to engage the children in map-making related to the project, she decided to take them outside for the next few days during her little time for science and social studies. Her friend, Mrs. Little, relayed a warning to her about going outside: "Last year, one of my friends who isn't here anymore wanted to teach about signs of spring and how leaves begin to form. She went outside and had her children observe the changes that spring brings. Unfortunately, some of the kids got dirty and Mrs. Strictman told all of us that no one else could go outside!"

Now the little hill of enthusiasm that Elizabeth had began to crumble and erode further. When she finally mustered the courage and asked about going outside, Principal Strictman promptly and emphatically told her to "complete the required permission form with the specific time, date, and purpose" and to "make sure to justify the activity by stating the state course of study objectives that would be met." Was this project worth the time, effort, and perceived professional and personal risk associated with it? Days later, permission for going outside was finally granted, yet Elizabeth wondered and worried at what cost.

Specific to the education of elementary teachers, Nichols and Tippins (2000) asserted that elementary teachers' personal and professional identities emerge through biomythical constraints. Elementary teachers, who are predominantly female, often embody feminist ways of knowing (Grumet, 1988; Lather, 1991). As learners, who are products of modernist schooling and science education, they are entangled in a myriad of social and political structures, which are perpetuated through science teacher education. Disengaged from their ways of knowing, they assume their places in patriarchal workspaces of elementary schools (Barton, 1998; Kincheloe, 1993; Nichols & Tippins, 2000).

Present-day classrooms have tended to echo a patriarchal perspective that extends from adult male conceptions of life. At the turn of the twentieth century in the United States, men walked away from agrarian work to take up vocations on factory floors. Simultaneously, bureaucratic managerial relationships within industries were superimposed upon schools, wherein teachers became assembly line workers, manufacturing future workers for productive and economic gain. As Barrie Thorne argues "both feminist and traditional knowledge remain deeply and unreflectively centered around the experiences of adults. Our understanding of children tends to be filtered through adult perspectives and interests...their full lives, experiences, and agency obscured by adult standpoints" (Thorne cited in Kurth-Schai, 1997, p. 194).

The bureaucratic management organization within industries assumed a static, one directional flow of power from the leader to the led; in schools, this relationship translated into a hierarchy of power from the school administrator to the lower ranks of teachers and students (Foster, 1989). Corporate curriculum designers have done their homework. Like cultural and feminist pedagogues, they share our interests to capture children's imaginings, play spaces, and dreams. Feminists would want the capture to result in freedom for children through creating "a world both responsive to children's needs and receptive to their contributions" (Kurth-Schai, 1997, p. 208) the result of which would be the creation of their own identities. Antithetically, corporatists, capture these as raw materials, viewed as "natural" resources to be made marketable and ready to use. Steinberg and Kincheloe (1997) warned: "In the interest not only of our children, but of the larger society we must exercise our personal and collective power to transform the variety of ways corporate power—gained via access to media [e.g. school science curricula]—oppresses and dominates us" (p. 5).

Historically, curricula designed by males has been male centered; "it banished the body and the intimacy of real family" (Grumet, 1988 as cited in Pinar, Reynolds, Slattery, & Taubman, 2000, p. 361). We recognize elementary educationis a predominantly female profession in that it is dominated by a patriarchal structure in which teachers are forced to subject learners to the same forms of oppression that they experience (Grumet, 1988). Madeleine Grumet, alternatively underscores the student-centered nature of feminist pedagogies as "grounded in an inherently feminine [way of knowing], and emphasize the educational worthwhileness of using students' personal experiences as a basis for learning" (as cited in Middleton, 1993, p. 114). We conceptualize teaching as a socio-cultural endeavor moving beyond mere corporeal constraints of thinking and learning. If elementary teachers were to be in school spaces envisioned as places of life learning, they may embark upon journeys with children creating new pathways of knowing in science education.

ROCKY SCIENCE BEGINNINGS

Growing up in family of six girls, our mother tried to encourage each of us to take up a hobby. With some prompting by my father, I decided to collect rocks. Living in Florida meant that most of my rock finds looked quite similar—white, limestone "gems" great for making hopscotch squares on the driveway. I was given a rocks and gems field guide and studied it often. I longingly looked at the pictures of opals, black onyx, and tiger eye topaz hoping I might happen to find one of these lovely objects. I picked up rocks of all kinds, carefully comparing my finds to the pictures and notes. Again, most seemed to be white limestone, but I was hopeful. Frustrated at the lack of variety, I resorted to shop for rocks at local stores. With my rock book in hand, I would compare labeled and unlabelled rocks to those in the guide. I found that if the rocks weren't labeled, I had little certainty about properly identifying what kind of rock I had in hand. Gradually, I became disenchanted as I could rarely identify rocks properly, and was depleting my monthly allowance with my purchases of "real" rocks. At the age of 8, I quit being a rock collector.

When I was 30, I had the opportunity to visit Australia. With two friends, I picked up many interesting rock specimens while on the beach in Darwin one early evening. We were three women from the United States connected to our home through the magnificent ocean sprawled before us. As we walked along, Jeannie Baker's (1987) book—*Where the Forest Meets the Sea* played over like a movie in my mind. I could see so clearly in my mind the strangler vines, the ghosts of the Aboriginal children, and crabs scuttling across the sand. I simply couldn't resist touching the beautifully layered old rocks, which were probably caressed by someone long ago. They would look interesting alongside the yellow pillar-shaped rocks I had gathered from Monkey Mia. As a science education doctoral candidate at the university, I had ready access to talk with scientists. Upon my return home, I excitedly presented my "Aussie rocks" to a geologist, "Bill", to get help accurately identifying my new finds. Bill made some general guesses about some being sedimentary and metamorphic rocks and said he really couldn't tell me anything more specific without more contextual information. His struggle only affirmed my own impression that rock collecting wasn't very fun. I again lost interest.

At the age of 32, a friend introduced me to Byrd Baylor's (1974) book for children—Everybody Needs a Rock. I listened to this lovely story about a child giving 10 ways to find a rock. It should feel good in your hand. It might look best under bathtub water. Like me in my youth, this child was so excited about looking for rocks if only to see and possess their beauty. I'd been looking through the categorical lenses of a scientist's field guide and missed out on knowing the world of rocks under my very feet! I continued to think about how a geologist might identify rocks found, but I didn't hesitate to call them by my own given names; sometimes describing their appearance, or perhaps named according to a related event—the "fun at Michigan lake" rock. I look at rocks everywhere. Often, instead of collecting them, I simply note where it rests in connection with everything around it. Leaving it where others might enjoy it too—an irresistible sunning spot for a lizard perhaps.

A few years later, now a science teacher educator, I met with a class of third graders to introduce them to earth science. I read *Everybody Needs a Rock* (Baylor, 1974) to the children, then invited them to find a rock in the schoolyard that they would like to get to know. The students looked with eyes anew at the playground that now seemed a different landscape offering irresistible treasures. We regrouped in the classroom and designed centers that would help us learn more about the selected rocks. There was a weighing station, a bathtub table—to not only see if their rock might float/sink, but also to check out rock colors underwater, sorting center, a the "good hopscotch" rock station where they would test to see if rocks could draw well on sidewalks and to test out their toss/roll properties. After a couple days of exploration, the children wrote storybooks and shared about their special finds. There were many stories emerging, for children continued to bring in more rocks — there was the one of a very cool rock found beside the back steps of a friend's house, and another story of rock hunting which featured a rare and treasured walk with dad around the neighborhood. At one point, a moratorium was declared on bringing any new rocks to the classroom as the collection was beginning to overflow and create cleaning challenges for the custodian! Eventually, we returned all rocks to their outdoor spaces but we continued to share rock stories for sometime thereafter.

Patti Lather (1991) has argued: "To put into categories is an act of power" (p. 125). In the narrative above, the naming of rock types became the means for alienating the child whose own language and experience of the earth was deferred to the presumed "proper" language of geological science. As teachers and learners, many buy into the myth that only "real" scientists created the "proper" language of science and have retained the requisite authority and skills to name things. As science educators, we carefully consider the role that language plays in our conceptions of being scientists. Clearly, we see that there is a need and place for scientific language; however, we strive to expand the spaces where the personal language of people being scientists is valued. In our meaning of being scientists we are not superimposing the image of the stereotypical image of a formal career scientist, rather philosophically we recognize that humans of all ages are enacting and being scientists continually.

The ways young learners are introduced to science as a discourse practice is important to consider the ways language reflects our conception of ourselves and our world. Sanchez (as cited in Adams, 1993) claims:

Most EuroAmerican or EuroWestern peoples tend to separate themselves from "nature" and to rank humans above animals, plants, and minerals in hierarchal fashion, and so it is not easy for them to perceive or accept a personal relationship with what they describe as the "natural world" (p. 211).

Language not only becomes a means of separation from the "nature" that we are—which as in this case, the discipline of earth science creating the biomythical separation of the abiotic from biotic. Ultimately, the conceptual reification of an object through language (e.g. rock) enables the physical separation and becomes a means for human domination of nature.

This story begs the question as to why the little rock collector above was so willing or unconscious of deferring her knowledge to that of the imagined geologist. Acts of collecting and naming serve as the physical and conceptual means for human domination over objects—"women, other human Others, and non-human nature" (Warren, 2000, p. 43). Additionally, through the process of our own collaborative composition, we realized that during our graduate studies an encounter with Belenky, Clinchy, Goldberger, and Tarule's (1986) notion of a received knower provided the language for recognizing our learned subordination as young learners of science. Presently, ecofeminism provides alternative ways for critiquing our own practices as science teacher educators as we consciously recognize and embrace our interconnectedness with all living and non-living things.

Thinking about the idea of collections, makes one ponder why humans appear to have a need to collect "natural things" as if they are separate from, above, or owners of nature. Many elementary science teachers promote collecting leaves, insects, and rocks. As science teacher educators, we engage our prospective teachers in experiences where they may recognize and embrace the interconnectedness among all living and non-living things. For example, Shel Silverstein's (1964) story of *The Giving Tree* is often read with a sense of romance in that the tree would willingly give its life limb by limb as the human required and requested. From an ecofeminist perspective, however, this story is read with disdain as there is lack of the recognition and respect for the very being of the tree. In science methods classes, we teach prospective teachers that in Alabama, because forestry is one of the top industries, hardwoods and old growth forests are clear cut and replaced by pine plantations; this is the cost of separation from nature and the lack of understanding notions of being.

Understanding of lived experiences, including but not limited to the physical, and the construction of meaning, occurs through embodied actionssuch as walking on the beach, touching other life forms, imagining the accompaniment of an Aboriginal child, and feeling a sense of wonder. Ideas of being and ecofeminism recognize and embrace the interconnections among all living beings and non-living entities. Warren (1993) acknowledged that "relationships are not something extrinsic to who we are...they play an essential role in shaping what it is to be human" (as cited in Kronlid, 2003, p. 127). We recognize that science is the study of the physical world, however, there is increasing recognition that science does not reside in a body of knowledge, it is not a mere construction of knowledge bound within the corporeal provinces of humans. Rather, we envision science as a matter of being.

EMBODIMENT—*BEING* SCIENCE

As seen in the previous stories, what we refer to as being science may be interpreted as a corporeal sensory experience, as the females in the stories experience the surrounding "natural" world through their physical senses. We recognize that others such as Allan Feldman (2002), study teaching as a way of being, yet for usthis concept retains a corporeal orientation. However, we offer an intercorporeal idea of embodiment—a central concept is the idea of being, meaning more than just corporeal experiences or reconnections between a brain and body and a separate natural world. In our view being includes corporeality, yet it is also continuously on-going action in a spatio-temporal realm of existence involving consciousness, perception, feelings (both physical and emotive), and the body

(Spencer, 2005). We also believe that individual beings do not exist alone, isolated, and untouched by anything or anyone. Notions of being suggest interconnections among all living and non-living things—the idea of "individual" as separate from others or from socio-cultural context does not exist. For us, meaning is created through what Merleau-Ponty referred to as "embodied action" (Strathern, 1996, p. 187). As such, the phenomenon of being and understanding science continues backward through memories, continues presently and mindfully in lived experiences both with others and alone, and in the future through imaginings and dreams.

PATHS OF CONTEMPLATION

The meaning we make of these experiences is important to our work as science teacher educators and researchers as we further expand possible pathways for our prospective teachers. In our courses we do not simply focus on corporeal teaching of science, rather we embrace and teach through intercorporeal experiences. We are constantly and consciously aware of environment and our places of being in and to the world. Through the collaborative efforts of this writing endeavor, we have experienced once again being science both corporeally and intercorporeally as we shared remembrances, thoughts, and emotions.

One of the myths we avoided was writing our lives framed as "biographies" as if one were capable of being extracted and represented as a singular being. As ecofeminists, we firmly situate ourselves and our work among the intricate interconnections of all living beings and non-living entities. The science within our view expands in many possible directions. For some, they interact with science as a cognitive adventure. For others, while the science may remain cognitively placed, they engage in the struggle to participate despite their apparent gender and race. For us, the science we envision is not a cognitive endeavor alone. Science, when seen an expression of being in and to the physical world and making sense of it, opens up possibilities for all to engage in creating and being science. As elementary science teacher educators, those traditionally viewed as deficient knowers of science are seen as they are—science creators.

REFERENCES

Adams, C. J. (1993). *Ecofeminism and the sacred*. New York: The Continuum.
Baker, J. (1987). *Where the forest meets the sea*. New York: Scholastic.
Barton, A. C. (1998). *Feminist science education*. New York: Teachers College Press.
Baylor, B. (1974). *Everybody needs a rock*. New York: Aladdin.
Belenky, M. F., Clinchy, B. M., Goldberger, N. R., & Tarule, J. M. (1986). *Women's ways of knowing: The development of self, voice, and mind*. New York: Basic Books.
Britzman, D. P. (1991). *Practice makes practice: A critical study of learning to teach*. New York: New York State University Press.
Clandinin, D. J., & Connelly, F. M. (2000). *Narrative inquiry: Experience and story in qualitative research*. San Francisco: Jossey-Bass.
Foster, W. (1989). Toward a critical practice of leadership. In J. Smyth (Ed.), *Critical perspectives on educational leadership* (pp. 39–62). New York: Falmer Press.

Grumet, M. R. (1988). *Bitter milk: Women and teaching*. Amherst, MA: The University of Massachusetts Press.

Harding, S. G. (1986). *The science question in feminism*. Ithaca, NY: Cornell University Press.

Kaplan, C. (1998). Resisting autobiography: Out-law genres and transnational feminist subjects. In S. Smith & J. Watson (Eds.), *Women, autobiography, theory: A reader* (pp. 208–216). Madison, WI: The University of Wisconsin Press.

Kincheloe, J. L. (1993). *Toward a critical politics of teacher thinking: Mapping the postmodern*. Westport, CN: Bergin & Garvey.

Kronlid, D. (2003). *Ecofeminism and environmental ethics: An analysis of ecofeminist ethical theory*. Doctoral dissertation, Uppsala University, Sweden. Dissertation Abstracts International, 64, 03.

Kurth-Schai, R. (1997). Ecofeminism and children. In K. J. Warren (Ed.), *Ecofeminism: Women, culture, nature* (pp. 193–212). Bloomington, IN: Indiana University Press.

Lather, P. A. (1991). *Getting smart: Feminist research and pedagogy with/in the postmodern*. New York: Routledge.

Merchant, C. (1980). *The death of nature: Women, ecology, and the scientific revolution*. San Francisco: Harper and Row.

Merleau-Ponty, M. (1962). *Phenomenology of perception* (C. Smith, Trans.). New York: Humanities Press.

Middleton, S. (1993). *Educating feminists: Life histories and pedagogy*. New York: Teachers College Press.

Milne, C. (1998). Philosophically correct science stories? Examining the implications of heroic science stories for school science. *Journal of Research in Science Teaching, 35*, 175–187.

Nichols, S., & Tippins, D. (2000). Prospective elementary science teachers and biomythographies: An exploratory approach to autobiographical research. *Research in Science Education, 30*(1), 141–153.

Nichols, S., & Tippins, D. J. (2006). Prospective elementary science teachers and biomythographies: An exploratory approach to autobiographical research. In W. M. Roth (Ed.), *Autobiography: Praxis of research method* (pp. 261–276). Rotterdam, The Netherlands: Sense Publishers.

Pinar, W. F., Reynolds, W. M., Slattery, P., & Taubman, P. M. (2000). *Understanding curriculum: An introduction to the study of historical and contemporary curriculum discourses*. New York: Peter Lang Publishing, Inc.

Roychoudhury, A., Tippins, D. J., & Nichols, S. E. (1995). Gender-inclusive science teaching: A feminist-constructivist approach. *Journal of Research in Science Teaching, 32*(9), 897–924.

Silverstein, S. (1964). *The giving tree*. New York: Harper Collins.

Spencer, M. E. (2005). *Exploring elementary science teaching and learning through an eco-feminist perspective: Narratives of embodiment of science*. Unpublished doctoral dissertation, The University of Alabama, Tuscaloosa, AL.

Statham, A. (2001). Environmental awareness and feminist progress. *National Women's Suffrage Association Journal, 12*(2), 89–104.

Steinberg, S. R., & Kincheloe, J. L. (1997). Introduction: No more secrets—kinderculture, information saturation, and the postmodern childhood. In S. R. Steinberg & J. L. Kincheloe (Eds.), *Kinderculture: The corporate construction of childhood* (pp. 1–30). Boulder, CO: Westview Press.

Strathern, A. J. (1996). *Body thoughts*. Ann Arbor, MI: The University of Michigan Press.

Warren, K. J. (1990). The power and promise of ecological feminism. *Environmental Ethics, 12*(2), 132–146.

Warren, K. J. (1993). A feminist philosophical perspective. In C. J. Adams (Ed.), *Ecofeminism and the sacred* (pp. 119–132). New York: The Continuum.

Warren, K. J. (Ed.). (1997). *Ecofeminism: Women, culture, nature*. Bloomington, IN: Indiana University Press.

Warren, K. J. (2000). Ecofeminist philosophy: A western perspective on what it is and why it matters. Lanham, MD: Rowman & Littlefield.

Zell, S. K. (1998). Ecofeminism and the science classroom: A practical approach. *Science and Education, 7*, 143–158.

AFFILIATIONS

M.E. Spencer
College of Education,
University of Montevallo

Sherry Nichols
College of Education,
University of Alabama

JANET BOND-ROBINSON

15. THE SITUATED POWER OF MENTAL MODELS

The difficulty of being a woman in science is not a lonely situation. It has many
analogs throughout the history of relationships and hierarchy. Diversity is seldom a
favored commodity. At any time and place only some kinds of people and
characteristics are favored. Many people are the favored few; a paradox, but there
are always plenty of favored people who have the characteristics that are valued.
I remember being 17 and somehow determining that I should never compete in the
areas that everybody else wanted. Some unknown occasion drove home very
clearly that I would have to be unique to be really successful. Uniqueness has the
potential of becoming favored. But how does anyone hold on to her own set of
uniqueness's in the face of the overwhelming push to be normal? The struggle to
retain and develop uniqueness necessitates resistance to a culture in which women
are the "other." It takes a lot of energy to resist. Where does that internal power
come from to actively resist?

DIVERSIFYING NORMALITY

We are all creatures of our family life, an effective form of situated learning. I have
my dad's sense of integrity and justice in business situations. He was for the
common man rising. I'm advocating for the common woman arising: basic
feminine traits, not just those of exceptional women who may have had to change
themselves to fit. I am not expounding for the exceptional woman or the women
who got ahead early. I am speaking of the common woman becoming as frequent
in chemistry as the common man. By the common person I am not excluding
intellect, however, I mean common man in the sense that Aaron Copeland's
"Fanfare to the common man" written in 1943, which expressed common in the
sense of salt of the earth, full of spirit and competence (and able to pay taxes)
("Fanfare for the common man", 2008).

    I have found that I have many opportunities to help "the common human" now
that I am often in leadership positions on grants, in programs, and as a professor.
The norms and standards of acceptance are so ingrained in the way they constrain
our thinking that I am probably less equitable than I think I am. Diversification of
the normal implies that the norms and standards of acceptance be more variable. In
the meantime I have to be able to take a chance on all kinds of people, which is a
risk. It seems less risky when I pick people like me. Since I hate to be judged
without actually having a chance to show what I can do, however, I take people at
face value and let them show what they can do. I am comparatively lavish in

K. Scantlebury, J. Butler Kahle and S. N. Martin (eds.) Re-visioning Science Education from Feminist
Perspectives: Challenges, Choices and Careers, 165–175.
© *2010 Sense Publishers. All rights reserved.*

support, positive, open, and verbally not judgmental, perhaps to a fault. The beauty in giving people latitude is that, over time, I can tell who each is. Some rise to the occasion; in fact, some of my most unusual workers clearly rose with responsibility and resources. Others go beyond, producing things I never would have thought of doing. This is the group that micromanaging would have frustrated. Lastly, a few people "hang themselves" because they don't believe I'm paying attention. They underestimate me. No snap judgment was necessary when I decided there was a long-enough track record to provide plenty of evidence. I have been learning to take less time in reaching a decision, but it still seems important to give every person a chance to do what he or she can do. The outcome afterward is clear when there are products to be evaluated.

CULTURAL THINKING CONSTRAINS WHAT IS NORMAL

My science discipline is chemistry. Chemistry is a representation of male culture, White Anglo Saxon, Northern European male. Its history documents Lavoisier, Mendeleev, and even Madame Curie, but its culture is predominantly White, male, and Anglo Saxon. The disciplinary personality is serious, reserved, precise, and definite. The main value that infects everything else is the worshipping of the work ethic. The spirit is one of competition, one directly related to capitalist society, which may be one reason why science doesn't flourish under communism (Polanyi, 1936). American chemistry, after World War II, deepened the participation of the White male through the GI Bill, moving away from much of the elite nature of European science. The prestige was no longer tied to the upper class; the common man had access to higher education. It was no longer class but intelligence and general capability, defined as men who do well in the courses that mattered. Chemical researchers arise in the field after long years of intense work, during which time they have experienced continuous scrutiny of the work and judgment of their adequacy by research directors, advisors, and reviewers in the field. These advisors determine whether the newest scientists are satisfactory.

It is the work ethic that makes a chemical research career more difficult for women. Not because women don't have as strong a work ethic as men but because of the timing of the most intense work. Once arriving at their first university position after graduate school and 2-3 years as a post doctoral researcher, they exist at the juncture of their professionally demanding years of proving themselves and the waning child-bearing years. It is no easier to mix motherhood and academe now than it was in 1975; I assumed there was now a mechanism for maternity leave as part of university policy in 2005, and was stunned when a younger colleague found herself in a bind. I didn't even pretend to meet these career hurdles. I quit working in clinical chemistry two weeks before my first son was born. My husband was in graduate school, so those were lean years. Somehow I knew that I could only do one really important thing at a time and still be content. My second son was born in 1979 during my husband's post doc position. I took five years to be home with my children; those were the years we lived in four different states: Utah, Oregon, Wyoming, and finally Iowa where my husband began his career at a liberal arts college very similar to the one from which we had graduated in Texas. Entirely new sides of me emerged in this freedom that I took to stay home with my children. I was able to take the time necessary to gauge my reactions to all kinds of feelings and events. I had time to ponder my future in ways that my husband couldn't do as respectably. The affective side of me developed along with cognition and motivation and allowed me to run confidently with my intuition. I developed confidence that was hard to shake. If it is true that we develop our sense of adult identity in the late 20's, then I did the one thing that really mattered to me personally.

When my older son entered kindergarten nothing mattered as much as the education my children would be immersed in. I decided after an unsuccessful run for the School Board that my interests showed I should become a teacher and participate in the educational system with my children. I began as a chemistry TA part time at the liberal arts college over a number of semesters, which seemed to reinforce the idea of teaching. The only kind of teacher I could rapidly become was a science teacher, so I pursued the Iowa requirements and student taught in high school chemistry and physics. Chemical education is a re-representation, a reflection, of chemistry as a discipline. The personality of the undergraduate chemistry course tends to be serious, reserved, precise, and definite. It is very often authoritative and judging. The main course value is that of the work ethic, augmented by intelligence. If students don't succeed it is because their work ethic is poor, they do not have the intellectual capability, or both. The spirit is one of competition and high workload, which is believed to bring out the best in students. These conditions support rigor in the discipline. It appears to be crucial to determine which students are best. Chemistry as a discipline continually expands; since looking for the best students is a primary goal; chemists are not generally interested in the expansion of the student population in undergraduate chemistry.

Situated learning has its dark side. It didn't seem as odd then as it does now when women aren't represented in a field. Theories of situated experience in a cultural group (Lave, 1988) focus on agency and intentions of people who must coordinate with others and with activities. These cultural activities support the status quo in traditional society. Meaningful actions and relationships build identity for the group and its members (Wenger, 1998), but it may not be the identity an individual is craving. Meaning is engendered in the interactions (Mead, 1934); but when those interactions leave an individual with a bad taste in her mouth, that is a part of the learning about whether one does or does not fit in. Fortunately and unfortunately, this daily back-and-forth of talk and relationships as we carry out valued daily tasks influences who we are and what we learn (Clancey, 1997).

I feel my real story is about the resistance and energy needed to sustain my identity as an idealist and with it a sense of personal power. Early on I noticed seeming contradictions when something happened that wasn't supposed to occur. My parents were absolutely the least bigoted individuals of their age I have ever met— even to this day. Their beliefs and assumptions were deeply embedded in the culture, but they insisted that all people should be treated the same. That argument, if I could get to it, was always the one on which my dad had to concede. But they were still products of their culture, living inside a set of cultural attitudes that weren't just, fair, and surely not diverse about the role of women. Another example of entrenchment in a culture comes from American history played out in my own high school. It wasn't odd to me that nearly all the Black students went to a high school on the other side of town. Since it was not talked about, my assumption was that the school was built where the students lived. I didn't know that the schools weren't the same. I don't recall ever wondering about it. During my senior year six black students entered my class of 600 students. We had just desegregated but most of us had never known we were segregated; despite hearing about segregation constantly on the news! I have never been able to forgive myself for being so undiscerning. It goes to show the power of cultural assumptions that squelches questioning.

As an adult I have more experience dealing with what is not said, i.e., tacit rules of action and relationship. Where does that capacity for resistance come from on a day-to-day basis? What is the source providing the power and wisdom to actively resist yet show diplomacy rather than emotional reactivity? What sustains people who are struggling for change when to the majority of people the need for change is not obvious? Most of the time struggles for change seem to occur at the level of individual people. I have discovered that my personal mental models have the capacity to nurture me so that an emergent power-from-within motivates me. A vision empowers me to strive for challenges and choices that go beyond my present capacity.

MENTAL MODELS DRIVE ME.

My mental models are grounded in my own experiences and in research literature in science education and cognitive science. My interest in implementation of reformed practices led me to graduate school with Bob Yager, a spirited and committed constructivist. I had previously left high school teaching disillusioned with the quality of administration and lack of depth in the thinking of school board members. I spent two years as president of the District's teachers. I left teaching first to do a fellowship at the Wright Center for Innovation in Science Education in Boston. I had begun *Pre-Columbian Chemistry: A history of the chemical technology of the Aztecs, Incas, and Mayas* (Robinson, 1995). I thought then that the production of innovative curricula and implementation of reformed practices was the areas in which I should specialize in a Ph.D. program. My dissertation, however, ended up in chemical education using evaluation methodology. I wanted to see if I could determine why the dissatisfaction of students in general chemistry was so high and had been for nearly a decade according to the Advising Office. Because of many academic difficulties in the course for science majors, many freshmen were channeled into preparatory chemistry in the first semester; then they enrolled in general chemistry for science majors. My discovery was that the best way to create havoc among students was to keep firmly constant the number of As, Bs, Cs, Ds, and Fs, preserving the average grade point at 2.0-2.1. Due to the Advising office the population of students had changed over time in terms of preparation, but the rigid grading practices didn't allow the preparation to show. Secondly, this population of chemistry students had higher ACT scores than the average college course but a mean grade point of 2.1 versus 2.7 in the college. It makes sense thinking of the discipline's culture: One way of achieving the rigors of intellectual capability and the work ethic desired by the chemistry discipline is by restricting grade inflation.

Over the years in graduate school, I was unclear about what kind of job I wanted. Finishing in May I looked for a post doc position that would help me find direction. The one I originally wanted was working with a program in the Chicago Public Schools. The one that I got was in chemical education, working on inquiry labs. Since I had already written The Chemical Analysis of Water Pollution through an American Chemical Society (ACS) minigrant, this kind of post doc experience seemed useful, a continuation of curricula work, and grounded in effective learning environments. I did not realize it would alter my life permanently; that my identity would shift to becoming specifically a chemical educator. The following January I was offered a faculty position in the same department and my new career began in August.

Situated in a chemistry department I had to figure out what my place would be as a chemical educator. What could an idealistic science educator uniquely do with this new, unsought situation? It began with a first attempt at a new course on Teacher Assistant (TA) Training. The importance of TA Training readily evoked a vision of change. I had been a TA in chemistry labs for five semesters and had experimented with TA training during my dissertation. I decided to use my experience and further development in constructivism as the basis for designing a program for TAs as well as a way for them to teach chemistry students. I envisioned TA training as the best way to change the kinds of teaching that occurred in college chemistry. Since few TAs had experience teaching high school, few had educational courses in their background. This TA experience could be a situated learning experience as they taught. The vision was one of constructivist learning environment. For five years we built a course that studied GTA development in teaching in a pattern we attribute to 'design research' (Brown, 1992; Cobb, Confrey, diSessa, Lehrer, & Schauble, 2003), which investigates how people function in a real learning environment. The purpose of a set of design experiments is to achieve an effective course (or other product). Those findings lead to successive course revisions. We built two instruments to drive and assess constructivist laboratory teaching by GTAs. Due to the advent of remotely acquired audio-video observations using the local area network (LAN), research investigations of laboratories became easier, produced higher quality data, and were less distracting to lab workers. The reliabilities of the instructors' and UGs' instrument reached a high Cronbach alpha of .86 and .95, respectively, in the 4th course iteration. The understanding gained in the experience of teaching, the structure of the teaching context, and the coaching that occurs by others created a cognitive apprenticeship in a model we call the "Laboratory Teaching Apprenticeship" (Bond-Robinson & Rodriques, 2006). This work developed a strong conception for pedagogical content knowledge (PChK), in the chemistry laboratory (Bond-Robinson, 2005). I believe this model could be a vision of how to prepare teachers at all levels for inquiry teaching. I was very pleased with this work, but its publication generated no comment by the chemical community!

A second vision became not only possible but very opportune in a chemistry department—although I thought it was the riskier research venture, which turned out to be true. I had philosophy of science with George Cossman during graduate school at Iowa City. I wondered what kind of a learning environment could explain the growth of a scientist from novice to "certified" as a scientist with a Ph.D. degree. Eventually, I came to see this as further examination of situated learning in a research community. National Science Foundation (NSF) sustained my visions in my second try for an Early Career Grant. Once I explained it well, I think it was easy for reviewers to see the benefits inherent in studying how scientists become scientists and how TAs can become more effective with undergraduate chemistry students. Further, there had never been any explicit research on the development of graduate students in their teaching or research roles.

Next to no detailed studies had been done that examined the issue of learning and reasoning in scientific work in the laboratory (Chinn & Malhotra, 2002). My vision, as a science educator, was to: provide detailed studies of scientists' actual reasoning processes in 'doing inquiry'. Situated cognition provided the framework for us to investigate. According to Greeno (1998) the way practice in using situated cognition was to find out how the learning and reasoning were coordinated in the activity of the community. Thus, an ethnographic study looking for the manner of situated learning seemed the ideal route. We found support for these approaches in both the sociology of science and the newer field of psychology of science. Problem solving and discovery processes have been the focus of the psychology of science. (Klahr & Simon, 1999) identified four approaches to scientific studies of science emerging in recent decades: (a) Historical accounts of scientific advances, (b) psychological experiments of non-scientists on structured and ill-structured problems, (c) observations of researchers' daily work in science, and (d) computational modeling of scientific discovery processes. Our study fits as (c) observations of daily work in organic synthesis laboratories as others have done in biomechanical engineering. (Dunbar, 1995) looked at analogical reasoning in three different molecular biology laboratories. Nersessian, Newstetter, Kurz-Milcke, and Davis (2002), taking a situated cognition approach, looked for evolution of the distribution of reasoning in biomechanical engineering.

The overall model for the study was Latour and Woolgar's entitled Laboratory Life (1979). Although their perspective and goals for learning were different, many features were very similar in both our studies. See Table 1. Many people are familiar with Latour and Woolgar's study of the Salk Institute in the late 70's as part of the new sociology of science. They took an ethnographic approach of an outsider coming into a new culture as is common in anthropology research Table 1 shows the important relationships between the research that we do and the research that Latour and Woolgar did. One of the largest differences is that as ethnographers we were not outsiders but observers with "interactional expertise." This is the designation that Harry Collins (Collins & Evans, 2002) gives to those who can understand the research as it is expressed but do not do this kind of research.

Table 1. Laboratory Studies

Method	Similar Yes/No	Latour & Woolgar	Bond-Robinson & Stucky
Type of Ethnography	Yes	Study of a laboratory culture in science	
Length of Study	Yes	Several Years of Participation	
Dates of Study	No	1975	2000
Type of Observation	No	Stranger	Interactional Expertise
Data Collection	Yes	Observations of daily work, field notes, conversations, interviews with researchers	
Technology	No	Audio-tape recordings	Video-audio recordings
Type of Data	Yes	Importance of conversations among researchers	
Theoretical Approach		Anthropological Science Study	Situated Cognition
Focus of Study	No	Making sense of the laboratory	Coordination of reasoning and learning
Scientific Thinking	Yes	Important to show when scientific thinking connects with everyday thinking	
Reality	Yes	Material world of the laboratory	
Kind of laboratory	No	Molecular Biology	Organic Chemistry
Type of Institution	No	Research Institute	University Research
Number and Type of Researchers	Yes	13 Ph.D.s and technicians	15 Ph.D.s and Graduate students
Group Approach	No	Assembly line approach	Individual projects

We found that science had a "normal" character similar to Kuhn's views (1970) and those of Polanyi (1962) about tacit learning through intense work on problems (Bond-Robinson, Stucky, & Robinson, 2008; Bond-Robinson & Stucky, 2005a, 2005b; Bond-Robinson & Preece, 2002). The graduate research experience is one where researchers and apprentices interactto practice organic synthesis in a specialized laboratory. They are not just immersed in the work; they are surrounded with accoutrements of organic synthesis whose use they must master in order to produce valued products. The standardized practices place constraints on reasoning and subsequent action. Infrastructure and constraints influence judgment and subsequent decisions. Community constraints guide and coordinate reasoning. There are norms and standards for behavior, practices, and interpretation of data. The intention to meet the goals in a culture doing organic synthesis leads to at least five necessary constraints on all graduate researchers' reasoning. (a) Mechanical skill and mechanical reasoning to produce and troubleshoot reaction systems; (b) Macro-level work based on nano-level understanding; (c) Grasping and aligning with tacit and explicit community norms and rules for work and its products. (d) Using and reasoning in the language and symbolic chemical representations of organic reactions; and (e) Learning to accurately interpret feedback from mechanical systems, data, and instrument reports/spectra in the same manner as other community members.

We found that we could account for much learning through enculturation into ways of thinking, practices of specialized work, norms and standards for work production, and language development in the scientific community. Our efforts to publish an ethnographic study have been daunting because we are still learning how to break our findings down into relevant, theoretical, and practical chunks.

THWARTING –ISMS

My progress as a chemical educator has been continually hampered by something I assume is ageism: "Now that you're here we have to call the young faculty junior faculty." Until that was said, I thought I fit in because my age group was very common in the faculty. I felt comfortable socially. As time went on, however, it seemed as if my similarly aged peers were not comfortable with me acting as if I was their peer. The young faculty, of course, didn't consider me a peer; no invitations to their lunches. The term, peerless, usually has a positive connotation in the direction of making unique contributions. My uniqueness in this situation corresponded to being different and perhaps possessing no significant expertise. This is where "educatorism" seemed to hit me hard. They simply didn't know what my expertise was if it wasn't specifically in a research area of chemistry. Even being awarded a NSF-Career grant, which surpassed all my own expectations, couldn't get me past that chemistry research hurdle. Getting the award was a wonderfully insightful event; nothing I could have ever done would allow me to achieve genuine favor.

Perhaps worst of all, I exercised my unknown expertise in the 500-seat and 1000-seat lecture halls. I was very comfortable teaching, attempting to incorporate my conceptualization of effective teaching to a lecture hall of 250 or 300. The first hurdle was managing the educational technology in a classroom for 500. It took a semester to feel comfortable with garage-door sized screens above my head on which I could orchestrate PowerPoint or use an ELMO document camera projector to illustrate problem solving. I chose to incorporate online homework in order to provide the missing feedback in traditional courses. My conceptual style of teaching was difficult for many students to fathom. They didn't seem to think that I was explaining (Bond-Robinson, 2004). Generally, my teaching evaluations were lower than the department average. Teaching evaluations were considered the word of God in evaluating my scholarship. My colleagues were frustrated because they couldn't figure out how to change the student evaluations. I suggested support of me as a colleague to students, to TAs, and to the dean. The chair was determined I should teach like everyone else. I was about to become convinced as well. Then I realized I didn't know how to teach in the standard, normal way that chemistry faculty did. "Peers" came in. It was unclear to others why many students didn't like my teaching. I was "enthusiastic" and "articulate;" I invited participation as I walked away from the podium.

My department chair commented that my teaching generated more opinion than anyone else's did. Semesters came and went. My evaluations plateaued off at a level below that of the faculty average.

My teaching and learning strategies are still designed to foster deeper understanding. I don't want students to use memorization strategies to do well on a test. So I actively thwart that kind of behavior by the strategies I put into operation. The current course is highly participatory and highly structured with weekly online homework of 18 problems, weekly recitation problem sets, and the Classroom Performance System (CPS) response questions given during the lecture. The grade distributions show that students make good grades overall because I consistently work to intertwine my goals for learning with their grades. Focusing on strategies for understanding allow more students to be successful than are traditionally. Poorer students learn how to study and learn for the longer term as a result of the structured activities and my focus on understanding over memorization. They do not know their final grade, however, when they evaluate me.

Evaluating constructivist teaching fairly requires a paradigm shift that students cannot seem to make. The way I teach doesn't match what students expect. It doesn't match what students expect because I am implementing a constructivist learning theory. Research on student evaluations has shown a 0.87 correlation in ratings when the teaching style or model used by the college instructor is the same style or model expected by students (Armstrong, 1981). The more the teacher follows the expected style, the higher are the ratings. I believe the following evidence from student evaluations supports the fact I don't do what students expect: My students don't like the organization of the course even though in the syllabus and frequent reminders reinforce that it is organized for their long term benefit. In the written statements on evaluations the students' tones are often upset and indignant as if I violated rules. Even people who think I am very nice and that I care about them and other students seem to believe that I don't really know how to teach. Since I have been a teacher at many grade levels, university and graduate, it must be because I don't do what these student believe I should be doing. When the class is not operating as expected, students are more critical of everything, and thus all the ratings they give are lower. Populations of student vary and evaluate differently. For example, the fall 2006 class at 8:40 in the morning was a majority of freshmen and sophomores. The spring class at 5:40 pm was a mixture, including many more nontraditional students. The younger student population was much more critical of the technology use than the more mature spring class even though I had many more problems with new technology during the spring 2006.

A successful approach to ameliorate the negativity has been to give an online survey in the week the course ends in which I state my goals once more from the syllabus and ask them to rate how each specific tactic affected them personally. Doing this just before the more general evaluations seems to remind them that my goals are related to their learning and that all my practices are specific intentions rather than disorganized attempts to be like the other professors! The last two semesters of the same second semester chemistry class have been good. Students have begun to recognize my intent is maximizing their learning. One student's comment was the following: "I recommend this teacher to all students who really want to learn." I'm pleased with that.

INCLUSIVENESS REQUIRES RISK-TAKING & ASSESSMENT

If we want to be inclusive science educators then we have to take career risks. Focusing on strategies that promote understanding allows more students to be successful than many traditional pedagogical strategies, such as lecture. Constructivist teaching meant culling the course content to include only the most significant concepts and conceptions. Poorer students learn how to study and learn for the longer term as a result of the structured activities and focus on understanding over memorization. I don't like feeling like a prophet with an unpopular message. Poor teaching evaluations hurt. But as a professional it's even worse teaching in a more predictable way that isn't as effective for long-term understanding by students. Part of the situated difficulty in selling constructivist techniques is that what I use for evidence that my students are learning more than others is my own exams.

Our latest project seeks to address this lack of standardized assessment by incorporating a longitudinal assessment system throughout the chemistry undergraduate (UG) curriculum. It also generates a way for me to show increased student learning at the end of one semester and longer-term retention of understanding in the set of prerequisite questions in the next course. An established common pre and post assessment system will allow individual faculty to make innovations and test student learning.

I have discovered that my personal mental models have the capacity to nurture me so that an emergent power-from-within tempers discouragement. A vision empowers me to strive for challenges and choices that go beyond my present capacity. The models that inspire me are varied: Mental models of what I want the world to be like, who I want to be, and what I can produce. I entertain possibility models of what I want the college and K-12 educational environments to be. No matter how discouraged I get today, the vision is still there tomorrow. For the optimist, sleep is like plugging in.

REFERENCES

Armstrong, N. (1981). The relationship between learning preference style and student evaluation of teaching. *Journal of the Association for the Study of Perception, 16*(1), 27–30.

Bond- Robinson, J., Stucky, A., & Robinson, R. (2008, April 1). *What can a laboratory study of chemistry tell us about learning? Epistemological and reasoning practices.* Paper presented at the National Association of Research in Science Teaching, Baltimore.

Bond-Robinson, J., & Stucky, A. P. (2005a, July 21–23). *Grounding scientific inquiry and knowledge in situated cognition* (pp. 310–315). Paper in the Proceedings of paper in the Twenty seventh annual meeting of the Cognitive Science Society, Strasa, Italy.

Bond-Robinson, J., & Stucky, A. P. (2005b, July 15–18). *In the genre of laboratory studies: A model of day-to-day authentic inquiry for science educators* (pp. 1–10). Paper in the Proceedings of Eighth International History, Philosophy, Sociology & Science Teaching Conference, Leeds, UK, alphabetical.

Bond-Robinson, J. (2004). Paradoxical perspectives: Seeming or real contradictions in the nature of explanations, relevance, and organization. In J. Eddy (Ed.), *Reflections from the classroom: A collection of essays on teaching written by notable teachers at the University of Kansas* (Vol. 6, pp. 11–16). Lawrence, KS: Center for Teaching Excellence.

Bond-Robinson, J. (2005). Identifying pedagogical content knowledge (PCK) in the chemistry laboratory. *Chemistry Education Research and Practice, 6*, 83–103.

Bond-Robinson, J., & Preece, A. B. (2002). *Learning by doing: Cognitive apprenticeship in research as a template for teaching inquiry.* Paper in the Proceedings of the Sixth International History, Philosophy, and Science Teaching, November, 2001, Denver, CO.

Bond-Robinson, J., & Rodriques, R. B. (2006). The science of design research used to catalyze graduate TA performance. *Journal of Chemical Education, 83*(2), 313–323.

Brown, A. L. (1992). Design experiments: Theoretical and methodological challenges in creating complex interventions in classroom settings. *Journal of the Learning Sciences, 2*(2), 141–178.

Chinn, C. A., & Malhotra, B. A. (2002). Epistemologically authentic inquiry in schools: A theoretical framework for evaluating inquiry tasks. *Science Education, 86*, 177–218.

Clancey, W. J. (1997). *Situated cognition: On human knowledge and computer representations.* New York: Cambridge University Press.

Cobb, P., Confrey, J., diSessa, A. A., Lehrer, R., & Schauble, L. (2003). Design experiments in educational research. *Educational Researcher, 32*(1), 9–13.

Collins, H. M., & Evans, R. J. (2002). The third wave of science studies: Studies of expertise and experience. *Social Studies of Sciences, 32*(2), 235–296.

Dunbar, K. (1995). How scientists really reason: Scientific reasoning in real-world laboratories. In R. J. Sternberg & J. E. Davidson (Eds.), *The nature of insight* (pp. 365–396). Cambridge, MA: MIT Press.

Fanfare for the common man. [Electronic (2008). Version], 1. Retrieved January 7, 2008, from http://lcweb2.loc.gov/diglib/ihas/loc.natlib.ihas.200000006/default.html

Greeno, J. (1998). The situativity of knowing, learning, and research. *American Psychologist, 53*, 5–26.

Klahr, D., & Simon, H. (1999). Studies of scientific discovery: Complementary approaches and convergent findings. *Psychological Bulletin, 125*(5), 524–543.

Kuhn, T. S. (1970). *The structure of scientific revolutions* (3rd ed.). Chicago: University of Chicago Press.

Latour, B., & Woolgar, S. (1979). *Laboratory life: The social construction of scientific facts.* Princeton, NJ: Princeton University Press.

Lave, J. (1988). *Cognition in practice: Mind, mathematics and culture in everyday life.* New York: Cambridge University Press.

Mead, G. H. (1934). *Mind, self, and society.* Chicago: University of Chicago Press.

Nersessian, N. J., Newstetter, W. C., Kurz-Milcke, E., & Davies, J. (2002). *A mixed-method approach to studying distributed cognition in evolving environments* (pp. 307–314). Paper in the Proceedings of International Conference on Learning Sciences.

Polanyi, M. (1936). *USSR economics.* Manchester: Manchester University Press.

Polanyi, M. (1962). *Personal knowledge: Towards a post critical philosophy* (paper back, 1974 ed.). Chicago: University of Chicago Press.

Robinson, J. B. (1995). Precolumbian chemistry. *Journal of Chemical Education, 72*(5), 416–418.

Wenger. (1998). *Communities of practice: Learning, meaning and identity.* London: Cambridge University Press.

AFFILIATION

Janet Robinson-Bond
Arizona State University

SECTION V: SISTERS ARE DOING IT FOR THEMSELVES

The fifth section explores some of the ways in which women are working to define new expectations for themselves, their colleagues, and their institutions, through scholarship and the development of supportive networks of between colleagues, students, families, and friends. The three chapters collected for this section of the book focus on challenges women face in academia as related to their careers as well as choices that impact their family lives. While previous sections have focused on issues women face, they have mostly done so as a biographical account of the lived experience/s of the author/s from which the reader has been invited to extrapolate the significance of the challenges the authors have faced and the choices available to them at different times in their careers. This section, while continuing to employ autobiography as a narrative format, offers the reader more than a recounting of the ways in which women's choices have impacted their careers as the authors explicitly detail how they have transformed their place and identity in the academy through their actions as mothers, mentors, and by engaging with academe's formal structures by becoming administrators.

In the first chapter in this section (Chapter 16) Angela Calabrese Barton, Margery Osborne, and Rowhea Elmesky examine the issue of balancing family and motherhood in academia. They do so, first from a historical perspective, providing an overview of the feminist literature framing the family-work conflict for women in academia and then by providing individual vignettes from their lived experiences describing the strategies they have each employed to "craft or author a life" in academia which merges family with work. Barton, Osborne, and Elmesky offer the reader a fresh perspective on this issue by choosing to focus not on the barriers they have as women with families in academia have faced, but rather, they present their experiences building a life "with/in academia with/for" their children and families. Finally, the authors draw together their individual stories within the socio-historical context of women/mothers in academia through the use of analytical metalogues, wherein, they invoke bell hook's (1990) notion "homeplace" as an argument for women creating utopias in the academy, in the larger science education community, and in the world.

In Chapter 17, Kathryn Scantlebury, Judith Meece, and Jane Butler Kahle provide a feminist critique of the hierarchical nature of mentoring relationships in academia. An examination of the traditional concept of having a "senior" person support a "junior" colleague invites critical discussion about power structures within traditional mentor/mentee relationships in which there is a tacit, sometimes overt, implication that the mentee has little to contribute in terms of knowledge or experience to the mentor. Historically, women have been poorly represented in positions of authority in academia, meaning women who join academia have been more likely to be mentored by men than women, therefore, complicating the issue of mentoring by including not only power differentials related to experience, but also gender. Building from the chapter title, "Wine and Whine", Scantlebury, Meece, and Butler Kahleutilize an interactive metalogue to examine the cross-generational friendship they have developed over time, during which they have mentored one another with regards to professional and personal issues that have influenced their academic careers. This chapter offers readers examples of the ways in which mentoring impacts women's entrance into the academy, the start and growth of academic careers, and the formation and sustainability of professional identities.

The final chapter (Chapter 18) in this section provides readers with a macro examination of some of the issues facing women in academia, including discrimination against feminists, from the perspective of an administrator. Writing autobiographically about her experience becoming a Dean at a large research institution in the South, Rosser explores instances in which her career as a feminist scholar have been perceived as a positive or negative attribute for a female administrator. Acknowledging the conservative political climate that prevails at the highest levels of academic administrative office, Rosser offers the reader a revealing look behind the scenes at the policies (explicit and implicit) that inform tenure and promotion decisions at many universities. From vantage point as a dean, Rosser provides particular attention to issues that may impact women negatively, relative to their male counterparts, examining issues ranging from the representation of accomplishments on curriculum vitae, to examining gender differences between males and females related to collaboration and sharing of research ideas with colleagues. Building from her scholarship in gender studies and her experiences as Dean, Rosser determined that women needed different supports than male colleagues to achieve in academia. The second half of her chapter is dedicated to describing the development and implementation of a National Science Foundation (NSF) funded comprehensive program, ADVANCE, which is aimed at improving mentoring as well as systems for promotion and tenure. ADVANCE provides institutions with macro-supports to implement transformative practices in mentoring, increase equitable allocation of resources and necessary structures to enable women to appropriate resources, alter leave policies to better support women and family planning decisions, and support global reassessment of administrative policies to remove subtle gender, racial, and other bias in the tenure and promotion process.

ANGELA CALABRESE BARTON, MARGERY OSBORNE AND
ROWHEA ELMESKY

16. CREATING NEW UTOPIAS IN THE ACADEMY:
SPACES OF FAMILY AND WORK

INTRODUCTION

Balancing family and academia, especially for women, is a chronic challenge. A review of the literature shows that women have been struggling with this issue since they were first "admitted" into academia (Astin, 1965; Glazer & Slater, 1987; Glazer-Raymo, 1999). For example, historical studies show that women who entered academia between 1890 and 1940 shouldered all the responsibility of family life while still working to meet the demands of the workplace. Current research reveals that little has changed over the past hundred years (Gatta & Roos, 2005).

Research and writing on women's experiences in the global economy make very clear, as we point out in this chapter, that while women have many barriers to overcome to meet the demands of work and home, they also have crafted strategies for being successful. These strategies are often situated within cultural systems, career domains, and national climates, e.g., the climate for women and work in the US still lags many other western countries in terms of maternity leave policies. The purpose of this chapter is not to focus on the barriers that we, as women with families in academia have faced. We view our own experiences as not about bumping up against and overcoming barriers (although this is a distinct part of what we do). Rather we view our experiences as more about "crafting or authoring a life" in the sense that overall, we each have sought to construct a "way of being" in academia that merges family with work, where each rely on and gain strength from the other.

Our chapter has three parts. First we provide an overview of the feminist literature that frames the family-work conflict for women in academia. We use this overview to highlight the challenges that women face and to make a case for why it is important to recast the family-work conflict as being about the authoring of new spaces. Second, we share snippets from our own personal stories of authoring new spaces – spaces of utopia – in the academy, as our own attempts to build a life with/in academia with/for our children and families. Third, we engage in a metalogue following our stories to flesh out the themes of home place and harsh world that help to deepen and nuance our argument around authoring new spaces of utopia.

K. Scantlebury, J. Butler Kahle and S. N. Martin (eds.) Re-visioning Science Education from Feminist Perspectives: Challenges, Choices and Careers, 179–190.

BACKGROUND

Academia has not always welcomes women into its professional ranks with open arms. Much research has demonstrated that women face inequalities in many areas of university life, such as earnings, tenure and promotion and access to resources. Years after women began to make greater inroads into the academy they remain underrepresented in many traditionally male fields, such as the physical sciences, mathematics, philosophy, economics, and engineering. They also are unrepresented at the highest professor ranks, on faculties in large and prestigious research universities and in academic leadership. (Gatta & Roos, 2004, p. 124).

The Masculine Culture of Academia

Feminists research into women and academia provide clear portrayals of the ways in which large universities are gendered institutions and rely upon the "male-model" of the ideal worker for their success over time (Acker, 1990). In this model, the professor is viewed as "unencumbered" by family responsibilities and free to "dedicate his time to the university" (Gatta & Roos, 2004, p. 126). This model separates the public and private spheres of the lives of academics (Glazer-Raymo, 1999), implies that the development of the scholarly mind is distinct from the demands of life (Aisenberg & Harrington, 1988), and sets up or supports inequalities in job expectation and performance. As Aisenberg and Harrington (1988) remind us, academia demands that scholars dedicate their lives to the pursuit of knowledge. This reinforces the family-work dichotomy, where "the demands of family, community life and leisure time are second to the demands of the intellectual life" (Aisenberg & Harrington, 1988, p. 107).

A review of the literature reveals that women in academia often face at least three kinds of family-work conflict, including: a.) Time; b.) Roles and Responsibility; and c.) Integration.

Time

Time conflict occurs when "time pressures from one role make it impossible to fulfill expectations of another role" (O'Laughlin & Bischoff, 2005, p. 80). Greenhaus and Beutell (1985), who write extensively on the time conflict for women and work report that the greater the number of hours worked per week, the greater level of work-family conflict. According to Duxbury and Higgins (1994), women feel this time conflict more, and compensate for it by minimizing their time spent in personal or leisure activities more so than do fathers or women without families. Similarly, Cole and Zuckerman (1987) found that women scientists were more likely to cope with time demands of the job and family by giving up discretionary time and flexibility in both their personal and professional lives. Giving up of flexibility can have negative consequences, however, because it can lead to a reduction in opportunities to travel, collaborate, or network (Tang, Fouad & Smith, 1999). In academia, where conference attendance and organizational committee work is highly valued, women can face criticism and penalties for their lack of visibility, especially when they experience the tenure review process.

Roles and Responsibility

Many studies show that women continue to carry the primary burden of childcare and household responsibilities (Bielby & Bielby, 1989; Gatta & Roos, 2004). This continued load impacts women's opportunities to craft roles and responsibilities. Like the time conflict discussed above, conflict in roles and responsibilities also emerges when the responsibilities one takes in a role are incompatible with those of another role, such as is often the case when family members become ill and the mother takes time off from work to care for them (O'Laughlin & Bischoff, 2005). It has been argued that academia's culture is liberal, allowing more freedom and autonomy in designing work schedules, thereby potentially reducing role and responsibility conflict. However, several studies have shown that even those fields that allow for flexibility, in for example, setting one's own hours and places of work, e.g., working at home, conflict can appear even stronger (Bailyn, 2003; Gatta & Roos, 2004). For example, as O'Laughlin & Bischoff, (2005) report, working at home may creates conflict "because the focus and energy needed to fulfill work expectations is likely to conflict with demands for attention from children and/or spouses" (p. 82).

Integration

Family-work integration is the major obstacle women in academic face (Gatta & Roos, 2004). Many women feel that they have to "choose" between family and work, marrying early or late, achieving tenure or having children, and her career or her husband's career (Gatta & Roos, 2004, p. 127). Women with children who do work to integrate family and work are often perceived has spending more time on family demands (Dressel & Clark, 1990; O'Laughlin & Bischoff, 2005; Piotrkowski, Rapoport, & Rapoport, 1987). Indeed, women experience more conflict between family and work than men, even though they may still be as productive as men in terms of tenure and publication (O'Laughlin & Bischoff, 2005; Sax, Hagedorn, Arredondo, & DiCrisi, 2002).

This point about integration is particularly salient to us because our efforts to build new ways of being in academia rely upon understanding integration in novel ways. We take up this point in the next section with stories of authoring spaces of utopia.

STORIES OF AUTHORING "SPACES OF UTOPIA"

In order to share the ways each of us have encountered and addressed the challenges noted in the literature we focus upon how we each have uniquely crafted our own personal utopian spaces in which we can integrate the worlds of work and family in academia. Why do we use this word, utopia? Utopia: an ideal and perfect place or state, where everyone lives in harmony and everything is for the best; is a fiction, a construct, an ideal. Our utopias are creations, spaces we create for ourselves because, frankly, no one else does or will. In trying to create these spaces, we negotiate, set limits, create rules of behavior and insist on living up to them. We dedicate ourselves to the care and maintenance of these spaces. We protect them by restricting membership, following all the rules and not acknowledging critique. We hold fast against the attacks leveled against them. And there are many! The boundaries of a utopia are battlefields or a thousand other metaphors evoking places of turbulence and struggle.

Angie's Story

I did not have children until I had been a professor for seven years, or in other words, until after I had received tenure. My decision was not fully a conscious one. In other words, I did not decide to "wait" until after tenure to have children. My husband and I simply refused to entertain the question until we had more stability in our lives, and until, of course, my own biological clock started to tick away. Once I became pregnant with my first child, I knew I was thrown into the world where I had to devote my energy to authoring a new life – and my children's lives – in the academy.

As I thought about how I authored this life, I found myself getting stuck on the details. On learning to type with one hand, or balancing myself with a baby on the front and a computer on my back as I walked to work or schools. But as I thought more about my experiences, I began to realize that blending motherhood with academia was about both my vision what I believe my place in academia is about (building a better world) and the details, however fragile they are, that made this life possible.

I have begun to see that I enjoy my life in academia because I actually believe that it puts me in a position to make a difference in the world. I want to help build a science education that fosters agency and social justice, and from this vantage point I can work with, learn from and help to effect teachers, children and their families. This ideal drives me. Having children only awakens this ideal more, and instills within me the desire to have my children participate, learn and contribute to this journey. Indeed I do not like to talk about blending family and career because I do not like to think about my job as career. Career suggests a path of progress in known direction. I am not so much interested in building a career as I am creating a space for helping to make change.

And so when I think about creating my own space of utopia and how it is made through the fragile details, I guess I am not surprised that most of these efforts have been about creating places of being rather than about keeping up. While most of what I thought I wanted for myself, my children and my work in academia remained somewhat of a hazy notion that these worlds could somehow be blended, my goals for making this so, were pragmatic and few.

First, I decided I wouldn't be afraid. I wouldn't be afraid of germs, of others' parenting styles, or our bodies greatest gifts and embarrassments, or of how people perceived the "new" me. Second, I knew that family and work would always be in conflict according to one or another's vision of life in academia, so I might as well make this space of potential conflict a productive one.

Not being afraid may sound like a corny goal, but the initial hurdles I, as a new mother, needed to jump over in order to blend my life at home with my life at school had a lot to do with being afraid. Would I expose my children to others' germs? Would my breasts leak noticeably if I nursed my daughter during a meeting? Who would care if I nursed my daughter during a meeting? How would I feel leaving my infant to wander the halls of Teacher's College (TC) with a colleague, a student, or a friend? Would I miss the chance to see her eat her first ice cream or take her first steps?

But, I also would not be afraid to create a new way of being in academia. I created play zones in my office and in our research space filled with children's books, toys, clean diapers and clothes. I brought my kids to conferences, like National Association for Research in Science Teaching (NARST) and held them while I talked. I snuck out of sessions to see insect exhibits at the local science museum and to walk around the nearby park. I accept compliments from others about how I am a good model for blending parenthood and academia while I feel like a fraud for doing neither well.

What I found was that my role as an academic transformed because it had to, if I was to survive as a mother and an academic, but it also transformed me and how I understand both of these roles. Besides learning to type with one hand, speaking about academic topics in a sing-song voice, or getting up at 4 am to read and write before my family awakens, I began to see even more clearly the politics of identity. Why did it bother me so much when I was referred to as "mom" by colleagues rather than Angie or professor or collaborator? Is this how the families I worked with felt when I described them as "urban, minority, high poverty" kids? I also learned to listen better to my students from those times I was holding or nursing my daughter – mainly because I couldn't "take charge" of the conversation and tell my students what they should be doing. In listening better, I built stronger relationships, and began to understand the nuances of my students' needs, interests and ideas. I also learned to praise my students more with word, song, laughter, clapping and spontaneity simply because of the presence of my children. I think it is not coincidence that my research group is so much more tightly knit personally and professionally now more than ever. I learned to see parenting as not about just giving myself over to my children but about helping them feel safe, well cared for in a variety of spaces, with a variety of people. While blending these roles complicated my life, it also gave me the space to simplify it: I began to learn how to let certain arguments fall to the side because they simply weren't worth the time or energy.

Margery's Story

Autobiographical statements are frequently arrogant, an apparent arrogance reflecting the hubris of retrospection, the surety of history. The truth is such arrogance often is just a thin veneer over deep uncertainties. The void waits beneath us. With a single miss step; we fall and are gone. Arrogance conceals fear—we have to act with certainty or we would be incapacitated, frozen in the headlights, waiting. I write this caveat as an excuse for the portrait I am going to draw of the life I have constructed. Unlike Angie and Rowhea my children are older—Cornelia is 13 and Larkin 24. I have been trying to combine the personal and professional for a while. I have tenure and the biggest debate for me, professionally, is whether or not to bother with promotion. Nothing for me will change if I get it, I will change nothing to get it. Is this hubris? Yes. What does it reflect? It reflects the fact that I have constructed a space where I do things the way I like them. I guard and protect this and irrespective of whether or not other people applaud or condemn it, I still like it. The reference point for judgment is within me. How un-ambitious, how un-masculine. How can I defend this stance of apparent selfishness? I don't really know and I struggle with this. Is a utopia a refuge, a private refuge? I have problems with selfishness; but let me describe the life I have constructed. Maybe that will help.

I have created my life by acting purposefully on my ideals. Again hubris! But just let me say in my defense here, I am more than aware of my limitations. As well as having children for 24 years, I have been a single mother for all of it. I think of myself as a problem solver—if I decide I want to do something like dig up my whole back yard and plant a rose garden, I figure out how to do it. That involves finding tools that allow me to dig huge holes even though I am not very strong, researching the types of roses that are hardy enough to grow in central Illinois, allocating the time to effectively kill the grass organically so I don't subject my children to herbicides, learning, learning from experience. And now, 12 years later, accepting what I've made, not trying to make it perfect and letting things grow to some extent they way they want to. And believe me they do, once you've prepared the ground, planted the plants and got it all going, changing things becomes very hard. For many reasons including, if you've thought it all out, worked and planned very hard and thoughtfully, it probably is foundationally what you really want and you should never wantonly change such a thing. I'm not talking about impulse buying here; I'm talking about the construction of a world.

So to some extent I feel like I have done that professionally. With my first child, and my first career I might add, I made a lot of mistakes. The one thing I did learn was that I needed to at least appear to have the skin of a rhinoceros as far as the public aspects of trying to integrate my professional and family life. For example, I learned to not apologize when people made comments about bringing my baby to my office. And then I learned to not even acknowledge the comments. I think in many ways this was the key, learning to not acknowledge criticism, or at least not publicly. I certainly heard all those comments and really they fueled the fire—they drove me to pretend even harder that what I was doing was right. I also learned to keep things private. I created the space where I could have my child at work and I maintained it. My child wasn't left crying while I wrote papers—I learned to write papers holding my child. My child wasn't entertained by secretaries or other faculty while I taught classes even when they offered to do it. But on the other hand, I let anyone who wanted to hold the baby, play with the baby, hang out in my office while I was working with their babies, do that. This was the beginning of my creating a space for other people with babies. Basically I learned to act under the conviction that what I was doing was right and also I learned that the only way to change the conditions where I worked was to act like the conditions were already changed. In other words I didn't set out to reshape the political and professional conditions of my professional life, I just acted like they were the way I wanted them to be. Strangely enough this worked.

So what is my justification for this? Shifting the norms of a society is difficult. It is atmospheric and subtle and the changes extend beyond the personal and private. I like to think that others can and have benefited. So anyway in constructing my world, writing my life as Angie says, for me means living the things I believe in. Not waiting for them to be there but living them as though they were there. And this, in effect causes them to be there for more than myself.

Rowhea's Story

As I tap away at my laptop, I look over to my sleeping sons and think about how I would love to be asleep. Yet, I also think about how much I love what I do, and specifically how important it is for me to share a window into my world for other females entering into and within academia. I remember the doctoral students whom have approached me over the years and asked my advice about starting a family and about the balancing of personal and professional realms. Unfortunately, years ago I did not really have any examples of other women's stories nor visions of how to negotiate life in academia and life as a mother/wife. Thus this narrative is to express solidarity with other women entering academia, as well as to provide an insider glimpse for males in academia who may have never had to choose between staying up all night with a child with the whooping cough and submitting a proposal whose deadline is the following day.

Reading Angie and Margery's stories, I feel like a breath of fresh spring air has swept through my room – like a sigh that I have been holding in for years has finally been released, allowing my feelings of loneliness as a mother in academia to surface and be acknowledged. In many ways, I have been so busy toughening my skin to counter the harshness in the world that I have not felt free to grow in my multiple identities as mother and science educator. Looking back, now finishing my second year as an assistant professor, I mostly recall negativity and discouragement of any sort of combination of personal and professional worlds. For instance, I still remember my initiation into the McKnight fellowship program at the start of my doctoral studies. The female coordinator loudly warned the new fellows several times over the course of two days, "Don't get married while doing your PhD!" While I obviously didn't adhere to that advice, it clearly communicated an incompatibility between academia and family.

I gave birth to Hadi during my final years of graduate study and Mumin during the third year of my post doc, my other two sons have been born during my pre-tenure years. Throughout that period of time and until now, I have learned through trial and error to create spaces where my work and family could exist simultaneously; however, the spaces I have created in public often do not feel very ideal or safe. Unlike Angie and Margery, I do not and have not felt very comfortable bringing my children into the university, although I have attempted to do so occasionally. When I was working on my first book project, for example, I remember bringing Mumin who was two or three months old to a workday with the other editors on the book, and although the editors are dear friends and colleagues, I was constantly worried about being able to nurse Mumin and put him back to sleep without excessive disruption or time loss.

As I contemplate upon my fear and uneasiness to challenge the status quo publicly, I believe two issues primarily shape my actions. First, I lack confidence to bring my children into academia because I do not have tenure and feel my actions are always under constant scrutiny. Secondly, I have concentrated my efforts on creating a more private utopia away from the academia's eyes because I wear hijab (full body covering) and am consciously aware of the common stereotypes associated with Muslim women as being oppressed individuals who presumably only have identities of mother and wife. In other words, in my interactions within academy, I already must struggle against labels and expectations regarding my ways of being that will only become more intensified as my children are increasingly visible. Hence, over time, I have worked to create a private space at home where my two worlds can meet and flourish in some sort of harmony. In fact, my husband Ahmed has been my strongest support with our sons and in helping me to be well situated in my home utopia. I remember when he first insisted to buy me a wireless card for my laptop years ago when I was pregnant with Mumin. At the time, I wondered whether it would be a useful investment – yet, many a day I found myself working away online while sitting on the edge of the tub as Hadi splashed happily in a bubble bath. The guiding goal for me over the years has been to accomplish what I need to, while also providing my children with important experiences and being part of their happiness. He has been my backbone of support for ensuring that I have all of the latest resources to make my accessibility with the academic world complete. Because he has been a work-at-home dad for much of our marriage, he takes care of our sons when I am at the university or in schools doing research. We travel together to conferences when possible and he keeps the boysat home when I need to go alone. I have learned to accept that I will not always be there for every important event that takes place in my children's lives and that is never easy to swallow, yet I make sure that there are others to be there instead – from my husband to our families and friends. Importantly, I have also learned that no matter where I am, I can create a new space for my productivity to flourish and for family to be content – thus, a utopic space can be fluctuating and flexible in nature. Certainly, the spaces we create as working mothers in academia are constantly shifting and must be (re)created depending upon different circumstances that we encounter.

Although I have often wondered and asked myself whether I have made the best personal and professional decisions, I know I have persevered in trying to establish safe spaces where I can both be a mother and a science educator because I have hope that the ripples of my focus upon social justice will positively impact my children and other children's lives.

DISCUSSION

We construct personal spaces that value things different than perhaps what drives the academy as an institution but very in tune with what drives the academy as a place of learning. What we mean by that is that our choices take us out of networking loops and opportunities for national level committees sometimes, but not all of the time—we still participate in the academy but in ways that rewrite the rules. Our spaces allow us to pursue the ideas and values we believe in, in ways that stretch us intellectually but also allow us to try to live out those values. The conflicts that we feel are both internal to our situations of being mother/professor, but also external to the challenges faced by universities today as they become more and more business like. We are reminded of Margaret Eisenhart's book on women in science where she describes women doing the work on science but viewed as living lives on the margins of science because what they value in doing science does not align with the values of science-career.

Also, we like to think of these spaces that we construct – our utopias – as hooks' does with her notion of homeplace. We have often talked about our teaching goals through this ideal (Calabrese Barton & Osborne, 2001), but we also believe that it is what undergirds our efforts to build spaces for being in academia. hooks writes about homeplace as:

> Historically, African-American people believed that the construction of a homeplace, however fragile and tenuous (the slave hut, the wooden shack), had a radical political dimension. Despite the brutal reality of racial apartheid, of domination, one's homeplace was the one site where one could freely confront the issue of humanization, where one could resist. Black women resisted by making homes where all black people could strive to be subjects, not objects, where we could be affirmed in our minds and hearts despite poverty, hardship, and deprivation, where we could restore to ourselves the dignity denied us on the outside in the public world (hooks, 1990, p. 44).

In Black Feminist thought, homeplace is built upon the tension between solidarity and difference. At times, homeplace anchors; it is a safe community. Such a community is built upon solidarity, and is a place where people who may or may not be "relatives" come to know and rely on each other. This vision of community is important, especially in terms of how we think about young people, because it acknowledges that relationships between parents and children go beyond children as property or possessions of parents, to children and parents as members of a larger caring community of on-going relationship, friendship and sites for change. This notion of safe community was especially important to Angie in how she and her colleagues at the Urban Science Education Center learned to pass Bee and Frankie around during meetings as different voices, different soothing techniques, and different touch mattered to the girls comfort. For Angie and Margery it meant learning to understand who became part of our utopia's and when and how. Learning to build a safe community was, in part, predicated upon recognizing the roots of a shared history and a common anguish among different individuals.

In piecing together the details that make our visions possible, we began to see that we had allies in individuals we had rarely interacted with, and that some of our closest colleagues did not understand our new actions. Seeking this common history as a support for building these safe communities helped us feel part of larger solidarity in a struggle to be heard and treated fairly outside the homeplace.

Yet this very notion of homeplace as anchor or safe community is also supported by grounding in difference. Homeplace as community teaches, and requires participants, to relate to a wide variety of people and backgrounds. This point of difference is also important to our efforts to create our own utopias in two ways. First, it speaks to the validity of the "voice" carried by the spaces we construct. In writing about the importance of difference in homeplace, hooks calls upon the value of "unassimilated otherness." In other words, when someone or something deviates from the norm, even the norm of the margin, then that voice is important because it deconstructs the ideal of homogeneity and fosters change through the recognition of difference. Second, these utopias are a balance of difference – of the ideals which drive our lives with fragile details that make up those lives and constantly change, break down, are built up. How we craft our spaces of utopia are situated, and we draw strength from such. To extend this point, too, our homeplaces shift across our day and our spaces of family/work, accommodating and challenging the demands of the family and workspace. We may at times, as Margery writes in her story, follow certain rules and deny certain membership to our homeplaces, but we may change these rules for our own needs at a moment's notice.

Homeplace is also marked by an articulation of remembrance and a dynamic understanding of knowledge and values. By remembrance we mean a critical and creative articulation and reflection on the homeplace, its members and their experiences. We think what is important here, in our own stories, is that in different ways our efforts to build a homeplace is grounded in a focus on a way of being and a vision for creating a world rather than a focus on career. Remembrance is critical to our efforts because it takes into account how an articulation of how we come to know the world is historically situated (in both what we know and how we know it), and that the articulation of the historical brings with it a radical political dimension because it calls into question connections between position, power, and knowledge. In this sense, homeplace as the practice of remembrance also embraces acts of subversion: The very act of articulation, in remembrance, politicizes experience and the meaning of experience and opens up spaces for critique and revision of those experiences and the world which helped shape them.

Homeplace also carries with it its own orientation to knowledge and values. Homeplace challenges static representations of knowledge or space because the production of knowledge and space is connected to the social uses of and need for it. In building our utopias, our homeplace, this means starting from a belief that the knowing and the doing of our lives, both professional and personal are intertwined–historically, socially and politically situated processes influenced by external needs, and that these are also shaped through internal channels. Our lives are an outgrowth of those who create it, even when situated in historically sedimented institutions. Perhaps more important, though, is the political dimension to this construction. For us this means two things. First, because our values and beliefs are experientially based, the way we live our lives becomes a representation of one's reality and can be used as lens to understand, critique and revision the realities of the harsh world, be it the academy or larger social contexts such as the place of professional women in general. Second, this knowledge can be used for something, to understand and influence, to change one's physical or existential reality.

CONCLUSION

Together, these ideas about community, practices such as remembrance and subversion, and knowledge and values embracing cultural and political standpoint underscore the cross cutting theme that our utopias are ultimately about transforming the harsh world. Everything that happens in and about homeplace is centrally connected to the ideal of a fair and equitable world. This is why we refer to the idea of homeplace as radical and political. Homeplace exists through the efforts of those marginalized to create the physical, emotional, and intellectual space to understand, critique and recreate institutional and social practices based in the discourses of domination and control.

We believe that as we seek to built a more just world in science education for women/mothers/academics, we, as a larger science education community, must be attuned to how both the homeplace and the harshworld are situated within multiple contexts: the larger science education community, our various institutions, and our families, to name only a few. In this sense, homeplace is deeply personal – what do I need to create to sustain my family/work? – but also under public scrutiny – how I fashion these spaces of homeplace will be reflected in my efforts to contribute to the larger teaching and research communities. How we understand the multiplicity of homeplace, its role in the professional science education community, and how it transforms us as individuals, as researchers, and as members of a larger whole, are critical questions for the science education community to take up.

REFERENCES

Acker, J. (1990). Hierarchies, jobs and bodies: A theory of gendered organizations. *Gender & Society, 4*, 139–158.

Aisenberg, N., & Harrington, M. (1988). *Women of academe: Outsiders in the sacred grove.* Amherst, MA. University of Massachusetts Press.

Astin, H. (1969). *The women doctorate in America: origins, career and family.* New York: Russell Sage.

Bailyn, L. (1993). *Breaking the mold.* New York: Free Press.

Bielby, W. T., & Bielby, D. (1989). Family ties: Balancing commitments to work and family in dual earner households. *American Sociological Review, 54*, 776–789.

Calabrese Barton, A., & Osborne, M. (2001). Homeplace and the harshworld: A feminist re-reading of science and teaching students in poverty. *Journal of Curriculum Theorizing, 17*(4), 131–144.

Dressel, P. L., & Clark, A. (1990). A critical look at family care. *Journal of Marriage and Family, 52*, 769–782.

Duxbury, L., & Higgins, C. (1994). Interference between work and family: A status report on dual-career and dual-earner mothers and fathers. *Employee Assistance Quarterly*, *9*, 55–80.

Gatta, M., & Roos, P. (2004). Balancing without a net: Integrating family and work lives. *Equal Opportunities International*, *23*, 3–5, 124–142.

Glazer, P., & Slater, M. (1987). *Unequal colleagues: The entrance of women into the professions, 1890–1940*. New Brunswick, NJ: Rutgers University Press.

Glazer-Raymo, J. (1999). *Shattering the myths: Women in academe*. Baltimore: Johns Hopkins University Press.

Greenhaus, J., & Beutell, N. (1985). Sources of conflict between work and family roles. *Academy of Management Review*, *10*, 76–88.

Hooks, B. (1990). *Yearning: Race, gender, and cultural politics*. Boston: South End Press.

O'Laughlin, E. M., & Bischoff, L. G. (2005). Balancing parenthood and academia: Work/family stress as influenced by gender and tenure status. *Journal of Family Issues*, *26*, 79–106.

Piotrkowski, C. S., Rapoport, R. N., & Rapoport, R. (1987). Families and work. In M. Sussman & S. Steinmetz (Eds.), *Handbook of marriage and the family* (pp. 251–283). New York: Plenum.

Sax, L., Hagedorn, L., Arredondo, M., & DiCrisi, F. (2002). Faculty research productivity: Exploring the role of gender and family-related factors. *Research in Higher Education*, *43*(4), 423–446.

Tang, M., Fouad, N., Philip, L., & Smith, P. (1999). Asian Americans' career choices: A path model to examine factors influencing their career choices. *Journal of Vocational Behavior*, *54*(1), 142–157.

AFFILIATIONS

Angela Calabrese Barton
School of Education,
Michigan State University

Margery Osborne
College of Education,
University of Illinois at Urbana-Champagne

Rowhea Elmesky
Department of Education,
Washington University in St. Louis

KATHRYN SCANTLEBURY, JUDITH MEECE AND
JANE BUTLER KAHLE

17. "WINE AND WHINE": CROSS-GENERATIONAL
MENTORING IN ACADEME

INTRODUCTION

The 'hierarchical' nature of the mentoring relationship reflects the traditional definition of the concept; that is, a senior person supports a junior colleague who often is expected to take on the values and practices of the mentor. Feminists have critiqued this model because it reinforces the existing power structures and implies that senior person does not, or cannot, learn from her 'junior' colleagues. Ideal mentoring can be reciprocal and focus on career development, personal development, and professional identification. Also, it is important to have multiple mentors, because different mentors may have different areas of expertise and knowledge that can be of use to the mentee. Our story illustrates how we three have served—at various times—as both mentors and mentees for and to each other; it is truly a story of the importance of cross-generational friendships and mentoring in academe.

Using a metalogue, our chapter will focus on the importance of cross-generational mentoring in women's academic careers. A metalogue allows us to keep our individual voices and perspectives. Although we are all, White middle class women, we have had different academic and mentoring experiences (Roth & Tobin, 2004). For over two decades, we have 'wine and whined' together, regarding the professional and personal issues impacting our academic careers; we have supported each other in good, bad, sad, and happy times; we have challenged each other; and we have enjoyed the strong professional and personal relationships that produced and supported our cross-generational mentoring experience.

The metalogue begins with a brief introduction to the chapter's co-authors focusing on our education background, current status, and research interests. Then, we focus on how mentoring has impacted our entrance into the academy, the start of our academic careers, our growth as researchers, the formation of our professional identities, and, finally, how it has sustained us in our academic careers.

WHO WE ARE AND HOW WE MET

Kate was Jane's doctoral student at Purdue University and has been in academe for 15 years. She is currently a professor in the Department of Chemistry and Biochemistry at the University of Delaware. Her research interests focus on gender equity in science teacher education and urban schools.

K. Scantlebury, J. Butler Kahle and S. N. Martin (eds.) Re-visioning Science Education from Feminist Perspectives: Challenges, Choices and Careers, 191–200.

Judith has been in academe for 25 years. Trained as an educational psychologist at the University of Michigan, Judith is currently a full professor and chair of Human Development and Psychological Studies in the School of Education at the University of North Carolina-Chapel Hill. Her primary research focuses on gender differences in motivation, and she has applied motivation theory to understanding women's achievement in mathematics and science. She first met Jane when she was interviewed for a position at Purdue University, and Jane was on the search committee.

Jane, who originally formed the connection for Judith and Kate, started her career as many women her age did, by teaching high school biology. The opportunity to earn a master degree at Purdue University as a participant in a National Science Foundation (NSF) Teachers Training Institute led to her eventually completing a doctorate in science education at Purdue (Kahle, 2007). Her career in academia has spanned 35 years. She recently retired as Condit Endowed Professor of Science Education at Miami University. Jane's research has focused on gender equity in science education as well as the systemic reform of science and mathematics education.

ENTERING THE ACADEMY

Kate: Unlike many of my female peers, I was fortunate to connect with a proactive and caring mentor during my doctoral studies – Jane Butler Kahle. I met Jane when I was teaching high school chemistry and enrolled in a Master of Science Education degree. My research focused on the enrolment patterns of women in undergraduate science. I was drawn to this topic, as the first international women's conference was held in 1976, my first year as a chemistry major at an Australian university. The next conference was held in 1985, I had graduated, embarked on a teaching career and had enrolled in a masters' degree program. I connected with feminist research. One of my male professors encouraged me to enroll in a doctoral program and advised I should consider "good schools with strong science education programs" and 'good scholars in my chosen area of research'. In an ideal world, those two things should overlap and for me they did. Jane Butler Kahle was a professor of science education at Purdue University. I had read Jane's research and Purdue was considered a top university, I placed its name on my list. Around this time, Jane came to Australia on a sabbatical leave as the Haydn Williams Fellow at Curtin University of Technology (Perth, Australia). Before she gave a conference keynote talk, I introduced myself to her. We talked non-stop, and she offered to assist me in the pursuit of my doctoral studies.

Judith: My commitment to a career in academe occurred in two phases. As a graduate student, I worked in the research laboratory of Jacque Eccles. At that time, Jacque had a grant from the National Institute of Education to study why girls discontinued their mathematics study after one year of high school mathematics. With Jacque and a group of graduate students we developed the expectancy-value model of academic choice to predict the differential course selections of boys and girls in high school. I thrived in this research environment, and I did not find it again until I went to Purdue after a three-year postdoctoral fellowship. Jane was a member of my search committee, and we met for the first time during my interview trip. We had lunch, and I remember being very impressed that this woman had read all the articles I had submitted with my application. There was an immediate connection, and later I learned that Jane had played a very instrumental role in my recruitment and selection for Purdue position. I stayed at Purdue for only two years, and I found a home in Jane's research laboratory. I joined Jane's graduate seminar on gender and science. The seminar provided a place where I felt safe to contribute and discuss ideas, and where my ideas would be heard and respected. Jane also shared her personal life with me. There was very little for a single woman to do on weekends in Lafayette. I spent many Friday evenings with Jane and her husband, Floyd, watching videos. There were also parties for graduate students and guests from Australia. These events provided a glimpse of academic life I had not seen as a graduate student. Unfortunately, my own home department, educational psychology, was less supportive. I received very few social invitations, and a senior professor, who was a prominent scholar in motivation, was critical of my research on gender. When I learned from one of his graduate students that he did not support my candidacy for the Purdue position, I quickly realized that attaining tenure was going to be difficult, unless I moved to another university.

Jane: My story varies from those of Judith and Kate, because I had few women mentors. In fact, my entrance into academe was almost accidental. In 1972, after completing my Ph.D., I accepted a position as temporary lecturer at Purdue, teaching methods courses and supervising student teachers. However, the federal government was reviewing major research universities for discriminatory practices affecting women and minorities. Federal research funds were withheld if discrimination was found—as happened at the University of Michigan. Without any notice or discussion, I received a letter retroactively appointing me to a tenure track assistant profession position. During my early years, my only recollection of a women mentor was another graduate of Wellesley, who was a full professor of entomology at Purdue. As one of the few women in the Department of Biological Sciences, I was asked to serve on several prestigious committees. Her advice: don't serve on committees and, above all, don't serve as the secretary. She added that her career was at the stage that it would not be hurt by time devoted to service, not research, but that I had to focus on research that would lead to tenure. It was sage advice that I have repeated to Judith, Kate, and many other young women.

BEGINNING AN ACADEMIC CAREER

Kate: One aspect of becoming a professor is the thrill and expectation of crafting others to follow in one's research path. In my first academic appointment, university budget cuts and internal politics lead to a freezing of the doctoral program in science education. Three years later, when I left that university, I accepted an appointment where I would have little or no interactions with graduate students.

Judith re-framed the 'myth' about working with graduate students. Although my mentors have had extensive experience as directors of doctoral research, Judith talked about the drawbacks of working with graduate students and the advantages of working with colleagues. When one works with colleagues on research and design a program of work, set deadlines and assign duties, my experience is that those responsibilities are met. Working with graduate students is a major tenet of academic life, and while my academic position did not promote the opportunities for me to do so through the usual channels, my mentors have crafted ways for me to experience this role by engaging me in various projects where I have served as a mentor to junior colleagues at different institutions. However, Jane and Judith's mentorship allowed me to continue a different academic path using different strategies. Jane and Judith set up structures such that I could interact and work with graduate students. Although not quite the same as directing one's own students it has been a very good experience.

However, it has also made me privy to the nuances and issues in working with and promoting graduate students. In working with my senior colleagues, the focus is on the research, not oneself. That is not to suggest personnel issues or life events are ignored but we make sacrifices to meet the agreed upon deadlines, respond to email inquires, and assume the agreed upon responsibilities. Jane and Judith do not go AWOL from all forms of electronic communications, they do not miss deadlines because it was a weekend, or decided to a take a 'mini' vacation or did not feel like getting the work done.

Jane: As I mentioned, external events affected the start of my academic career; I just thought that I was lucky to have a lectureship. However, the experience made me wiser concerning the politics of academia and the lack of support from many male colleagues. I also found that as a single woman, I was considered a 'threat' by many of my colleagues' wives. One particular incident stands out. Several science education colleagues, who had grant money, arranged for a car to take all of the science educators, but me, to a national meeting in Chicago. For the first time, I spoke out about the discrimination and how it could affect my career, particularly my path to promotion and tenure. One of the five, responded to my memo, thanking me for writing and saying that he had never thought about such effects. Through a female colleague in speech communication, I became aware that I had many typically female speech patterns. I quickly became more assertive, dropping such phrases as 'I would like to say,' 'Have you thought about?' 'What do you think?' for simple declarative statements of my thoughts and ideas. Eventually, I instituted a seminar on female speech patterns for all my graduate students. The women needed the guidance—and the men were alerted to a gender difference before the popular book, *Women are from Venus; Men are from Mars.*

BECOMING A RESEARCHER—FINDING A RESEARCH PATH

Kate: When I began my graduate career at Purdue University, Jane's mentoring immediately become evident. Through the large international student community, I met graduate students from many other departments. I quickly learnt that having a desk, let alone an office of one's own, was most unusual. Jane's ability to secure external funds meant that as her graduate student I had research assistantships, summer support, and other resources, such as 'magic' numbers for photocopying. Those perks often were not available for my friends.

Jane had spent her sabbatical in Australia learning the nuances of qualitative research and she arranged to have a symposium on the subject my first spring at Purdue University. It was at this event, I met Judith and began another professional mentoring relationship that enriched my career and personal life. Judith has strong quantitative skills and in the ensuing years she has taught me to 'find the story' in the data – whether quantitative or qualitative – find the story. And while I had excellent professors in my graduate statistics courses (the first of whom was Ken Tobin), the analysis, which I worked on with Judith and Jane and which produced a paper focusing on African American children in urban schools, gave me a deep appreciation for a methodological approach to preparing quantitative data sets.

Jane and Judith are excellent role models that an academic is a life long learner. Jane was in Australia to learn about qualitative research methodology and when Judith and I collaborated with Jane on her Discovery (Ohio's Statewide Systemic Initiative for which Jane was the principal investigator) research, Judith identified that we should use HLM (Hierarchical Linear Modeling) for the analysis, and she enrolled in a short course to learn the technique.

Judith: Before leaving Purdue, I became interested in studying exemplary science teaching on students' motivation and achievement. At the time, effective teaching was defined in terms of increases in student achievement. One of my advisors at Michigan, Phyllis Blumenfeld, was interested in the effects of tasks on students' motivation. In science, a variety of tasks could be found. Phyllis and I wrote a NSF grant together to study exemplary science teachers. Through this project, I became interested in how teachers create different motivational environments in their classrooms. I was influenced by Jane's qualitative analysis of science classrooms, and the study included a qualitative component. In 1989, Jane invited me to spend part of my pre-tenure leave at Miami University, where I completed an analysis of the qualitative data. Because I had chosen to work with a professor at Michigan, I was experiencing difficulty establishing myself as an independent scholar. While at Miami, I received the advice and support I needed to find my own path. I also had a chance to observe Jane make a transition to an endowed chair position, a new path in her own career. As before, this experience provided a preview of what my professional life could become post-tenure.

Jane: My early mentors were men, one of whom advised me to prepare a five year plan for reaching my career goals and to identify an area of research and stick with it. Good advice on several accounts. I prepared a plan that would lead to tenure and promotion in spite of my commitment to two children, whom I raised alone. And I began to focus my research on barriers to girls and women in science. I avidly read the research on girls in mathematics that Jacque Eccles and Elizabeth Fennema were publishing, and met two social psychologists, Alice Eagley and Kay Deaux, at Purdue who were developing models for gender research. Eventually, Judith arrived for an interview, and I knew that I had found a colleague with wonderful skills, a keen intellect, and similar interests. Later, I met Kate in Australia. She was accepted as a doctoral student at Purdue, where she completed her degree, but she followed me to Miami University for her final year.

FORMING A PROFESSIONAL IDENTITY

Kate: Other women cite the difficulty of balancing a career with child-raising and mothering, that was not an issue for me but my challenge was articulating and crafting a single, solo life in an adopted country without familial supports or close friends. Judith, like myself, was a feminist, single, heterosexual and did not have children. Her mentorship of my academic career became important in several ways. First, when I met Judith she was an assistant professor. She had more recent experiences than Jane of the transitions from pre-post tenure, power dynamics played on junior, and female, faculty, and the navigation of one's academic career.

As a feminist, and a female without children, I have talked with Judith about the assumptions and expectations that young women make of senior faculty. If young women fail to attain academic standards, due to demands from their personal lives, such as motherhood, spousal work demands or parental care-giving, they assume that as female professors we are more lenient, affable, and flexible than their male colleagues. In some cases, this is taken for granted. Women graduates only view female faculty mentors in a positive manner if the faculty are supportive of family issues.

Judith: My professional identity evolved gradually from graduate school to the present. It was a male mentor who first told me I had the ability to complete a Ph.D. program at the University of Michigan. My main mentors in graduate school were young female professors who were untenured at the time. They both provided room in their research projects for me to work with them side-by-side. I felt like an equal, and made major contributions to each project. This experience provided the confidence and skills I would need to enter a research career. At the end of graduate school, I decided not to follow a male partner to Boston and pursue my own career. It was my first major step toward forming a professional identity. When I was awarded the tenure track position at Purdue, it affirmed my decision to make my career a priority. By the time I arrived at UNC-CH, I was determined to get tenure and stay. For me, it involved limiting my social life to stay focused on research and writing. During this time, I depended a great deal on my women friends and sister to provide the support I would need to reach tenure. I was awarded tenure at age 39, and resumed a social life. Five years later I was asked to follow another male partner to a new position in Mexico. This decision was difficult, but I realized that my professional identity was too important to me to walk away from a professional career. Jane and I discussed my decision to stay at UNC-CH and she was completely supportive. Looking back, I realize that support was important for solidifying my professional identity. From that point on, I sought out friends and partners who would support my career. From Kate, I have learned it is possible to have a full life as a single woman, and she has become an important mentor in that regard.

Jane: My professional identity really began with what I call, my first 'big time' consulting job. Paul DeHart Hurd put together a team of biology educators for a major NSF grant, Project Synthesis. Teams were formed for each of the sciences. In addition to Paul, my colleagues were Bob Yager and Rodger Bybee. We studied 20 years of NSF-funded projects, synthesizing the findings and preparing scholarly papers and policy statements. It introduced me to leading researchers in all the discipline areas of science and hooked me on large studies and the importance of reaching the public with findings. My gender research led to the receipt of the National Association for Research in Science Teaching's (NARST), highest honor, the Distinguished Contributions through Research award. The best part of receiving the award was the public acknowledgement that gender studies were a legitimate area of research!

I also have had opportunities to serve on many National Research Council committees, finally realizing that I was not the 'token woman' but an equal. On one of those committees, I worked with a physical chemist (Steve Berry, University of Chicago) who later facilitated my research shift to systemic educational reform. When I moved to Miami University, Steve alerted Ken Wilson (Ohio State University) of my move. Ken, a Nobel Laureate in physics and I joined forces to write the proposal and to provide leadership for Discovery. My final identity has been one of a major player in reform and in research about reform. And, I consider my most important research study as the one that led to the paper co-authored with Kate and Judith. We brought divergent strengths to that research, and its findings provide guidance for future researchers, reformers, and politicians.

SUSTAINING AN ACADEMIC CAREER

Kate: I came to the United States with a purpose of studying science education from a feminist perspective throughout my doctoral coursework my research papers had that focus. During my first position at the University of Maine, a colleague, Dr. Susan Laird, willingly engaged me in discussions about feminist philosophers during hikes through the Maine woods and over many meals. While I began to establish a research identity away from Jane, I also began to experience the challenges of an academic career. However, Jane was always a phone call away and we worked together to on getting papers from my dissertation published. Towards the end of my second year at the university, I questioned if I could have a successful academic career in a college that overloaded junior faculty with service and teaching commitments, when Susan announced she was leaving for another institution I decided my time at Maine while educative, should end. I accepted a position at the University of Delaware, in a chemistry and biochemistry department, which offered a very different challenge to a feminist scholar. Through Jane and Judith's support, I maintained the focus of using feminist theories to underpin my research and attained a NSF grant to conduct research that built upon my doctoral studies. The University of Delaware, the administrators in the college and department, and several faculty provided mentoring and support which I had not experienced in Maine.

Judith: Like Jane, I was advised early in my career to find a focus and stay with it. That has been a somewhat of challenge for me. Although my research focuses on gender differences in motivation, I moved away from Jacque Eccles' research to strike out on my own. I focused on classroom environments, and used goal theory to guide my research. In retrospect, it was a poor decision and it made it difficult to sustain a program of research. An important turning point was going to Miami University as a visiting professor for one year. Jane invited me to Miami to direct her research projects while she was at NSF. At Miami, I had an opportunity to work with Kate, until she returned to Delaware. She was eager to learn about quantitative research and to share her knowledge about qualitative research. We also developed a friendship outside the office, in which talked about future plans, family, and life of single women in academe. It was my first experience of working with a competent junior colleague. Meanwhile, while directing Jane's research projects, I was learning about working with a research team and conducting large-scale studies. Jane had also agreed to help me learn more about funding opportunities. With her assistance, I was asked to be a part of two proposal panels, one of which was Research on Learning in Education (ROLE). When I returned to UNC-CH, I invited two mathematics educators and a new junior colleague to write a grant to examine the influence of reform-based teaching on middle school development as learners and knowers of mathematics. We were successful, and this grant work has sustained my interest in research for the past five years. With the support of a Spencer grant, we are following the students into high school algebra. For me, this work has brought my research full circle to examining gender differences in mathematics achievement—now almost 30 years later.

Jane: I can truly say that externally funded research has been my passion and has sustained my career. From the beginning, I have had at least one externally funded project throughout my career. And my research stayed focused: first, on economically disadvantaged students in Gary and Chicago; second, on girls and women (combining when possible the dual effects of gender and race); and, last, on systemic reform of science education (with a strong emphasis on equity). Through research, I was able to continually grow. A sabbatical with Joe Novak allowed me to explore Ausebelian theory; another sabbatical at Curtin University of Technology with Barry Fraser and Ken Tobin developed my skills as a qualitative researcher; my friendship with Judith has taught me (and many of my graduate students) skills in quantitative analysis; and Kate has opened doors to a new type of research, which I would call holistic and Kate would call by some unpronounceable name!

I made two important career moves—one to Miami University and the challenge of a Endowed Professorship (the first in science education in the US, I think) and the second to the National Science Foundation as Division Director for Elementary, Secondary, and Informal Education (ESIE). At Miami, I was principal investigator of the Ohio SSI, learning the skills of lobbying the legislature and working cooperatively with both the Ohio Board of Regents and the Ohio Department of Education (who frequently fought with each other). Those skills helped me negotiate the larger bureaucracy of the NSF (and Congress) and re-establish the importance of research in all projects, whether the primary focus was teacher professional development, curriculum development, or informal science education. In addition, with a talented group of colleagues at NSF, I initiated a program to rebuild the human infrastructure in science education. One aspect of that program, Centers for Learning and Teaching, was a focus on educating a new generation of researchers in mathematics and science education.

WHAT MAKES A GOOD MENTOR?

Kate: Researchers note the importance of mentors on one's academic career and that same sex mentors are often more effective. Women are often disadvantaged compared with men, as there are fewer females in academic positions, especially those who are in positions to provide opportunities for junior colleagues. Jane takes her role and duty as a mentor seriously; she is often placed in positions for recommending junior colleagues and ensures that others are included in the many opportunities that come to someone of her status and achievements. But Jane and Judith are also proactive in their mentoring efforts – offering to read and critique grant proposals, manuscripts, beginning conversations regarding the next steps for one's career. And also, how to avoid situations that can detract from academic advancement – committee work that is service orientated, rather than focusing on policy-making or budgetary review are some examples.

Judith: What makes a good mentor? For me, mentoring occurs on many levels. Both Jane, Jacque, and Kate were important role models. In psychology, we have a theory of called "possible selves" developed by Hazel Markus. Because Jane was 15 years older, she provided images of "possible career selves" for later stages of my career. Kate provided a "possible self" as a single professional, living happily without a partner or children. Mentoring also involves developing an apprenticeship relationship. By participating in this relationship, certain skills are developed. But more importantly, as one participates in research with a mentor, a professional identity begins to form that transcends this relationship. Additionally, mentoring involves opening doors. Jane played an important role in helping me to obtain my first tenure track position and my current research projects. Finally, mentoring is providing support and asking the critical questions. Over the last tenyears, Kate, Jane, and I have met in various cities and used our "wine and whine" times to discuss research, careers, and important decisions that need to be made. Our interactions are supportive, but critical questions are raised as needed. These sessions are important for clarifying issues, finding solutions, and balancing personal and professional lives. In my view, it is these relationships that enable women in academe to sustain their careers.

Jane: My early mentors were Mary Budd Rowe, Joe Novak, then Jacque Eccles and Elizabeth Fennema. They all had or have a passion for research, they were open with their ideas and thoughts about research and they provided me access to different resources. For example, Mary Budd Rowe, invited me to serve on review panels at the National Science Foundation that expanded my access to researchers in science and mathematics education. Jacqui and Elizabeth were doing innovative gender research in math education that led me to ask what were the issues in science. All were generous with their time, advice, and expertise. All slipped in personal messages among the professional advice they generously gave. Likewise, Kate and Judith's friendship as equal professional colleagues has added dimensions to my research and my interests. I admire and follow Judith's example in data analysis and interpretation and Kate's thoughtful expansion of feminist theory intrigues and challenges me.

SUMMARY

We respect and value each other as researchers, scholars, friends, and women. That mutual respect for our contribution of professional and personal knowledge to the group has produced a strong, cross-generational mentoring relationship in both the private and public spheres. We have learnt from each other, learnt together and provided solicited and unsolicited advice on our academic careers. Effective mentoring is proactive, caring, critical and supportive. It provides career opportunities and a sharing of knowledge on a multitude of topics, and sometimes it involves wine.

REFERENCES

Kahle, J. B. (2007). The road to reform. In K. Tobin & W.-M. Roth (Eds.), *The culture of science education. Its history in person* (pp. 25–25). Sense Publishers.

Roth, W. M., & Tobin, K. (2004, September). Cogenerative dialoguing and metaloguing: Reflexivity of process and genres [35 paragraphs]. *Forum Qualitative Sozialforschung/Forum: Qualitative Social Research [On-line Journal]*, 5(3), Art. 7. Retrieved November 9, 2004 from http://www.qualitative-research.net/fqu-texte/3-04/04-03-07-e.htm

AFFILIATIONS

Kathryn Scantlebury
Department of Chemistry & Biochemistry,
University of Delaware

Jane Butler Kahle
School of Education and Allied Professions,
Miami University

Judith Meece
School of Education,
University of North Carolina-Chapel Hill

SUE V. ROSSER

18. CHALLENGES AND CHOICES ADMINISTRATORS FACE:

Perspectives from a Feminist Dean

INTRODUCTION

My experiences as a feminist and a scientist, including twenty-three years as Director of Women's Studies in three quite different institutions, with my tenure home in departments ranging from biology through family and preventive medicine to anthropology, provided me with positive preparation for most challenges that dean's face. Understanding and dealing with diversity, looking at situations through the intersections of race/ethnicity, class, gender, sexualities, and other forms of identity, and understanding systems, power, and hierarchy along with other feminist baseline educational knowledge prove useful on a daily basis for dealing with the diverse constituencies such as faculty, staff, students, peer deans, the Provost and the President within the institution with whom the dean interacts, as well as donors, alums, and community leaders outside the university. My background as a scientist, including managing a laboratory, writing grants, and analyzing data, prepared me well for understanding the culture of a technological and scientific institution and making data-based decisions. Directing Women's Studies taught me to understand the perspectives of colleagues, tenure and promotion committees, and the dean and to learn to package non-traditional and even radical approaches and ideas in acceptable categories and language familiar to academia.

As a director, understanding the perspective of the college on hiring, tenure and promotion, budget resources, indirect cost revenues, priorities, interdisciplinarity, collaborations, and all other matters proved key to making the case for women's studies on these issues. The more that the Director could do to present Women's Studies in the categories, language, and ways that the Dean understood and defined these issues and that the other departments/units in the College presented them, the better the chances were for Women's Studies to receive appropriate resources and treatment. My background as a scientist experienced in writing grant proposals to appeal to the priorities of funders taught me that another way to consider issues and requests was to cast them in ways that demonstrated how they solve problems the College or Dean faces. Just as federal and foundation funders find proposals that include more than one institution or educational level easier to fund, explaining how helping Women' Studies often helps two departments served as another useful strategy, since often faculty hold joint appointments or affiliations.

K. Scantlebury, J. Butler Kahle and S. N. Martin (eds.) Re-visioning Science Education from Feminist Perspectives: Challenges, Choices and Careers, 201–213.

For example, in cases of promotion and tenure, as Director I needed to demonstrate how the cases in Women's Studies fit the classic criteria of research, teaching, and service valued by the college. I provided the acceptance rate or listing of top tier journals in Women's Studies, since that was standard practice in science and other departments for judging the quality of refereed publications. I explained how supervision of the Women's Studies internship students or practicum in activist service constituted teaching similar to that in schools of social work, nursing, or education where supervision of students who work under the guidance of professionals in the community has a longer tradition of counting as teaching. I drew parallels between a faculty member in Women's Studies who served on the executive board of the local battered women's shelter to faculty members in business who serve on the board of a local hospital in terms of real-world expertise and knowledge gained or to faculty serving on boards of their professional societies. My colleagues recognized that these years of experience in making some of the non-traditional aspects of women's studies fit the criteria of academia helped me as dean to see issues from a variety of perspectives and present them in ways likely to garner the resources and acceptance that benefited both individuals and the College. In these ways, they viewed my feminism as a positive contribution to my administrative skills as dean and scientist.

NEGATIVE FALLOUT FROM FEMINISM

In contrast, I was not too surprised at some of the negative reactions from some faculty, staff, peer deans, and other administrators when they learned not only that I was a feminist, but also that my research focused on women, gender, feminism and science, medicine, and technology. They expected me automatically to favor all women and discriminate against all men. I had to prove that such behavior would not constitute my approach to dealing with individuals or groups.

A graphic example of the distorted assumptions about me because I was a feminist emerged in the conservative campus newspaper of a prestigious Big Ten institution when it was announced in early 2006 that I was one of two finalists for Provost. They took out of context and distorted comments I had made some eight years earlier when interviewed about the potential value of single sex classrooms for women in science. Please note that I removed the names of the institution, newspaper, chancellor, and other candidate, substituting X instead.

But according to some university officials, Rosser is considered the favorite. Rosser, a one-time candidate for U of X provost in 1995 and a U of X alumnus, said in a phone interview she was "encouraged to send an application" by U of X representatives. Before becoming dean of the College of Liberal Arts at Georgia Tech, Rosser served for four years as the director of the Center for Women's Studies and Gender Research at the University of Florida. While at Florida, Rosser made some controversial statements in regard to the role gender plays in the learning environment.

In an April 9, 1998, article in the Independent Florida Alligator — a Florida student newspaper — Rosser was quoted as saying in reference to separating men and women in the classroom that "it comes down to the fact that the students and faculty can concentrate on the subject matter in the classroom." In an interview with this newspaper, however, Rosser said she does not advocate single sex education in large public universities, but said "in certain instances it can have real value" and "can be helpful." Single-sex education, she said, is not something she would pursue at U of X. "I believe there should be a place for such an institution," Rosser said. "But it's not something that should be going on at a large public institution like U of X" X, the other remaining candidate, has been part of the U of X College of Engineering since 1982, first as a member of the mechanical engineering faculty. He was named the associate dean for academic affairs for the College of Engineering in 2001 and became executive associate dean last year Understanding the field to be limited to these two candidates, we endorse Mr. X. (Pazuniak, January 15, 2006).

In the editorial in the same issue of the newspaper, they made the following remarks:

> Sue Rosser, another one of the finalists, strikes us as deeply troubling. Though she has, as dean of the Ivan Allen College at Georgia Tech, helped build a solid liberal-arts program, Ms. Rosser holds some unconventional — if not radically backward — views on methods to increase female participation in the sciences. In 1998, the Independent Florida Alligator, a student newspaper, reported that Ms. Rosser believes men can pose an academic distraction and single sex learning environments may be preferable, quoting her as saying, "It comes down to the fact that students and faculty can concentrate on the subject matter in the classroom." The controversial administrator reinforced this notion in a 1999 panel discussion at Colorado College. Recently, she discussed such beliefs in an interview with this newspaper, though she stated she would not seek such reforms at U of X if hired.
>
> A brief perusal of Ms. Rosser's post-doctoral work reveals little more than a litany of books dedicated to the advancement of women in the sciences, including, "Teaching the Majority," "Female-Friendly Science," "Re-Engineering Female Friendly Science," "Women, Science and Society: The Crucial Union," "The Science Glass Ceiling" and "Feminism and Biology: A Dynamic Interaction."
>
> Among her suggestions to help further women in the sciences, according to the aforementioned Colorado College transcript, is this little gem: "Use less competitive models to practice science." (Editorial Board, January, 15, 2006)

In a later editorial, shortly before the decision was made, the other candidate (a White male, associate dean) and I were portrayed as follows:

> A competent dean known for his intellect and generally respected by his peers, Mr. X will ably occupy the second highest office at U of X with a brand of dignity and professionalism this school deserves. He has both a

bachelor's and doctoral degree from the University of Michigan, a master's from the University of California–Berkeley and a solid administrative record that includes his current work within U of X's School of Engineering.

Mr. X stands in stark contrast to the attributes of Ms. Rosser, a fringe feminist whose ideology could further embattle the administration building's already-sullied reputation. The Georgia Tech administrator has openly advocated for single sex classrooms in higher education — a notion perhaps best relegated to the early 20th century — and sought to further various other gender-based policies that universally treat the sexes as fundamentally different within an education context. She seeks to draw vast contrasts between men and women seeking a higher education, and in the year 2006 such is a dichotomy that any civilized university ought to reject.

Indeed, in stating the qualifications of Mr. X for this weighty job, it must be recognized that one of the many reasons he ought to receive this promotion is simply because he is not Ms. Rosser. To be sure, this is not a contest between two suitable individuals — Mr. X is as qualified as Ms. Rosser is troubling. And given the extraordinary nature of those qualities, the chancellor's forthcoming decision ought to be a relatively simple one. (Editorial Board, March 6, 2006)

Mr. X received the Provost position at U of X. Although many issues no doubt played into the decision, it is difficult to assess the role of the conservative student newspaper in branding me as a "fringe feminist", particularly at a time when the U of X faced withdrawal of funding from a Republican legislature:

A number of issues will be awaiting X, when he assumes the provost position, with a constrained budget situation being among the most critical, according to the chancellor. "We're all concerned about the extent to which the state is withdrawing our budget," the chancellor added in a phone interview. "This trend can't continue." (Parzuniak, March 9, 2006).

The most egregious use of my feminism against me on my home campus came from a disgruntled employee who tried to get the college and university to give him $800,000 when we terminated him and sought to fill his position after more than one year's medical leave after which he refused either to come back to work or provide the documentation from the health care provider demonstrating his eligibility for disability. He filed a complaint with the Office of Human Resources and then with the Equal Employment Opportunity Commission, claiming I discriminated against and terminated him and another male staff member who I perceived as "threatening my authority as dean". All levels of both the University and State grievance and appeals processes found no grounds for the grievance and ruled against him at every level. Still, the whole procedure required substantial time and caused me considerable worry. The employee was eventually shot and killed by the police at his home where they had been called to investigate a threat of domestic violence, where allegedly the employee threatened to kill his mother with a knife.

POSITIVE BENEFITS OF FEMINISM

In contrast to this very negative use of my feminism against me, most faculty, staff, and other deans appreciated my background and held expectations that I would use it to help the institution. When I became the first woman academic dean at the public technological institution where I was hired in 1999, I wondered whether they really knew what they had gotten. Although my curriculum vitae, which at that time included seven books and eighty articles on women and science, not to mention more than twenty years as director of women's studies, provided clear clues, I wondered if they understood the implications of that.

During the interview process, I tried to determine this by asking questions of different individuals and groups, in ways that I hoped were discreet: Do you think the institution is ready for a woman dean, I inquired of the other deans? What strategies has the institution developed to attract and retain women faculty, I asked the Provost?

Keenly aware that being the first woman dean obviously focused their attention on gender, I did not want to overemphasize my own research interests on science technology, women, and gender. But I did want to ascertain their readiness to engage in institutional transformation to create a comfortable climate for women, including me. With my questions, I attempted to walk the fine line between appearing obsessed and focused only on women's issues and finding out what I needed to know. I did not want to take a job at an institution where they would be upset when they learned about my work on feminism and science or on development and implementation of policies and practices for women, since one of the many aspects that attracted me to the position of dean was the possibility of continuing this work at a different level in the administrative hierarchy.

The reassuring answers to my questions convinced me to take the position. When I arrived on campus, several of the women faculty, including some in other colleges, made it very clear that not only did they know what they were getting, but that they also had pushed hard for me. They were thrilled I was here because of my background and anticipated great advances for the campus as a whole to come from my leadership on women's issues.

As part of my start-up package, I negotiated three years of funding to support a Center for Women, Science, and Technology; during the first year, I convinced Housing to provide a dorm for sophomore women in science, as a variation on a learning community. Pleased with our initial progress, the other women faculty and I began to strategize about ways to insure the permanent future of these efforts, as well as a much larger project to advance women faculty to senior and leadership positions.

Since this larger effort would focus on promotion, tenure, and hiring for the entire institution, success would not be possible without support of key male top administrators, especially the deans, Provost, and President. Very aware that this would serve as the real test of how committed the institution was to advancing women, I approached the most powerful male dean of the largest college.

His response stood as some of the strongest institutional and personal support I have ever felt. He not only agreed enthusiastically to support the proposal, but he also offered to approach the Provost to see if he would serve as the principal investigator (PI) on the grant. Known for his conservative views, the Provost would be more likely to endorse the project if approached by the powerful male dean than by me. Although my fellow dean didn't say so, he recognized this immediately and offered to obtain the Provost's endorsement to serve as PI. Centered on issues nearest and dearest to faculty purviews and power such as promotion, tenure, hiring, and collecting data on sensitive issues beyond salaries, including start-up packages, space, and salary supplements, the Provost had to serve in the critical role of PI to obtain these data and to insure genuine transformation of the entire institution.

By the time the grant funding arrived, the powerful dean had become Provost and served as the PI himself. Working with him in that position allowed us to push institutional advancement of women beyond my hopes and expectations. His confidence and support of me also enabled the college to accomplish outstanding achievements, unrelated to gender, while I was dean.

GENDER DIFFERENCES IN CURRICULUM VITAE

My vantage point as a dean provided me with a perspective to see some issues that may arise in the tenure and promotion process that may impact women particularly negatively, relative to their male counterparts. These issues had not been evident to me either as a faculty member who had successfully negotiated the tenure and promotion process at a few institutions or as a chair who had shepherded faculty in their bids for tenure and promotion.

As a dean, I see hundreds of curriculum vitae each year from faculty at different stages of their careers, ranging from applicants for tenure track and research positions at all ranks, faculty in the college for which I serve as dean during annual evaluations, as well as all faculty from all colleges within the institution each year who come up for tenure and promotion. Recommending individuals at other institutions for positions, promotions, and professional awards each year assures that the issues do not reflect peculiarities for women at my home institution.

The relative similarity or uniformity of the men's curriculum vitae (CVs) compared to those of women struck me immediately when I began to see large numbers of curriculum vitae from both men and women. Of course, the CV's of men varied in their content in terms of research and teaching focus and included some variety and variance in numbers and quality of publications, teaching evaluations, and service. Although an occasional outlier among the male CVs stood out as especially strong or unusually weak, most of the men fit a bell curve without too much variation from the mean.

In contrast, the CVs of the women showed much more variation and could be described most accurately as a bimodal distribution. Many women substantially out-performed both their male and female peers in at least one, and often all, areas of teaching, research, and service. Other women remained at the other tail of the distribution, lagging considerably behind both their male and female colleagues.

Because I knew many of these women, I realized that most of them had no idea how far they deviated from the norm of their professional peers. Neither the superstars nor the women at the other end of the spectrum recognized how much their CVs differed from the bulk of those of their peers and the impact this would have on their promotion and tenure potential. The women whose CVs fell on the left tail of the curve faced the most immediate problems likely to derail their promotion and tenure, and I considered what supports, structures, and programs might be implemented to facilitate their cases in time for promotion and tenure. I also recognized that the unaware superstars might benefit from a reality check, since they might not be seeking and receiving the same awards, rewards, and recognition as other individuals achieving at their level.

I then contemplated the broader questions of why the curriculum vitae of the men fit a bell curve while the CVs of women fit a bimodal distribution and what, if anything, explained the extreme differences between these two groups of women faculty. In short, why did the men appear to be getting and responding fairly uniformly to the messages about expectations for promotion and tenure, while women seemed not to receive the message or at least responded in widely disparate fashion to the messages?

Although I realized that possible differences in background training upon hiring, start-up packages, reactions to failure, and even outright discrimination might contribute to such differential responses, I tended to eliminate these, knowing the culture of our institution and the desire to consider an explanation that could be addressed at this stage of their career. Differences in mentoring received by men and women faculty came to mind as a possible explanation, since receiving and comprehending messages about expectations appeared to characterize the difference. Somehow, most men seemed to get it and many women appeared not to get it, either wildly exceeding or falling quite short of the norm.

Both male and female faculty at our institution in most colleges and certainly in the college where I'm dean, are assigned a faculty mentor. However, I had observed on many occasions, and encouraged new hires to take advantage of, the numerous opportunities for informal mentoring that occur through social interactions, research collaborations, and service on key committees. I recognized that the many valuable tidbits about "what really counts around here" conveyed and absorbed during these informal occasions often proved more insightful and accurate than the information conveyed by formal mentors.

Aware of the national research documenting that gender differences are greatest at medical, Research I, and Research II institutions (Long, 2001), I also knew of climate surveys indicating that women talked with colleagues about their research less frequently than their male colleagues did. I also knew the evidence indicating that although women on average serve on more committees than their male peers, that the committees on which the women serve may not be the important or key committees. This information, coupled with the knowledge that like most Research I institutions (Long, 2001), the percentage of tenure track women at our institution remained at about twenty percent, made me wonder about the number and quality of social interactions that our women faculty had with their male colleagues.

Piecing this information together, I suspected that our women faculty did not receive the same quality and even quantity of informal mentoring as their male peers and wondered whether this might be at least partially responsible for why men got the message about expectations for tenure and promotion and women might not.

Simultaneously with my considering the overall differences in CVs of men and women faculty, I worried about another phenomenon that I had witnessed at the level of the institution-wide promotion and tenure committee. Occasionally, I had been present at discussions of cases of promotion and tenure where I had questioned whether subtle instances of racial and/or gender bias had influenced the outcome of the case. All of these cases were borderline, required considerable discussion, and resulted in relatively close votes. I should emphasize that in no instance did I witness overt sexism or racism, nor did such subtle factors ever emerge in a clear-cut case or one in which an individual of another race or gender with a very similar record had received a different vote or decision.

At times, in a very difficult case in which an individual came up for tenure in the seventh year or later than the norm, having taken a leave for family reasons or to pursue a project in a developing country or Historically Black College or University, I had wondered whether this had influenced the evaluation and votes by my colleagues on a subtle level. Did they accept such leaves or question them as indicators that the individual might not be committed and focused as a scientist, engineer, or scholar? Did they genuinely understand that stopping the tenure clock meant that year(s) should not be counted, or did they unconsciously increase their expectations and add another year(s) to the denominator when calculating the quantity of publications since the PhD or post-doc? I wondered if the deans, college promotion and tenure representatives, and members of the department promotion and tenure committees needed exposure to the research documenting how subtle biases, stereotypes, and messages from broader society can influence discussions and decisions in professional situations in unconscious ways.

ADVANCE

In 2001, during my second year as dean I saw an opportunity to obtain some resources that might enable Georgia Tech to develop a comprehensive set of programs that would improve mentoring, as well as the system for promotion and tenure, thereby enabling the women. In fiscal year 2001, the National Science Foundation (NSF) launched the ADVANCE initiative, initially funded at the level of $17 million. ADVANCE has two categories to include institutional, rather than individual, solutions to empower women to participate fully in science and technology. NSF encouraged institutional solutions, in addition to the individual solution permitted under the category of Fellows Awards, because of "increasing recognition that the lack of women's full participation at the senior level of academe is often a systemic consequence of academic culture" (NSF, 2001a, p. 2). Under ADVANCE, Institutional Transformation Awards, ranging up to $750,000 per year for up to five years, promote the increased participation and advancement of women (NSF, 2001a).

In October, 2001 the first 8 institutions receiving ADVANCE awards were announced (NSF, 2001b): Georgia Tech, New Mexico State, the University of California—Irvine, the University of Colorado—Boulder, the University of Michigan, the University of Puerto Rico, the University of Washington, and the University of Wisconsin-Madison. Hunter College joined the first round of ADVANCE awardee institutions in early 2002.

To initiate the institutional transformation necessary to advance women to senior ranks and leadership positions, Georgia Tech's proposal to ADVANCE included five major threads. These five major threads also exemplify the steps the Provost PI and I thought would be useful for solving some of the issues I had observed:

Termed Professorships to form a Mentoring Network:

One tenured woman full professor in each of four colleges with disciplines funded by NSF became the designated ADVANCE professor. The title and the funds of $60,000 per year for five years associated with the ADVANCE Professorship conferred the prestige and funds equivalent to those accrued by other endowed chairs at the institution. This sum also meant that $1.2 million of the $3.7 million grant went directly to support the ADVANCE Professors in keeping with the NSF notion that the ADVANCE grants should be substantial to recognize the importance of activities to build workforce infrastructure. Because Georgia Tech is a research university, the PIs of the grant particularly recognized the necessity for ADVANCE professors to sustain their research productivity while undertaking this mentoring role. ADVANCE Professors often used funds to pay for graduate students or post-docs to support their research.

Each ADVANCE Professor developed and nurtured mentoring networks for the women faculty in her college. The focus of the mentoring activities varied among the colleges, depending upon the numbers, ranks, and needs of the women. In the College of Engineering, a large college with about 42 women out of 400 tenure track faculty, isolation constituted a primary issue in many departments. The lunches arranged by the ADVANCE professor with women faculty from the College provided an opportunity for them to meet women in other departments and develop social and professional networks. A popular professional networking opportunity included evaluation of the curriculum vitae of junior faculty by senior colleagues to assess their readiness for promotion and tenure and/or gaps that must be addressed for successful promotion to the higher rank. The ADVANCE professor often helped to explain and mediate problematic issues in some schools with the chair and dean.

In the smaller College of Computing, with eight of 60 women as tenure track faculty, many of the women had young children, so many of the lunches and activities focused on explication of family friendly policies and strategies to balance career and family. In the College of Science, lunches and activities centered on grant-writing workshops and other means to establish successful laboratory research. In Ivan Allen College, where 40% of the tenure track faculty are women, the ADVANCE professor chose luncheon themes on publication and scholarly productivity.

Although all four ADVANCE professors held luncheons and mentored individual women faculty, each focused the initial activities upon those issues she perceived as most problematic and/or critical for achieving tenure, promotion, and advancement to career success for the women in her particular college. By the fourth year of the grant, the professors evolved more cross-college activities, expanding programs and initiatives particularly successful in one college to women from all colleges on campus.

Collection of MIT-Report-Like Data Indicators:

To assess whether advancement of women really occurs during and after the institutional transformation undertaken through ADVANCE, data must be collected on indicators for comparison with baseline data upon grant initiation for several indicators. Georgia Tech proposed in its grant to collect data on eleven of the following twelve indicators that NSF eventually required all ADVANCE institutions to collect by gender: faculty appointment type; rank; tenure; promotion; years in rank; time at institution; administrative positions; professorships and chairs; tenure and promotion committee members; salaries; space; and start-up packages.

Family-Friendly Policies and Practices:

Recent studies document that the balancing career and family constitutes the major difficulty for tenure track women faculty in general (Mason & Goulden, 2004), and women science and engineering faculty in particular (Rosser, 2004; Xie & Shaumann, 2003). Competition between the biological clock and the tenure clock becomes a significant obstacle for women faculty who have delayed childbearing until they receive a tenure track position. For women faculty in science and engineering, significant time away from their research makes it less likely they can successfully achieve tenure in a research institution. The dual career situation becomes an additional complicating factor for women scientists and engineers, 62% of who are married to men scientists and engineers (Sonnert & Holton, 1995). Given the dearth of women scientists and engineers, the reverse situation does not hold since that would mean few men scientists and engineers would be married. To facilitate the balancing of career and family, perceived overwhelmingly by women scientists and engineers (Rosser, 2004), particularly those of younger ages, as the major issues, Georgia Tech instituted the following family friendly policies and practices: stop the tenure clock, active service- modified duties, lactation stations and day care. The specific details of these policies can be accessed under Family and Work Policies at http://www.advance.gatech.edu.

Mini-Retreats to Facilitate Access to Decision-Makers and Provide Informal Conversations and Discussion on Topics Important to Women Faculty:

Research has demonstrated that women faculty tend to have less access and opportunities than their male colleagues to speak with the decision-makers and institutional leaders (Rosser, 2004). Often this unintended discrimination and lack of access results from women's absence from informal and social gatherings. To insure access of tenure track women faculty to the senior leadership of chairs, deans, provost, vice presidents, and president, the Georgia Tech ADVANCE grant organized two-day mini-retreats during each year of the grant. Focused on topics of interest and concern to all faculty, such as case studies of promotion and tenure, training to remove subtle gender and racial bias in promotion and tenure decisions, and effective strategies in hiring dual career couples, these retreats have provided opportunities for the tenure track women faculty to interact with the institutional leadership and express their opinions/views on matters of mutual interest.

Removal of Subtle Gender, Racial, and Other Biases in Promotion and Tenure:

In my role as dean, my close involvement with the promotion and tenure process provided insight into ways in which unintended subtle biases might influence decisions on promotion and tenure. For example, I observed that in some cases when the tenure clock had stopped for a year for a valid reason such as childbirth, the clock appeared not to stop in the heads of colleagues, as they considered the individual for promotion and tenure. They seemed simply to expect an additional year's worth of papers, talks, and productivity to be added.

To address this issue, the Principal Investigator who was the Provost appointed a Promotion and Tenure ADVANCE Committee (PTAC) Committee to assess existing promotion and tenure processes, explore potential forms of bias, providing recommendations to mitigate against them, and to elevate awareness of both candidates and committees for expectations and best practices in tenure and promotion. After one year of studying the research documenting possible biases due to gender, race/ethnicity, ability status, as well as interdisciplinarity, the committee developed nine case studies with accompanying sample curriculum vitae. Each illustrated one or more issues or areas where possible bias might impact the promotion and tenure decision. After discussion of these case studies at a mini-retreat, the refined versions served as the basis for an interactive web-based instrument, Awareness of Decision in Evaluation of Promotion and Tenure (ADEPT), designed by colleagues in the College of Computing. Individuals can use ADEPT[1] to participate in a virtual promotion and tenure meeting, where depending upon her/his response, the meeting takes different directions and generates different outcomes in promotion and tenure.

As I write this article, (note that the grant ended in 2006) we enter our fifth and final year of the $3.7 million National Science Foundation (NSF) ADVANCE grant. Preliminary data and results suggest that the activities associated with the five threads of the ADVANCE grant may have helped to make distribution of the curriculum vitae and tenure and promotion results for the male and female faculty more similar. Although mentoring activities of ADVANCE and the ADEPT tool addressed this directly, the other three threads facilitated these objectives indirectly. The long term impact and true test will come in future years, after the NSF funding ends. For now, both male and female faculty and administrators view ADVANCE as positive and recognize that having a feminist dean can provide new perspectives and initial valuable transformations for the institution.

Because my scholarly work for the last quarter century has focused on the intersection of women, feminism, science, health and technology, people tend to be aware of my background and hold expectations of how it will influence my approaches and decisions as an administrator. In a few instances when individuals had a personal political agenda or grudge, they could appropriate my words from my nine books, 120 articles, and hundreds of speeches I've given on these topics, take them out of context and use them to paint me as a "radical", "fringe" feminist and to suggest that I would discriminate against men. More commonly, people see my background and work in feminism and science as providing expertise in building bridges across disciplines, dealing with diversity, and initiating programs to attract underrepresented groups to science, technology, mathematics, and engineering in ways to benefit women, the institution, and science and engineering as a whole. On balance, I believe my background as a feminist and a scientist has provided more opportunities and positive choices than challenges and problems for me as an administrator.

NOTES

[1] The web-based instrument, along with best practices from PTAC, and resources on bias can be accessed at www.adept.gatech.edu/ptac.

REFERENCES

www.adept.gatech.edu. Retrieved June 23, 2005.
http://www.advance.gatech.edu. Retrieved June 23, 2005.
Badger Herald Editorial Board. (2006, January 15). Opinion and editorial. *The Badger Herald.* Retrieved (n.d.) from http://badgerherald.com/oped/2006/01/15/sapiro_for_provost.php
Badger Herald Editorial Board. (2006, March 6). Opinion and editorial. *The Badger Herald.* Retrieved (n.d.) from http://badgerherald.com/oped/2006/03/06/farrell_for_provost.php
Long, S. (2001). *From scarcity to visibility: Gender differences in the careers of doctoral scientists and engineers.* Washington, DC: National Research Council.
Mason, M., & Goulden, M. (2004, November/December). Do babies matter (Part II)? *Academe, 90*(6), 11–16.
National Science Foundation. (2001a). *ADVANCE. Program solicitation.* Arlington, VA: Author.
National Science Foundation. (2001b). *ADVANCE Institutional Transformation Awards.* Retrieved October 1, 2001, from http://www.nsf.gov/advance
Puzniak, A. (2006, March 9). Provost. *The Badger Herald.* Retrieved (n.d.) from http:// badgerherald.com/news/2006/03/09/chancellor_names_pat.php
Puzniak, A. (2006, January 15). Provost search narrows. *The Badger Herald.* Retrieved (n.d.) from http://badgerherald.com/news/2006/01/15/provost_search_narro.php
Rosser, S. V. (2004). *The science glass ceiling: academic women scientists and the struggle to succeed.* New York: Routledge.
Sonnert, G., & Holton, G. (1995). *Gender differences in science careers.* New Brunswick, NJ: Rutgers University Press.
Xie, Y., & Shauman, K. (2003). *Women in science.* Boston: Harvard University Press.

ACKNOWLEDGEMENTS

Parts of this chapter were taken from a previously published article:
Rosser, S V. (2007). Levelling the playing field for women in tenure and promotion. *National Women's Studies Association Journal 19*(3): 190–198.

AFFILIATION

Sue Rosser
Ivan Allen College,
Georgia Institute of Technology

KATHRYN SCANTLEBURY AND SONYA MARTIN

19. LAUGHTER, SOLIDARITY, SUPPORT AND LOVE:

Looking Back and Moving Forward in Academia

We have organized this book to reflect the perspectives and experiences of women in science and science education across time, space, and geographic location. Through these chapters, we have explored some of the individual/collective challenges faced by women in science and science education to contextualize the role, careers and trajectories of women in academia over the last four decades. We have examined how women moved geographically from the homes of their youth to take up the challenges of being an academic, and for some of us, those journeys also meant leaving the values and philosophical stances of one's family. Some of these challenges include personal life events, such as choosing to marry or not, be involved in personal partnerships or not, raising children or not. Examples of public life issues include discussions about the courses which women faculty are assigned to teach, the research they conduct, and whether their academic appointments are in colleges/schools of education, science content departments or joint appointments between faculties. In each instance, we find women's identities in science and science education are shaped by the relationship between their personal/public life decisions, both of which inform women's individual and collective experiences and achievements in academia.

The autobiographies and perspectives provided in this book illustrate many areas in the academy in which women and minorities continue to face challenges. This is especially true in the fields of science and science education, where historically and culturally constituted practices still limit opportunities for scholarship for them. For example, existing hierarchies within academia, such as the divisions between science and science education or elementary and secondary science education, continue to impact career trajectories of women and minorities in academia. In the sections that follow, we revisit some of the challenges posed in the earlier chapters in an effort to advance the discussion about how women and men can work collaboratively to actively and consciously address inequities in academia that will expand opportunities for researchers, teachers, and students at all levels and in all fields of study.

Ongoing Issues for Female Science Educators in Academe

The perceived value of science as a discipline in education, both as teaching and research, continues to impact women scholars' power and status within their departments, college and universities and has an impact on their ability to receive

K. Scantlebury, J. Butler Kahle and S. N. Martin (eds.) Re-visioning Science Education from Feminist Perspectives: Challenges, Choices and Careers, 215–220.

grants, engage in particular types of research, publish their work in top journals, and, as a result successfully attain tenure. In their chapter, Mary Spencer and Sherry Nichols (Chapter 14) remind us how important it is to have people who have taught children, not just science, to be elementary science educators. However, they provide the argument that since elementary teaching is not privileged or valued then why would someone who is prepared in science choose to teach elementary school science or elementary science teachers. Their observation makes clear why it is important for us to encourage the academic community to value science education in the K-12 and tertiary levels as legitimate and significant areas of scholarship. Otherwise, women and men will continue not to be supported to engage in research in K-12 teaching and learning and may decide to pursue careers in other disciplines.

Even within K-12 education, teaching small children science is often undervalued compared with teaching high school science and these inequities in power and status continue to be replicated at the college level. Universities are highly structured entities with an individual's symbolic capital impacting her/his power and status. For example, consider Rose Pringle's (see Chapter 3) concern that her administrators and peers did not value her teaching of elementary science education majors or that this assignment was not viewed as being significant as "teaching science". Moreover, her administrators interpreted Rose's commitment to excelling in teaching as evidence that she enjoyed her assignment and did not want to teach other science education majors in middle or secondary science. Rose viewed herself as "stuck" in teaching elementary science education majors, and with the larger number of students compared with her colleagues involved with secondary education science and/or graduate education, more of Rose's time went to nurturing activities such as interacting with her students rather than to focus on research. In order to maintain a research agenda, Rose synergistically re-allocated her time teaching and focused her research on elementary science education, an area of study also devalued by the administrators, because she had limited time for other research projects.

Rose's experiences raises an important on-going challenge for scholars engaging in education research, obtaining external funding. Education as a research field continues to lag in funding, and while other monies in science education are available in the USA, researchers must negotiate how to conduct their studies in the context of curriculum reforms or programs focused on teachers' professional development. While, making a recent speech at the National Academy of Sciences, US President Barack Obama made a commitment to a renewed focus on funding for science research. In his speech, he indicated he would commit increased funds towards science and mathematics education targeted towards standards, revising curriculum, improving physical facilities in schools and the use of technology, and teacher preparation. Thus, research in science education was not included in Obama's priority list (Obama, 2009). In addition, current trends in funding tend to favor research projects that adhere to positivistic paradigms of research, which are at odds with many of the participatory research methodologies employed by those who are informed by feminist theoretical frameworks. As a result, many researchers who are committed to engaging in transformative participatory methodologies in science education are marginalized in their attempts to gain funding as the reviewers are looking for examples of empirical evidence for claims, which may be valid, but tend to obscure the socio cultural aspects of teaching and learning which are salient for feminist scholars and researchers. This is particularly salient in the USA, as the criteria for tenure and promotion in colleges/schools of education are shifting to include an expectation of attaining external funding.

However, that funding is granted based on reviews by peers in the field speaks to the need for colleagues to become better informed about different research methodologies and be open to how differing epistemologies concerning what it means to learn or know science can contribute valuable knowledge to the field. The added politics of peer review for grants and the negotiation of a substantive role on large collaborative grants are new challenges for all, but as we are reminded by the stories of several women in this book, the challenges are unique for women academics in science education, who often carry heavier teaching and service loads than their male peers, who have reproductive choices that may impact research productivity, and, especially for those researchers who use research methodologies and theoretical frameworks that lie outside of the mainstream practices. The science education community as a collective has a responsibility to individuals, both females and males, to support research initiatives that will expand our current understandings about how people teach and learn science in varying contexts. For example, what knowledge would science education researchers produce if they considered the gender dynamics between the researcher and researched when collecting data or how might we consider the impact of social experiences within a classroom on the leaner's cognitive understanding of science? A feminist re-examination of science education research may result in new questions and methodologies to connect the personal aspects of learners' lives to scientific knowledge (Scantlebury & Martin, 2010). Finding ways to value difference, as well as supporting and encouraging faculty to engage in scholarship that differs both methodologically and theoretically is an on-going challenge in academia, which if met, can only serve to enrich our research communities and to expand opportunities for teachers and students in science.

Contextualizing Women's Careers and Experiences from Science to Science Education

This interesting book section traces the career trajectories for women who have made or are making transitions from research science into science education. The identity of these women shift as they negotiate different research paradigms, theoretical frameworks, and re-evaluate what counts as 'data', in their new field. Moreover, they have dealt with the loss of status and power as they transitioned from a discipline viewed as high status (i.e. masculine) to one that is more people orientated, that is, more feminine. The women who trod this path, perceive that their colleagues do not value their research, their teaching or the ethic of care they show for students, through advising sessions and/or improving one's teaching.

Administrators often discourage junior professors from spending too much time on these activities in lieu of conducting and publishing research. This particularly impacts science educators with appointments in content rather than education departments and often can be in conflict with the feminist ideology and pedagogy that may frame academics' research and teaching practices. Another challenge for women science educators in science departments is whether colleagues who are participants on peer review committees for tenure and promotion value science education scholarship. For many science educators, their research trajectories are shaped by the recognition of what their peers perceive as 'acceptable' research which may favor quantitative data over qualitative and may find positivistic paradigms for research more acceptable than research methodologies that stem from feminist frameworks encouraging more ethnographic and qualitative examinations of teaching and learning. As a result, many women are forced to make decisions to either limit their research to areas which they feel their colleagues will understand and accept as evidence of scholarship or to make only minor alterations to their teaching methods until after they attain tenure. Such scenarios may lead pre-tenure faculty to feel discouraged in their academic career, resulting in attrition from the academy. Thus a re-envisioning science education from feminist perspectives may be empowering for women and men who want to transform the academy by embracing differences rather than excluding those people who bring different values, expectations, and intentions to their scholarship and teaching.

Feminism, particularly for women, provides space from which to consider new and different identities in science. Women who lie outside of science, in comparison to those who assume science identities as a way of being/seeing the world, often must cut ties with other identity markers such as woman, mother, etc. Although Brickhouse (Chapter 6) and others (Seiler and Blunck, Chapter 5) have described science as a "way out", this perspective also raises questions about the role of science in isolating young people, especially women and minorities, from their identity and membership to their community/family (see Carlton Parsons and Moore Mensah, Chapter 2). This issue of identity and membership in communities and science is further complicated for immigrants who are racial minorities as discussed in the chapters by Rose Pringle and Rowhea Elmesky (Chapter 3) and Karen Phillips (Chapter 9). The socio-historical context of racial relations in the United States for minorities creates a different relationship for American minorities than immigrant minorities with regards to expectations and experiences in academia. As Black women from Jamaica, neither Pringle nor Phillips placed race as a central issue in describing their experiences in academia in the US. For Carlton Parsons and Moore Mensah, being African American women working in American institutions, race has played a prominent role in shaping their career trajectories in science education. Both women discuss their decisions to situate their career experiences in Predominantly White Institutions (PWI) as a conscious choice to bump up against long-held expectations for women and minorities to engage in stereotypical roles in academic settings. Using Black Feminist theory as a framework for examining their experiences, these scholars pro-actively implement an aspect of feminist praxis and research that expands opportunities for future scholars.

Conscious and Unconscious Feminist Praxis, Pedagogy, and Practice

The chapters in this section offer examples of how individual women are making a difference in their lives and the lives of the students and the communities in which they conduct research by consciously enacting feminist theoretical lenses to shape their pedagogical practices and to frame their research agendas and methodologies. Kirch and Martin (Chapter 12) and Spencer and Nichols (Chapter 14) discuss the role of feminist pedagogical practices in teaching preservice and inservice elementary science teachers. Their contributions make salient the transformative potential for consciously engaging their students in critical discourse about the role individuals play in shaping students' experiences in science. Each chapter offers readers a thoughtful analysis of different approaches for transforming elementary science teacher education that have important implications for how teacher education programs are structured as well as how the contributions of faculty in both science and science education could be re-envisioned to provide greater opportunities for collaboration and mutual appreciation for the value that each plays in the preparation of science teachers. Catherine Milne (Chapter 13) and Janet Bond-Robinson (Chapter 15) urge readers to consider employing different lenses to examine science education, what Rich (1979) called 're-vision', a looking back to discover new perspectives through discovery stories and mental models.

Sisters are "Doing it for themselves"

Penny Gilmer (Chapter 7) discusses how as a female academic in chemistry in the 70's, her colleagues viewed her decision to have children as an indication that she did not take her career seriously. While Calabrese Barton and Osborne (Chapter 16) show that some aspects of this strong held belief has changed in academe, Elmesky (Chapter 16) notes how uncomfortable she has felt in bringing her children into academic settings, either at an institution, meetings, and/or conferences. For Elmesky, as a Muslim woman who wears a hijab, her perception is that the academy is also not accepting of her religious affiliation. Other authors also discuss the role that religion of their lives and how that commitment influences their gender roles and the expectations they, and others hold, for them regarding traditional roles of motherhood and wife (see Carlton Parsons and Moore Mensah, Chapter 2; Brickhouse, Chapter 6).The advice that a woman should not have children until she attains tenure is still given to women academics. The career path and trajectory of academe is in conflict with a woman's optimal fertility time. As Sue Rosser (Chapter 18) notes that this and other issues related to combining career and family responsibility are particularly challenging to female academics. As new generations of women academics, such as Rosser assume administrative leadership roles in the academy, universities may begin to implement simple but effective strategies to support women.

Until academic institutions make serious and sustained efforts, both in policy and practice, to equitably support women and minorities to succeed in academia, women will undoubtedly continue to create their own supportive networks. Examples in this book include the development and nurturing of inter-generational friendships and mentoring relationships, as described by Scantlebury, Meece, and Kahle (Chapter 17) and by the intentional creation of spaces of utopia in the academy by women academics who attempt to build lives with/in academia with/for their children and families (Calabrese Barton, Osborne, and Elmesky, Chapter 16). These individuals' actions, coupled with institutional programs such as those developed through ADVANCE, will continue to transform the academy in the upcoming decades. Contributions from the women in this book demonstrate that when scholars bring a focused ethic of care to their research and teaching, they can create structures (enhanced and supported by laughter), which enable them to build solidarity with one another and maintain social networks. In turn, these structures, shared sense of solidarity and social networks can assist both women and men to address inequities in academia in an effort to minimize challenges and to offer individuals with a wider range of choices for a career in academe.

REFERENCES

Mason, M., & Ekman, M. (2007). Mothers on the fast track. How a new generation can balance family and careers. USA: Oxford University Press.

Obama, B. (2009). *President Obama addresses NAS annual meeting*. Retrieved May 4, 2009, from http://www.nationalacademies.org/morenews/20090428.html

Rich, A. C. (1979). On lies, secrets, and silence: Selected prose, 1966–1978. London: Norton.

Scantlebury, K., & Martin, S. (2010). How does she know? Re-visioning conceptual change from feminist perspectives. In K. Tobin & W. M. Roth (Eds.), *Re/structuring science education: Reuniting sociological and psychological perspectives*. Springer.

AFFILIATIONS

Kathryn Scantlebury
Department of Chemistry & Biochemistry,
University of Delaware

Sonya N. Martin
School of Education,
Drexel University

EDITORS

Kathryn Scantlebury is a Professor in the Department of Chemistry and Biochemistry at the University of Delaware and Coordinator for Secondary Science Education in the College of Arts and Sciences. Her research interests focus on gender issues in various aspects of science education, including urban education, preservice teacher education, teachers' professional development, and academic career paths in academe. She recently published book chapters on gender issues in the *Handbook of Research in Science Education* and *Second International Handbook of Science Education*.

Jane Butler Kahle recently retired from an endowed professorship at Miami University and as Director of the *Ohio Evaluation and Assessment Center for Mathematics and Science Education* that she established. Dr. Kahle has served as chair of CEOSE, *NSF's* committee on equal opportunities for women and as *Division Director for Elementary, Secondary, and Informal Education (ESIE)* at the NSF. She was principal investigator for Ohio's Statewide Systemic Initiative and has published widely on issues concerning girls and women in science.

Sonya N. Martin is an Assistant Professor in Science Education at Drexel University. Martin taught science at both the elementary and secondary levels in the Philadelphia public school district for five years, during which time she earned two graduate degrees in Elementary Education and Chemistry Education from the *University of Pennsylvania*. Her current research focuses on video analysis and cogenerative dialogues as tools for introducing pre- and inservice teachers to an effective means for catalyzing changes that benefit the learning environment for both teachers and their students. She has published articles in *Science Education, Journal for Research in Science Teaching,* and *Cultural Studies of Science Education*. She is an Editorial Board member for the *International Journal of Research in Science Education* and the *Journal of Science Teacher Education*.

CONTRIBUTORS

Bambi Bailey is an Associate Professor of Education at the University of Texas at Tyler School of Education. Her research interests include equity issues in science education focusing on the interaction of content and pedagogy at the preservice and inservice levels. Because of this interest she has served on the National Science Teachers' Association's Preservice Committee.

Angela Calabrese Barton is a Professor of Teacher Education at Michigan State University. She has been a chemistry teacher and has developed and taught in numerous after school programs for urban youth located in community centers, shelters, and schools. Her research, teaching and service intersect around two main themes: (a) science learning and frameworks for unpacking deep engagement, and (b) teacher learning around the intersections of science teaching and youth lives. Her work appears in books and journals including the *Educational Researcher, American Education Research Journal, Journal of Research in Science Teaching, Journal of Teacher Education,* and *Science Education.*

Susan Blunck is an Associate Clinical Professor at the University of Maryland, Baltimore County (UMBC) in Baltimore, Maryland. Dr. Blunck's professional efforts have been focused on promoting excellence in science teaching through the development of innovative, teacher-centered, and standards-based preservice and professional development programs for science teachers. Dr. Blunck is currently serving as the Director of the UMBC Teacher Education Graduate Programs as well as the UMBC Center of Excellence in STEM Education where she is researching K-12 STEM Academy building processes and K-12 STEM teacher development. She has authored numerous publications and made many presentations related to K-20 science teaching and teacher development.

Nancy Brickhouse is Professor and Interim Deputy Dean of the College of Education and Public Policy at the University of Delaware. She was the Editor-in-chief *Science Education* from 2001-2006. Her research interests have focused on issues of gender identity development in science education and on teaching about the nature of science. She has published widely in journals such as *Science Education, Journal of Research in Science Teaching,* and *Educational Theory* and has lectured internationally.

Rowhea Elmesky is an assistant professor at Washington University in St. Louis. Her research focuses upon understanding how science education can be a transformational force in the lives of culturally marginalized and economically disadvantaged children rather than contribute to the reproduction of their marginalized positions in society. Along with Kenneth Tobin and Gale Seiler,

Rowhea is an editor of their book entitled, *Improving urban science education: New roles for teachers, students and researchers*, which won the Choice Award for Outstanding Academic titles in 2006.

Penny J. Gilmer is a biochemist/science educator at Florida State University. She came into science education from her department of Chemistry and Biochemistry in the early 1990s. After switching her research from biochemistry to science education in the later 1990s, she decided to earn a second doctorate in Science Education by conducting action research in her own biochemistry classroom. She was the President of the *National Association for Research in Science Teaching* and on the Executive Committee of the Board of the *Association for Science Teacher Education*. Her research focuses on improving K-16 science education.

Jane Butler Kahle recently retired from an endowed professorship at Miami University and as Director of the *Ohio Evaluation and Assessment Center for Mathematics and Science Education* that she established. Dr. Kahle has served as chair of CEOSE, *NSF's* committee on equal opportunities for women and as *Division Director for Elementary, Secondary, and Informal Education (ESIE)* at the NSF. She was principal investigator for Ohio's Statewide Systemic Initiative and has published widely on issues concerning girls and women in science.

Susan A. Kirch is an associate professor of science education at New York University. Her current research consists of two related themes: investigations of teaching and learning science inquiry strategies in urban elementary schools, and studies of teacher learning in the areas of science and inclusion. Kirch has participated in a variety of initiatives designed to bring teachers, K-12 students, educational researchers and scientists together to study access to science and the nature of scientific inquiry. She recently served as a co-principal investigator on a National Science Foundation grant to disseminate research on gender equitable practices in science education.

Jennifer Lewis is an associate professor in the Department of Chemistry at the University of South Florida. Her research interests focus on current trends in the teaching and learning of chemistry at the undergraduate level, including the evaluation of curricular reform implementations with an eye toward both effectiveness and equity. Her research publications have appeared in *Chemistry Education: Research and Practice, the Journal of Chemical Education,* and *the Journal of Research in Science Teaching.* She recently served as a co-editor for two issues of *Feminist Teacher* designed to showcase disciplinary diversity in the interpretation and application of feminist pedagogies.

Sonya N. Martin is an Assistant Professor in Science Education at Drexel University. Martin taught science at both the elementary and secondary levels in the Philadelphia public school district for five years, during which time she earned two graduate degrees in Elementary Education and Chemistry Education from the

University of Pennsylvania. Her current research focuses on video analysis and cogenerative dialogues as tools for introducing pre- and inservice teachers to an effective means for catalyzing changes that benefit the learning environment for both teachers and their students. She has published articles in *Science Education, Journal for Research in Science Teaching,* and *Cultural Studies of Science Education.* She is an Editorial Board member for the *International Journal of Research in Science Education* and the *Journal of Science Teacher Education.*

Judith Meece is professor and chair of Human Development and Psychological Studies at the University of North Carolina-Chapel Hill. Judith is a nationally recognized scholar in the field of achievement motivation and her research focuses on the role of classroom and school environments in the development of adolescent's academic motivation and future aspirations, and she is especially interested in the influence of school transitions on achievement motivation, learning, and school adjustment.

Felicia M. Moore Mensah is an assistant professor of science education in the Department of Mathematics, Science and Technology at Teachers College, Columbia University. Her research interests focus on issues of diversity and social justice education in science teacher education and the support of science teaching in K-12 urban classrooms. One recent article in the Journal of Research in Science Teacher considers professional development and positional identity in science education.

Catherine Milne is an associate professor in the Department of Teaching and Learning in the Steinhardt School of Culture, Education and Human Development at New York University. Her research focuses on areas such as the nature of science and science education, the nature of teacher education, and multimedia education.

Colette Murphy is a Senior Lecturer the School of Education at Queen's University Belfast. She completed her PhD in science, became a science teacher and then a science teacher educator. Before Queen's, Colette was a Principal Lecturer at St Mary's University College Belfast for 10 years, where she ran the Continuing Professional Development program. Her current research focuses on the life and work of Vyogtsky, coteaching and cogenerative dialogue. She has led several research projects on coteaching science in primary schools (mostly funded by the AstraZeneca Science Teaching Trust). Colette is a member of the Editorial Boards of the *International Journal of Science Education* and *Research in Science Education* and reviews papers for several other journals, as well as research proposals for the *Wellcome Trust, ESRC, AERA* and *NARST.* She is Chair of the Irish Association for Social, Scientific and Environmental Education. Colette is also a published author of children's fiction.

Margery Osborne is a professor in the Department of Curriculum and Instruction, University of Illinois at Urbana-Champaign, USA, where she teaches early-childhood and elementary science education. Her research interests, located within the intersections between constructs of reflective practice and research in critical and feminist pedagogy, include exploring the dynamic and complex nature of teacher knowledge.

Sherry Nichols is an Associate Professor of Science Education at the University of Alabama. Her research interests focus on understanding science teaching as a community-based practice. She has drawn on case-based pedagogy, feminist perspectives, visual ethnography, and narrative inquiry to engage teachers and community members in rethinking science education. She teaches elementary and secondary science teacher education courses, and conducts research extended across a local middle school and public housing after school program.

Eileen R. Carlton Parsons is an associate professor in the School of Education at the University of North Carolina at Chapel Hill. She investigates the influences of context, culture, and race in the teaching and learning of science in K-postsecondary settings. Her present work focuses on African American students at the elementary and middle school level. She recently proposed a conceptual framework that accommodates the aforementioned; the model synthesizes the works of Michael Cole and Urie Bronfenbrenner with a customizing feature for African Americans–the triple quandary posited by Wade Boykin.

Karen Philips is an assistant professor in the Department of Chemistry at Hunter College of the City University of New York, and winner of Hunter College's Presidential Award for Excellence in Teaching. Her research interests focus on gender and ethnicity in urban science education, and on the development, implementation and assessment of innovative instructional methods that help students to gain a deeper understanding of chemistry. Efforts are targeted toward undergraduate organic chemistry as well as the high school chemistry curriculum, with an emphasis on issues related to group learning and laboratory design.

Rose Pringle is an associate professor in the School of Teaching and Learning at the University of Florida. Her research interests include preservice teachers' positionality as science learners, issues associated with learning to teach inquiry-based science and the translation of such knowledge into practice, and the impact of teachers', counselors' and parents' expectations on African American girls' self-perception as science learners.

Janet Bond Robinson is an associate professor of chemical education at Arizona State University. She began her postsecondary career as an assistant professor at the University of Kansas. Her research interests concern (1) identifying fundamental aspects of PCK enacted by an effective constructivist teacher in the laboratory and the scaffolding methods that will catalyze performance of PCK; and (2) characterization of the learning environment in a research laboratory and the kinds of reasoning acquired that spur development of a scientist.

Sue Rosser is the Dean of the Ivan Allen College of Liberal Arts at Georgia Tech in Atlanta, where she is also Professor of Public Policy and of History, Technology, and Society. Author of approximately 120 journal articles on women, gender, science, technology and medicine, she has also written or edited 11 books. Her latest edited book is Women, Science, and Myth(2008).

Gale Seiler was a high school science teacher for 16 years, teaching in a variety of settings from Montana to South America to Baltimore. She is currently an Associate Professor at McGill University in Montreal, Canada where she teaches science content and methods courses to elementary and secondary preservice teachers. Her research examines how curricula and classrooms can be restructured to provide access to science participation for groups traditionally excluded from science. She is interested in collaborative research involving multiple stakeholders and is currently engaged in identity and memory work with science teachers from underrepresented groups, exploring how and why they persisted in science.

M. E. Spencer is a Secondary Science Specialist with the Alabama Math, Science, and Technology Initiative at the University of Montevallo. She teaches graduate science education and environmental education courses. Her research focuses on embodiment of science and science education, ecofeminist thought, and environmental education with particular attention to teachers and middle school students throughout the state of Alabama.

Helga Stadler is an ex-physics teacher from a Viennese upper secondary school. Since 1992 she has been an Assistant Professor at the Department of Physics Education and eLearning at the Faculty of Physics, University of Vienna. Her research interests Areas are learning and teaching in physics class, gender issues in physics education and professional development of science teachers.

Molly Weinburgh is the William L. & Betty F. Adams Chair of Education and the Director of the Andrews Institute of Mathematics, Science, and Technology Education. She is an active member of numerous science education societies. Her service to these include: President of the ASTE, President of SW-ASTE, ASTE Board of Directors, Strand Coordinator of Culture, Social and Gender Issues of the NARST, Local Arrangement Committee for the NSTA, and Policy Committee of the SSMA. Her research interests include equity issues, inquiry science and professional development for teachers.

INDEX

CPSIA information can be obtained at www.ICGtesting.com
Printed in the USA
BVOW05s0745050514

352474BV00004B/25/P